WORL...
OSS
IN SLOVAKIA

Jim Downs

Liefrinck Publishers
1303 Crestridge Drive
Oceanside, California 92054
Tel/Fax (760) 439-3573
Downsjd@cox.net

Cover photo shows a group of American airmen with Slovak Partisans near Brezova in Western Slovakia, early September, 1944. The Americans had been released by the Partisans from a prisoner of war camp and were heading for a rendezvous with a rescue mission of the Office of Special Services (OSS). Photo courtesy of the Slovak national Uprising museum, Dr. Jan Stanislas. Cover designed by Bella Downs. Back cover photograph courtesy of Kathy Baranski Lund.

ISBN 0-971-7482-0-9.

Bound and printed by BookMasters, Inc.

*To the brave men and women of the
DAWES and WINDPROOF Missions; and also to my
lovely and patient wife, Patsy Downs.*

Contents

Foreword
Personalities

1	Blechhammer Raid	1
2	OSS Zeros In On Slovakia	11
3	Slovak Uprising Breaks Out	23
4	On The Loose	35
5	Dodging Germans	41
6	Holt Green	47
7	Rendezvous On A Grass Field	53
8	"Unbelievable Environment"	61
9	Krajne	71
10	Return to Tri Duby	77
11	"Carnival Atmosphere"	89
12	Going Home	97
13	Shaky Ground	103
14	More Airmen	111
15	Situation Becomes Desperate	117
16	"Imminent Catastrophe"	125
17	Maria Gulovich	137
18	Underground Courier	145
19	Rain, Fog, and Gunfire	151
20	Over the Precipice	151
21	*Rosauer Lände* Prison	173
22	Bad Luck On Dumbier	183
23	More Suffering	193
24	Betrayal	205
25	"Things Don't Look Right"	211
26	"Some Devil Is Coming"	225
27	Fleeing Once Again	233
28	Ludvik and Igor Nabelek	241
29	Mauthausen	247
30	Into Russian Hands	259
31	Evil Men	271
32	Murder, Wine, and Brandy	277
33	Berlin Communiqué	287
34	Freedom in Bucharest	293
35	"Our Best and Bravest"	299
36	The Drama Ends	307

Epilogue 317
Acknowledgements 327
Partil Bibliography 331
Index 332

Foreword

The story line in this book is not a neatly fashioned narrative with a few well-etched characters in a bucolic setting. Neither is it a simple tale of a few brave people. The reader will be challenged to follow a long parade of individuals, mostly American, a few British, and a number of Slovaks, who are caught up in a drama of secret missions, daring escapes, and in the end, tragedy. Two dozen men, and two remarkable women, struggle through frigid weather and rugged terrain to escape a German *Abwehr* unit led by an *SS* major, an Austrian noble. A half-century now has passed. Although this account is not intended to be the final word on the events in Slovakia in 1944, it is the most detailed account yet of the Anglo-American involvement.

Most of the American and British agents who heroically volunteered for the Slovak missions lost their lives, victims of bad luck, bad weather, and bad judgment. The author has opted to include what one editor described as an "overwhelming number of characters." Of course, he's right. Originally, the author agonized over attempting to tell the story through the personality of one participant, or perhaps three or four. In the end, he went for the mosaic, the whole, complex episode with the myriad of players of all nationalities. For the Anglo-American reader, the Slovak and Hungarian names alone can be semantic jawbreakers. The obscure towns and villages are little known outside of central Europe. But what emerges is the most complete account of two desperate groups, one American, the other British, fleeing through the mountains before their luck ran out.

A list of the personalities who played both large and small parts in the story follows the Foreword.

The story opens with American airmen, victims of the *Luftwaffe*, falling out of the sky. It continues with the OSS organizing plans to rescue them as the Slovak National Uprising erupts. The Slovak government, which has been a friendly partner to the Third *Reich*, suddenly finds elements of the population caught up in the revolt. Berlin recognizes the strategic reality of their threatened rear, and Hitler orders his *SS* storm troopers to crush the Uprising. Actually, the *SS* units are patch-work units hastily organized. Nevertheless, a succession of explosive events follows.

The OSS and the British SOE and the 15th Air Force in Bari, Italy, team up to land agents in two daring flights of B-17's behind German lines on a grass field near the Slovak rebel capital. Things soon go haywire. When it becomes clear that a retrieval mission is necessary, the 15th is grounded by bad weather and the personnel are marooned. The *SS* units subsequently overrun the airfield and the rebel capital as thousands of Slovaks flee.

A small party of Anglo-Americans joins the flight. The Yanks hike into the rugged mountains with their British allies just as savage winter conditions are about to occur. Frostbite and hunger nearly overwhelm the refugees. In hot pursuit is an Austrian nobleman, an *SS* major commanding *Abwehr 218*, a counterintelligence unit made up of Germans, some Slovak fascists, and a hundred turncoat Ukrainians.

By now, most of the Slovak army has been destroyed. Thousands have been captured, and others have melted away to return to their homes. Some join the Partisans while a few aid the Anglo-Americans. One, a young woman – a school teacher turned underground courier and later an interpreter for the Soviets — baffles her American friends as she repeatedly puts her life at risk to save them. Another woman, a Slovak-American citizen working for the British, is captured by the *Abwehr* and pays with her life.

Meanwhile, five members of the Anglo-American group avoid capture. Maria Gulovich, a Slovak multi-lingual school teacher, leads two Americans and two British through the German lines. Confronted repeatedly by retreating German troops, she survives through her quick thinking, wit and guile. Finally, Maria leads them to the Red Army lines, but their problems are not over.

Emerging Cold War attitudes complicate matters as the wartime entente between the Anglo-Americans and the Soviets is giving way to suspicion and hostility. But ultimately, Maria and the others escape and find their way to the American and British military missions in Bucharest, Romania.

During this time, the Soviets, the British and the Americans all had been giving minimal aid to the beleaguered Slovaks. Central Europe was not at the moment a significant Anglo-American concern although the Soviets were positioning themselves for a favorable geopolitical position.

By the fall of 1944, fighting was raging around the world. Paris had fallen. General Eisenhower's armies had reached the Rhine and were threatening to break into the German heartland. The *Wehrmacht* was retreating in Italy, and the Soviets had advanced into eastern Poland, poised to crash through to Berlin. In the Pacific, the Japanese were on the run as the U.S. Air Force began pounding their main islands. The U.S. Navy had sunk nearly the entire Japanese fleet at the Battle of Leyte Gulf, and the U.S. Marines were about to invade the islands of Guam and Saipan. General MacArthur was preparing to return to the Philippines.

Obscured by these larger events, desperate forces struggled in remote places. Partisan groups – as in Slovakia — engaged in bloody struggles to gain national independence in Eastern Europe and the Balkans. The British, American and Soviet intelligence services – each more aggressive than their own general staffs — inevitably intruded into these local conflicts from Greece, to Italy, and in western Europe. The reader, therefore, is again cautioned that this account is complicated by the number of personalities.

The author became interested in this story while working on an account of a B-17 pilot shot down in Slovakia. Two of the pilot's crew were rescued by the OSS. Supposedly, other American airmen caught with the OSS mission had been executed by the Germans, although in fact, they had not. The author began to track them down. Several – George Fernandes, Bob Hede, Jack Shafer, Ernie Coleman, and three others – were still alive. Their stories are told here.

Also, the author learned that Maria Gulovich Liu, the school teacher heroine, was living in California. She had told her story many times, and now she patiently worked with the author to tell it again in rich detail. Although over 50 years had elapsed since World War II, family members of the OSS victims were eager to talk about their men, and surprisingly would learn from the author the full story of what had happened to them. The OSS had not been forthcoming in providing information in those postwar years. When the records were declassified 35 years later, the families were no longer asking questions.

Joe Morton is a surprise participant in this story, an Associated Press correspondent who talked his way into flying into Slovakia with the OSS. As Morton feverishly took notes after the flight of six B-17 bombers landed on the grass airfield, *Wehrmacht* artillery fire in the hills nearby could be heard. Prepared for a quick getaway, the Flying Fortresses kept their engines running. In the air, P-51 Mustangs prowled the sky and buzzed the field, ready to keep the *Luftwaffe* at bay.

It was high drama. Morton was chasing what he earlier had told colleagues, was "the biggest story of his life." With a wife and an infant daughter back in Missouri, the popular and courageous writer would suffer the same tragic fate as the others. This book is the story Joe Morton planned to write. He could have told it best.

Jim Downs
February 15, 2002
Oceanside, California

SLOVAKIA

...1944

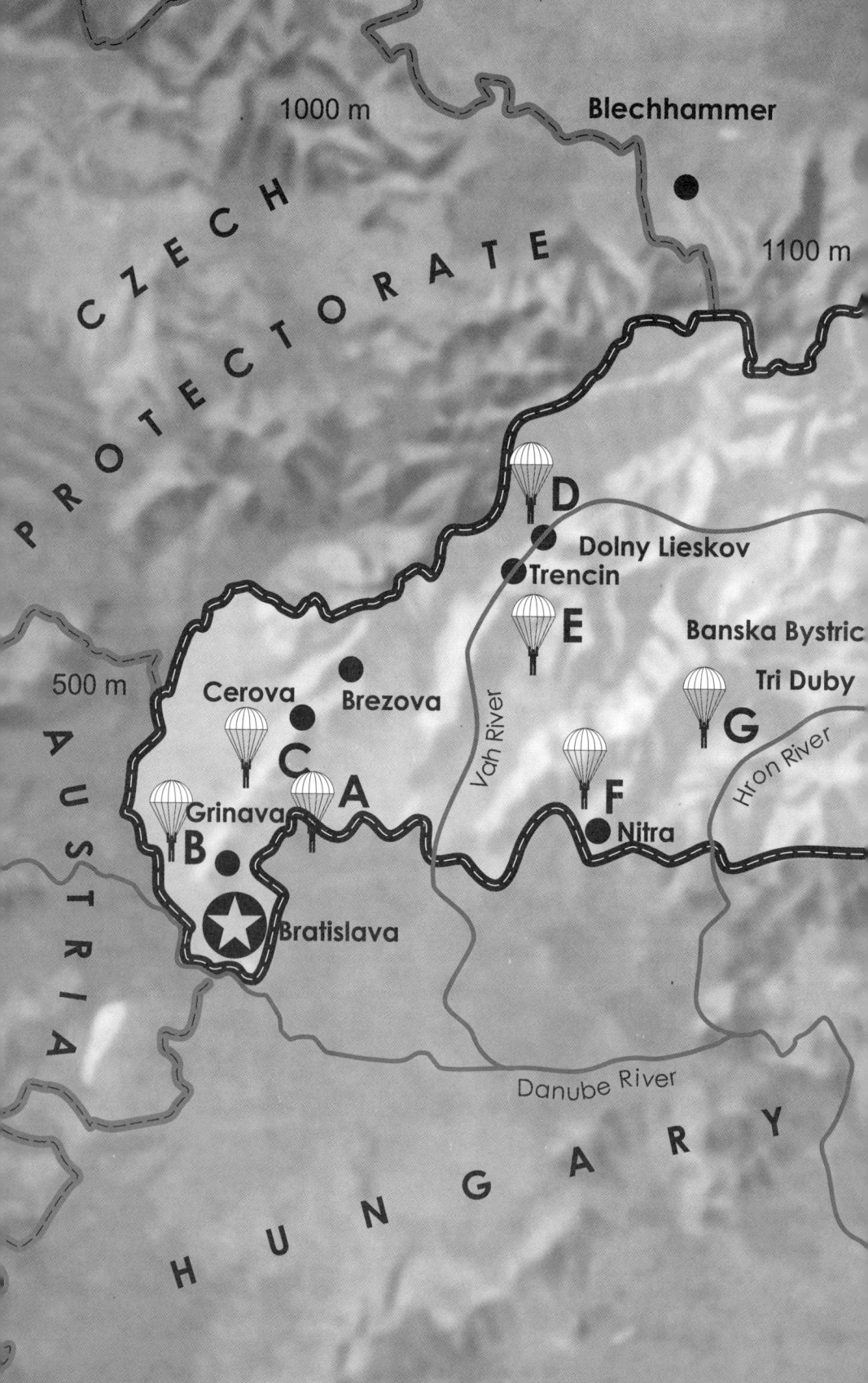

Young Slovaks today will not recognize their 1944 southern boundary. The Hungarians occupied land that today belongs to Slovakia. Flying out of Italy, the U.S. 15th Air Force crossed over Slovakia nearly daily in the summer of 1944 to bomb such synthetic oil refineries as Blechhammer. Over 60 Allied aircraft were shot down by the *Luftwaffe*. The reader can see where Richard Moulton (**A**), Manley Fliger (**B**), Ira Corpening, Jack Kellogg, Norton Skinner, and Virgil Stuart (**C**) parachuted out. George Fernandes, Bob Hede, and Nick Yezdich (**E**) bailed out on the same day, July 7. Within minutes of those men, Howard Coleman (**F**) in another plane was on the ground. Later, Jack Shafer, John Brinser, Theron Arnett, and Edwin Zavisa went down on October 13 (**G**), their 13th mission on an unlucky Friday.

Personalities mentioned one or more times.

* Downed airmen flown back to Italy on September 17 by OSS.
** Downed airmen flown back to Italy on October 7 by OSS.
x Downed airmen who fled into mountains with OSS, later captured.
y OSS and SOE men executed at Mauthausen concentration camp.
z OSS and SOE personnel who survived the war.

Altfuldisch, Hans	*SS* Officer, Mauthausen.
AMSTERDAM Mission	British SOE team, Jewish members.
Arndt, Heinrich	*Gestapo* interrogator, Mauthausen.
Arnett, Theron x	B 17 Radio Operator, shot down, October 13.
Artz, Lt. Lincoln	B-24 Pilot, shot down, June 26, 1944.
Ascani, Major Fred	B-17 Pilot, October 7 OSS rescue flight.
Bachmayer, Georg	SS Officer, Deputy commandant, Mauthausen.
Baranski, Capt. Edward y	OSS, DAY Mission leader, FALCON organizer.
Benes, Eduard	Czech Prime Minister in exile, London.
Ben-Yaakov, Zwi y	AMSTERDAM team member from Palestine.
Berdichev, Aba y	AMSTERDAM team member from Palestine.
Bodecker, Col. Charles	P-51 52nd Fighter Group Commander.
Brinser, Lt. John x	B 17 Co-pilot, shot down, October 13.
Brown, Robert y	OSS Radio Operator, DAWES team.
Bruce, Col. David	Commander of OSS Europe.
Bulfin, Frank x	B 24 Photographer, shot down July 7.
Carter, Colonel Harry	British military mission, Bucharest, Romania.
Catlos, Sgt. Steve z	OSS Hungarian linguist, DAWES Mission.
CFI	Czech Forces of the Interior (Slovak Army).
Chapin, Lt. Col. Howard	OSS Station Chief, Bari, Italy.
Chermesh, Chaim	AMSTERDAM team, survived.
Cheston, Charles	Deputy OSS Director, Washington DC.
Cinnaman, James	B-17 Pilot, October 7 OSS rescue flight.
Cobb, Lt. Neal**	B-24 Bombardier, shot down, July 7.
Cohen, Lt. Com. Edward	British SIS Officer, London.
Coleman, Howard x	B-24 crewman shot down, July 7.
Coloney, Bill	P-51 Pilot, 52nd Fighter Group.
Corpening, Ira	B-17 Pilot, shot down, July 7.
Cransac, Jaques	Captured French Partisan, executed.
Dallman, Howard	B-17 Co-Pilot, Tri Duby, Sept. 17 rescue mission.
Davies, Sgt. Bill z	SOE Agent, WINDPROOF mission.
Deranian, Lt. Nelson, USNR	Organized DAWES Mission, Bari.
Dirlewanger, Oskar Colonel	SS commander, "Butcher of Warsaw."
Dolna Lehota	Village where German attack occurred.

Donahue, Robert*	American airman, Banska Bystrica.
Donovan, General William	Commanding General, OSS, Washington DC.
Dumbier	Mountain on Prasiva Mountain Range.
Dunlevy, Kenneth z	Radio Operator, DAWES Mission.
Edelweiss Unit	SS Unit which tracked down DAWES team.
Eigruber, August	Austrian Nazi *Gauleiter*, executed, 1947.
Feemster, Clyde	B-17 crewman, October 7 OSS rescue flight.
Fernandes, George x	B-24 Navigator shot down, July 7.
Fliger, Manley**	B 24 Navigator, shot down, Sept. 13.
Follas, Gordon	New Zealand escaped POW.
Galembush, Steve	OSS radio operator in Yugoslavia.
Gaul, Harriet	Lt. Jim Gaul's mother.
Gaul, Lt. Jim USNR y	Deputy Commander, DAWES Mission.
Glavin, Col. Edward	OSS, Commanding Officer, Bari, Italy.
Golian, General Jan	Head of Slovak army at start of Uprising.
Gönder, Bandi	Possibly betrayed OSS at Polomka.
Gorman, Capt. Jack	B-17 pilot, Tri Duby, October 7 rescue flight.
Green, Daisy Holt	Lt. Holt Green's mother.
Green, Lt. Holt USNR y	Commander, DAWES Mission.
Grinava	Slovak POW camp north of Bratislava.
Gulovich, Maria	Slovak school teacher, courier, interpreter.
Habecker, Walter	*Gestapo* Interrogator, Mauthausen.
Hede, Bob x	B-24 Waist Gunner, shot down July 7.
Heinzerling, Lynn	Associated Press colleague of Joe Morton.
Heller, Charles y	OSS Radio Operator, HOUSEBOAT.
Hensen, Keith z	British SOE Radio Operator.
Hoefle, General Hermann	*SS* Commander, crushed Slovak Uprising.
Horvath, Anna	Joe Horvath's cousin, Polomka.
Horvath, Sgt. Joe y	OSS Radio Operator, DAWES team.
HOUSEBOAT mission	British SOE mission, Slovakia.
Hruby, Blahoslav	OSS Analyst, London.
Ingr, General Sergej	Czech Minister of Defense, London.
Jagger, Claude	Associated Press executive, New York.
Jakes, Otto	Head of Czech desk, OSS, Bari.
Jakubany	Maria Gulovich's hometown.
Joyce, Edward	OSS Political officer, Bari, Italy.
Kamenesky, Pavel	Escaped from the Polomka hut.
Kanduth, Johann	Mauthausen prisoner, crematorium.
Katek, Charles	Head of Czech desk, OSS London.
Kellogg, Jack	B-17 Co-pilot, shot down, July 7.
Keszthelyi, Lt. Tibor y	Hungarian linguist, DAWES Mission.
Kettgen, SS Major Hans	Captured Banska Bystrica, October 27.
Knap, Michal	Slovak who hid Americans, Krajne.
Kockanova, Anna Engler	Witnessed capture of Americans, Myto.
Kulka, Eugem	Jewish doctor hidden by Michal Knap.
LaFatta, Guy x	Airman shot down, September 13.
Lain, Lt. Ken z	Weapons expert, DAWES Mission.
Lannurien, Georges	Leader of French Partisans.
Loughner, Jim	B-17 crewman, October 7 OSS rescue flight.
Luzier, Howard x	B-24 crewman, shot down, August 27.

McGregor, Lt. Bill z	Weapons expert, DAWES Mission.
McSorley, David	British escaped POW, Grinava POW camp.
McSparren, Glen	B-17 crewman, October 7 OSS rescue flight.
Menzies, Stewart	Commander, British SIS, London.
Mican, M/Sgt Jerry y	OSS Czech Interpreter, DAWES team.
Miller, Lt. Lane y	DAY Mission.
Morton, Joe	Associated Press correspondent.
Morton, Letty	Wife of Joe Morton.
Moulton, Richard	Airman, shot down June 26.
Mueller, Werner	*Gestapo* interpreter, Mauthausen.
Muller, Charles x	Airman shot down, August 27.
Myto	Village where Mican, Keszthelyi captured.
Nabelek, Igor	Slovak, with brother, Ludvik, met captured
Nabelek, Ludvik	OSS personnel in Banska Bystrica jail.
Newton, Bill	B-17 crewman, October 7 OSS rescue flight.
Niedermayer, Josef	SS Officer, Mauthausen.
Norgaard, Noland "Boots"	Joe Morton's s AP Bureau Chief, Rome.
Novak, Tony z	Slovak member of DAY mission.
O'Neall, Lt. Kelly USNR	OSS War Crimes Investigator.
Ornstein, Wilhelm	Mauthausen prisoner in crematorium.
Papierski, Edward	OSS Radio Operator, Yugoslavia.
Paris, Nelson y	U.S. Navy Photographer, DAWES team.
Perkins, Lt. Colonel	Senior SOE Officer, London.
Perry, Lt. Francis (Frank) y	German linguist, DAWES Mission.
Piontek, Josef	Slovak interpreter for Joe Morton
Pittman, John x	Airman shot down September 13.
Polack, Milan Major	Slovak officer who recruited Maria Gulovich.
Prasiva	Mountain Range east of Donovaly.
Pritchard, Lt. Colonel Gil	B-17 Pilot, both OSS rescue missions.
Prykryl, Colonel Vladimir	Soviet commander of Czech brigade.
Raczka, Ben x	B 24 crewman, shot down Sept. 13.
Raubolt, Wesley x	B-17 crewman, Shot down, August 27.
Reik, Chaviva	AMSTERDAM mission, captured with Reiss,
Reiss, Rafael "Rafi"	executed near Banska Bystrica.
Repta, Jan	Slovak Partisan commander, Brezova.
Rider, Captain Don	Original OSS leader of DAWES Mission.
Rippon, Richard x	B 24 crewman, shot down September 13.
Ross, Lt. Colonel Walter	OSS operations chief, Bari, Italy.
Roth, Martin	SS Officer, Mauthausen.
Rowe, Hugh	B 17 Pilot, Tri Duby, October 7 rescue mission.
Ryan, Jack	Colonel, 15th AF Operations Chief.
Sasha	Russian who joined Maria and Others.
Schianca, John*	B-24 Tail Gunner, shot down, July 7.
Schmidke, Karol	Slovak Communist deputy.
Schoeneseiffen, Dr. Manfred	*Gestapo* interrogator, Mauthausen.
Schulz, Karl	SS Officer, Mauthausen.
Schwartz, Jan z	Commander, HOUSEBOAT Mission.
Sehmer, Major John y	Commander, WINDPROOF Mission

Shafer, Jack x	B-17 pilot, shot down, October 13.
Skalos, Josef	Polomka Slovak, saw capture of OSS.
Skinner, Norton**	B-17 crewman, shot down July 7.
Smith, Ethan Allen**	P-51 pilot, crash-landed, Tri Duby.
Soltesz, Frank**	P-51 pilot, shot down, July 7.
Souhrada, Colonel Jindrich	Slovak officer flown into Tri Duby.
Stanek, Major Jan	Slovak captured in the Polomka hut.
Street, Jim	B-17 Pilot, Tri Duby, October 7 rescue flight.
Strode, Sam*	B-17 Tail Gunner, shot down, July 7.
Stuart, Virgil	B-17 Radio Operator, shot down, July 7.
Studensky, Major	Leader of Soviet Mission, Banska Bystrica.
Surovec, Jan	Slovak soldier, Interpreter for DAWES team.
Tamara	Studensky's code clerk, Banska Bystrica.
Taylor, Lt. Jack	OSS Agent, DUPONT Mission, Vienna.
Thomas, Thayne*	B 17 pilot, Shot down, August 29.
Thost, Dr. Hans Wilhelm	*Gestapo* interpreter at Mauthausen.
Threlfall, Lt. Col Henry	British SOE commander, Bari.
Thun-Hohenstein, Major	Commander, *Abwehr* 218.
Tiso, Josef	President of Slovakia, World War II.
Tomes, Emil z	Civilian, DAY Mission.
Trumm, Andreas	SS Officer, Mauthausen.
Twining, General Nathan	Commanding General, 15th Air Force.
Velichko, P.A.	Soviet Officer, Commander of Partisans.
Veliteisvo	Slovak Army headquarters, Banska Bystrica.
Velky Bok	Location of SOE team above Polomka Hut.
Vesel, Lt. Col. Milan	Slovak Army, brother of Milos and Mirko.
Vesel, Lt. Col. Milos	Slovak Army, brother of Mirko and Milan.
Vesel, Lt. Col. Mirko	Slovak Army, brother of Milan and Milos.
Viest, General	Commanding General, Slovak Forces.
Volnuk, Lt. Dymko	Soviet officer with Czech brigade.
Vrto family	Family who hid DAY team members, Piest.
VRV	Slovak Underground military organization.
Watkins, Alex*	P-51 Fighter Pilot, crash-landed by Tri Duby.
Wilson, Arnold x	Member of Shafer's B-17 crew.
Wilson, Jack y	British SIS agent fleeing with OSS.
Winberg, George**	B-24 Navigator, shot down July 7.
Wisliceny, Dieter	Berlin *RSHA* Officer, Schoeneseiffen friend.
Witiska, Colonel Josef	*SS* Commander, Bratislava, Slovakia.
Wojewoda, Cecelia	Polish intellectual, Banska Bystrica.
Yeagin, Eugene x	B 17 airman, shot down, October 13.
Yegoroff, Igor	Soviet commander of Slovak Partisans.
Yezdich, Nick**	B-24 Waist Gunner shot down July 7.
Zavisa, Edwin x	B 17 airman, shot down October 13.
Zenopian, Lt. Stefan z	SOE WINDPROOF team member.
Ziereis, SS Colonel Franz	Camp Commandant, Mauthausen.
Zvara family	Hid the DAY team, Zvolenska Slatina.

Chapter 1

Blechhammer Raid

Cerova, Slovakia, July 7, 1944.

Jack Kellogg was getting edgy. With 37 missions behind him, the tension was taking its toll. He had lost several of his best friends, and he couldn't shrug off those images of crippled planes falling in spinning, flaming dives. He had seen too many four-engine bombers vaporized in fiery explosions, their crews to be "missing in action" forever.

Today the 15th Air Force was heading for Blechhammer in Upper Silesia, deep inside Germany. The roundtrip would take them through a maze of German fighters and murderous flak—500 miles each way from their Italian base – a voyage of special hell over Yugoslavia, Austria and Slovakia.

Kellogg looked out at the clear, blue sky 25,000 feet above the Czech Protectorate as he listened to the whir of the rotating top turret. Suddenly without warning, a *Messerschmitt*, diving out of the sun with guns blazing, hit their number-four outboard engine. The engine burst into flames, and Kellogg gasped as the engine cowling ripped off and, flapping wildly, wrapped around the wing.[1]

"Feather the prop," Pilot Ira Corpening shouted, as the propeller raced out of control. The wing shook violently. Stunned, Kellogg saw a piston burst out of the engine. And then another.[2]

The two pilots struggled with the controls and eased the B-17 into a wide turn. They salvoed the bomb load, and as they banked left, German fighters moved in for the kill. Luckily, an American P-51 fighter in the vicinity drove them off. But, it mattered little—the bomber was mortally wounded. And alone.

As they headed home, Sam Strode, the tailgunner, watched the rest of the formation fade away to the north. He looked around for the fighter escort.

The vibrations of the right wing increased as Corpening and Kellogg wrestled with the controls to keep the aircraft upright, although they were now losing altitude. Hearts raced and excited voices filled the intercom. Over enemy-occupied territory and hundreds of miles from their home base, the crew knew the deadly consequences of their situation. Looming in the distance, the Austrian Alps blocked their escape route. After twenty minutes, the plane had descended to 12,000 feet as the burning engine trailed smoke. The prop was running wild, and Corpening gave the command to bail out.[3]

Virgil Stuart, the radio man, was the first to jump. Corpening was the last, free-falling 10,000 feet before opening his chute. Ending up in an tree in the square of a small village, he was captured immediately.[4]

Norton Skinner, the flight engineer, watched his chute open and was surprised at how slowly he descended to earth. He looked at the countryside and saw several villages amid a panorama of irregular stands of dense woods and small farms. He could see the freshly plowed fields alternated with green crops. A few cows and sheep grazed leisurely. He had no idea he was looking down at Slovakia. He saw several chutes descending at lower altitudes to the north.[5]

Jack Kellogg, who jumped just before Corpening, also marveled at his quiet descent. He saw parachutes to the north at a lower altitude. He watched their circling plane, its engines howling and the right wing dipping, hit the ground a half mile away. The plane crashed in a cart-wheeling explosion, exploding in a boiling ball of flame. Black smoke billowed into the air. Moments later, Kellogg saw three parachutes land just north of the crash.

Kellogg saw he was going to drop into some woods about three hundred yards up the hill from the village. His chute snagged in the limbs of a tree. Hanging about eight feet above the ground, he struggled out of his harness and dropped easily to the ground and took off on the run.

Heart pumping and feet flying, Kellogg would be free for eight days in the foothills of the Male Karpaty (Lessor Carpathian) Mountains until he was captured by Hungarian militia. Two drunk Hungarians would nearly beat him to death before turning him over to German soldiers who took him to the notorious Hszalabyai prison in Budapest.

Kellogg endured 40 days of solitary confinement. His *Luftwaffe* interrogator suspected him of being an agent of the Office of Strategic Services (OSS) which puzzled Kellogg. He wouldn't learn why until years later.

Sam Strode, the tailgunner, had landed up the mountain several hundred yards from Kellogg. He would be free for three days until captured by Slovaks 15 miles south of the crash site.[6]

Norton Skinner dropped near some men working in an open field. When they saw him, they took off running. He went the other way. That night, a Slovak ran into him on a trail and took him to a house and fed him. An hour later, a policeman arrived and took him to a Slovak prison in Bratislava.

Virgil Stuart, the radio man, landed in a brushy area near some woods. He had seen German soldiers, and ran a short distance and then dropped to his hands and knees and burrowed into a thicket. The Germans ran through the woods, but couldn't find him. That night he was discovered by local villagers and spirited away to a private house. Stuart had no idea where he was, but he knew it wasn't Germany.[7]

The combat phase of the war was over for these ten Americans. The huge fleet of planes of the 15th Air Force, meanwhile, continued on. Blechhammer, a huge oil refinery complex, protected by a forest of anti-aircraft guns, awaited the Americans. *Messerschmitt* and *Focke Wulf* fighters raced through the skies, ready to take their toll of the intruders.

In tight formations the bombers doggedly stayed on course through the cruel sky as deadly flak fragments ripped through their planes, killing men and wounding others. When they passed over of the target area, desperate pilots struggled to maintain a level flight pattern in formation while their gunners braced themselves for the German fighters waiting outside the target area.

Burning planes soon filled the air, and others limped along with damaged control systems and crippled engines. The huge formation headed back across western Slovakia toward Italy. A few planes fell back, trailing smoke and falling to the earth. German troops waited on the ground, watching the chutes and biding their time.

Bombardier Neal Cobb had just dropped his ten 500 lb. bombs when flak hit the nose canopy of his B-24. A flak fragment smashed his bombsight and left a huge hole in the Plexiglas. Behind Cobb, his buddy George Wynberg was knocked against his shattered navigator's table.[8]

Coming Down At Dolny Lieskov.

Although gravely wounded, Earcel Green, Cobb's pilot, managed to pull the Liberator out of formation. He ordered Cobb, who had been wounded in the leg, to go to the back of the aircraft to man one of the guns.

Alone in the sky, the B-24 was an easy target for circling German fighters. Greene and the co-pilot managed to keep the plane flying although they steadily lost altitude. Cobb found tailgunner John Schianca lying on the deck, his leg had been broken by a piece of flak and was bleeding profusely.

Cobb remembers that the plane was flying below 1000 feet when Green finally ordered them to bail out. "Good luck to you boys" were his last words. Moments later, Cobb and the ball-turret-gunner, Andy Parker, helped Schianca out of the side hatch. Cobb shouted to Parker to bail out.

"I'm not going to go," Parker yelled back. Cobb didn't wait, and jumped clear, pulling his D-ring after a quick count of three. An instant after his chute opened, he hit the ground hard.

"I heard the plane crash and saw flames and smoke rising over a small hill a half-mile away," he remembers. "And I heard the strangest thing as I lay there – the Dolney Lieskov church bells ringing. I knew we weren't in Germany."

Unable to walk after he hit the ground, Schianca called for his friend, Parker, unaware he had died in the crash. A few minutes later, Schianca heard the voices of Slovak soldiers. They took him to the Catholic hospital in the city of Trencin, 20 miles away. Villagers buried Green, his co-pilot, and Parker near the smoldering remains of their aircraft.

Same Day, Nitra.

A few miles away in another B-24, pilot Jake Wilson and his crew knew their plane was doomed. They too had taken flak hits over the target and had fought off German fighters for 20 minutes. With only two engines still running, Wilson gave the order to bail out.

Because of a wound to his shoulder, waist gunner Bob Hede couldn't get into his parachute harness. Nick Yezdich, the other waist gunner, helped him, and then, unaware of his own wounds, Yezdich literally threw Hede out the hatch door. Tailgunner Archie LaFond went out the side hatch and was killed or knocked unconscious when he hit the tail assembly. Slovak farmers later found his body with his unopened chute.[9]

Wilson's bombardier, George Fernandes, bailed out around 5,000 feet. He landed near the edge of a small village on a mountain ridge, and almost immediately was surrounded by dozens of villagers. Fernandes saw that the people were friendly, although he was later taken into custody by a Slovak policeman.[10]

Hede and Yezdich were captured and taken to the Trencin hospital, joining Schianca and Fernandes. Slovaks buried Archie Lafond in the hospital cemetery.

The next day, Fernandes and Yezdich were taken by truck to a POW camp in Bratislava. Here they met Norton Skinner, Cobb, and approximately

20 other men. Several planes had been shot down within a 100-mile radius that day, including a P-51 piloted by Frank Soltesz. Sam Strode arrived three days later after his capture.

Howard Coleman, a tailgunner on another B-24, also remembers those dramatic events of July 7.[11]

> We were hit by flak 'real hard' over the target, then attacked by fighters. Fire started in the wings and then the intercom went out. I was the tailgunner. A shell burst knocked me into the fuselage area. My plexiglass bubble was shattered. We stayed in the air another 20 minutes, struggling to keep up with the formation but to no avail. I remember bailing out, although I don't remember pulling the D-ring. As I floated down, I saw four ME-109's in the area around me. One lined up and I thought he was going to shoot me. I was sure of it. I closed my eyes. But they left me alone.
>
> I landed in a small tree which bent to the ground like a sapling. I was free for three days—alone in the mountains. The crew landed over a 20-mile area near the city of Nitra, south of Trencin. Lying in a ravine, I heard a twig snap and saw a small boy tending to some grazing cows. Using sign language, I communicated that I was hungry, rubbing my stomach and opening my mouth. I gave him a five dollar bill and he left. Two women came back with a picnic basket filled with wonderful breads and cakes. Some men came and got me and took me to a doctor who said I needed to go to a hospital. I had been wounded in the eye. They fed me again, and I was surprised at the good treatment.
>
> The people brought two beautiful horses and a carriage and took me to an Army base. Everyone in Nitra lined up on each side of the street, it seemed, to come out to wave goodby. I thought this is what it would be like to come back to New York City. They were real friendly people. The army then took me to Bratislava. We traveled there in a wood-burning truck. Later they took me to the POW camp in Grinava where I saw some of my crew.[12]

Back in Bari, Italy, on July 8, Major General Nathan Twining had reviewed the report of the previous day's losses. The 15th Air Force had flown 35 missions with a total of 962 sorties. He had sent out 477 B-24's, 184 B-17's, 357 P-51 and P-38 fighters, most of them to Blechhammer. The *Luftwaffe* sent up 275 fighters in defense, mostly in the Vienna-Budapest corridor through which the Americans flew, going and coming. To the north over Slovakia, just under 100 fighters had challenged the American air fleet.

The day's losses included 17 B-17's and B-24's—a total of 170 men missing in action, not counting fighter pilots. For Twining, it was a routine day of high altitude bombing.[13] For Kellogg, Strode, Skinner, Fernandes, Hede, Cobb, Schianca, Coleman, and the others, the events of July 7 would never be forgotten.

When American and British airmen parachuted into Slovakia prior to September 1, 1944, they were imprisoned in Slovak, rather than German, camps. Some landed in the border region between Moravia and Slovakia and occasionally were caught in a tug of war between the Slovaks and the Germans. One might be captured by Slovak gendarmes, as Ira Corpening was, only to be handed over to the Germans. A garrison of German soldiers was near the Czech border. Norton Skinner also was captured by Slovaks, but other members of his crew who landed just a few hundred yards away were taken by Germans. A few airmen told stories of being whisked out the back door as Wehrmacht soldiers came in the front.

Near the village of Grinava in the Slovak POW camp, the prisoners settled in, hoping to sit out the war in what was, for the moment, a relaxed environment. The Soviet Red Army was advancing west, and the men believed the war would soon be over. They were unaware of the dramatic events about to unfold.

---

1 Jack Kellogg, Interview with the author, 1995.
2 Ibid.
3 Ira Corpening, Interview with the author, 1995
4 Ibid.
5 Norton Skinner, Letter to the author, 1995.
6 Juraj Rajnenic, Letter to author, 1995.
7 Clayton Metcalf, Telephone interview with the author, 1996.

8 Neal Cobb, Interview with author, August, 1998.
9 Bob Hede and Nick Yezdich, Letters to the author, 1997.
10 George Fernandes, Unpublished manuscript; Interview with the author, 1996.
11 Howard Coleman, Telephone interview with the author, 1998.
12 Ibid. Actually the Slovaks in Nitra remained loyal to the Tiso regime when the Uprising started.
13 15th Air Force Diary, Maxfield Air Force Base, Alabama.

Chapter 2

OSS Zeros in on the Slovaks

William Donovan, a prominent New York attorney and friend of President Franklin D. Roosevelt, made several trips to Europe in 1938-39. He became convinced that the United States would be drawn into the war which was about to break out there. A Medal of Honor winner in World War I, he was certain that the U.S. needed to prepare to deal with the oncoming crisis.

Donovan deplored the fact that the U.S. government had no central agency for collecting strategic intelligence. He lobbied Roosevelt early in 1941, and the President subsequently created the office of Coordinator of Information (COI), and gave the job of directing it to Donovan. This agency later evolved into the OSS.[1]

Early on, Donovan and the OSS faced several obstacles. General officers in U.S. Army combat commands, for example, traditionally were skeptical of cloak and dagger operations. This attitude was shared by the Joint Chiefs of Staff and the Army G-2 (intelligence) section. They also were not enamored with General Donovan because he was not a career officer. The officer class always was suspicious of politically connected generals. The mission of the Army, as the traditionalists saw it, centered on the infantry and the artillery. Even the Army Air Corps, for example, was suspect.

Donovan also had trouble with the British, who believed they alone among the Western Allies were able to run effective intelligence operations.

The British Secret Intelligence Service (SIS, also known as MI-6), had pre-World War I origins. Among its efforts in the 1920's, for example, was an attempt to overthrow the Bolshevik Revolution in Leningrad. The onus was on Donovan and the OSS, therefore, to prove themselves and measure up.

The British enjoyed their time-honored jests of labeling the Americans as "simple blokes" from the colonies. The SIS even viewed the newly formed British Special Operations Executive (SOE) with skepticism. The SOE was created to spread sabotage and chaos – Winston Churchill described its aims as setting Europe ablaze.

The SOE also was suspicious of the OSS. A SOE officer once grumbled that the Americans had their "God-awful academics rushing about. We have suffered more, have sacrificed more." Until they had shed blood, therefore, the efforts of the Americans would remain suspect.

Donovan in fact had recruited dozens of well-known university professors for the OSS such as William Langer and Arthur Schlesinger, Jr. Sensitive to this criticism, when the OSS personnel arrived in London throughout 1942 and 1943, the Americans kept a low profile and displayed a respectful attitude toward their hosts.

Led by Stewart Menzies, the mysterious "C," the SIS had scored a major coup by breaking the German codes with the amazing Enigma decoding device, probably the single most intelligence victory of the war. What the Americans and Menzies didn't know was that the Soviets had several espionage agents among the ranks of British intelligence. Stalin, therefore, was well informed throughout the war about what British and American intelligence operatives were up to.[2] The Americans would learn this years later.

The principal aims of the SIS, SOE and the OSS were to penetrate Germany and France, although central Europe also a prime concern. Donovan and the British eagerly sought to run missions in what was pre-war Czechoslovakia, keeping in constant contact with President Eduard Benes' Czech Government-in-Exile in London. The Czechs purported to represent all of what was pre-war Czechoslovakia, which included Slovakia, although the latter at the moment was an independent state with a government loyal to the Third Reich.

Benes' Czech Intelligence Service (CIS) regularly kept the OSS informed. In April, 1943, London OSS Branch chief, Colonel David Bruce, began meeting regularly with CIS chief Colonel Frantisek Moravec for briefings. When Captain Charles Katek arrived in London in November, 1943, to head the "Czech desk," OSS plans for Czechoslovakia began to take shape.

Katek, a charming and dynamic officer out of Northwestern University and a fluent Czech linguist, developed close rapport with Benes and Foreign Minister Jan Masaryk. Katek could approach Masaryk informally on any issue.[3] Soon after arriving in London, Katek reported that CIS personnel, including Moravec, were coming into his office two or three times a week with "various items," including German Order of Battle of information and "dossier information" on German, Polish and Czech individuals."[4] Moravec allowed Katek to read CIS radio messages from the Czech underground intended for Benes personally.[5]

February, 1944, London

Colonel Bruce saw the importance of the operations in the Mediterranean Theater of Operations (MEDTO), and ordered Katek to fly there and review plans and intelligence collection at the stations. Katek visited Algiers, Cairo, and Italy where he also met with officers of the 15th Air Force. Katek reported disappointment when his request for airlift support was rejected due to the "shortage of airfield space." Katek and the OSS would struggle continually with the Air Force generals to get adequate airlift support.

Upon his return to London, Katek began dealing with the proposed FALCON mission, determined to get agents into the Check Protectorate or Slovakia. Captain Edward Baranski in Algiers became Katek's man, drumming up support for FALCON. Lt. Colonel Edward Glavin sent him to see Colonel David Bruce in London, but here Baranski encountered problems with the British.

Baranski spoke fluent Slovak. As recently as August, 1943, he had been a lowly Air Force mess officer in Utah, overseeing menus and feeding troops. He was sent to Sicily in October, and the following month he was transferred into the OSS at Bari. As a linguist, Baranski had the ticket as well as being an aggressive, intelligent officer.

In London, Baranski discovered that the Czechs were wary about supporting the mission without the approval of the British. Baranski concluded that "British red tape" would effectively kill the mission. Frustrated, he returned to Algiers.

Operation FALCON was designed to insert two three-man teams into the Czech Republic in a joint mission. The OSS would furnish the communications set-up, signal equipment, planes, parachutes, special beaming equipment, clothing, food and medical kits needed by the field unit, as well as aid in soliciting supplies needed by the Czech underground. The CIS would furnish all conspiratory details, native clothes, passports, papers, initial reception committee, and local intelligence. The issue was whether all this coordination would come to pass.

May, 1944, Algiers, North Africa.
Returning to Algiers, Baranski lobbied vigorously for FALCON. In a lengthy memorandum, he stressed on 15 May that Czechoslovakia was the "hub of Europe" and that FALCON should be strictly an OSS operation. Lt. Colonel Glavin sent Baranski back to London a second time to meet with the CIS. Baranski was so confident FALCON would materialize that he began to draw equipment, including binoculars, Leica and Minox cameras, and a .32 caliber revolver.[6]

In London, Baranski found an enthusiastic supporter in Colonel Bruce. On 2 June, Bruce notified General Sergej Ingr, Minister of National Defense for the Czech government, that the OSS in Algiers, North Africa, desired to institute the FALCON mission with a joint Czech-American team. Bruce outlined the four objectives of FALCON: 1) To obtain Order of Battle Information on the Germans, 2) To appraise the strengths and weakness of the underground forces for the Allied commanders in order to coordinate joint military objectives, 3) To assist the Underground in soliciting supplies for the underground, and 4) To obtain political intelligence.

This discussion took place as the hectic preparations for the Normandy invasion occurred. Troops and supply convoys were converging on debarkation points along the English Channel, and all military commands were buzzing with activity.

For the OSS, Operation OVERLORD was the top priority. By the end of May, the OSS had notified Eisenhower's headquarters that 571 rail targets in France had been targeted for destruction. Also, in the days before and after the invasion, 13 so-called "Jedburgh" teams, each consisting of a Frenchman, an Englishman and an American, were dropped into France.[7] These teams had special sabotage missions designed to delay the movements of German troops once the invasion had begun. FALCON was shelved for the time being.

The OSS also was readying its teams for counterintelligence operations in Normandy to coincide with the Allied advances into France. Then on June 6, D Day, the biggest amphibious invasion in history was launched, and the OSS was running missions at a furious pace.

June 20, 1944.

Two weeks later, General Ingr finally replied to Colonel Bruce about FALCON, suggesting that Bruce notify "appropriate British circles in this matter," reiterating the Czech position which disappointed Baranski in March. As a small nation, Ingr wrote, "We must undertake nothing in the above mentioned matter without the knowledge of our other Great Allies."[8] Those were to become significant words.

Bruce reviewed with Baranski the issues relating to the Czech concerns while General Donovan was again in London. The Americans realized the

London Czechs dared not offend the British for getting them out [of Czechoslovakia] in March, 1939. A few days later Donovan left for Algiers and then returned to the United States. He was dealing with dozens of issues.

The formal British SIS reaction to FALCON was made by Lt. Commander Edward Cohen, one of the senior SIS officers. Cohen said the British opposed FALCON because it would jeopardize missions currently underway in Czechoslovakia. In all, the SIS and SOE currently had eight teams operating in the Czech Republic.

Colonel Bruce, meanwhile, enjoyed great rapport with his two British counterparts, Gubbins and Stewart Menzies. Bruce's diaries[8] refer to lunches and dinner parties with these men at such elegant spots as the Savoy, the Connaught, the Waldorf and Claridges. Although these were congenial social meetings, Bruce was not able to budge the British on key issues such as FALCON.[9]

In two successive days, Katek and Baranski met with SIS Lt. Commander Cohen and got a wavering response the first day and a negative one on the next. Katek grumbled in a memo that the British were exploiting to "full measure" the fact that the Czechs owe their lives to the British."[10]

Katek and Baranski, although both dismayed by the British, stubbornly refused to drop the plan. On June 22, Katek met again with General Ingr and Colonel Moravec. Moravec told Katek that the British suggested to him that he inform the Americans he disapproved of the mission.

As Baranski's frustration mounted, he suggested to his superiors that the OSS embark on the mission alone, arguing that the OSS would be burdened indefinitely with the British. The next day Katek and Baranski notified Colonel Glavin, now stationed in Caserta, that FALCON was still stalemated. Three days later Baranski left for Algiers after urging Glavin and his superiors to solicit General Donovan's help.

Donovan was furious. On 30 June, he wrote to Menzies, the SIS chief, "The [British decision] is incomprehensible and the reasons offered by Commander Cohen are [invalid]." Donovan's intemperate tone was characteristic of his aggressive style.[11] Baranski, fully aware of the intensity of Donovan's reaction, was energized again to save his mission.

July 7.

Colonel Bruce's staff was informed by Menzies that SIS did not oppose FALCON, but that the Czechs weren't in favor of it. "That sounds like hooey!" one OSS officer concluded. And, of course, he was right.

General Donovan had other problems. He was fuming over the French criticism of American aid to the French Underground. The hostile comments, direct from General Charles DeGaulle's headquarters, stated that British aid to the French Underground was "ten-times greater" than American aid. Although this was an exaggeration, the OSS indeed had been handicapped by inadequate airlift support by the 8th Air Force, although through no fault of Donovan.[12]

The peripheral impact of the stinging French criticism affected decisions regarding the Slovaks. Donovan was motivated to approve aggressive missions wherever and whenever in order to enhance the credibility and raise the profile of the OSS. Slovakia now was on the planning boards, and Donovan was determined to become a key player throughout Europe, especially in the Balkans and eastern Europe.[13]

Donovan's relations with the French had been exacerbated by the personal hostility between Roosevelt and DeGaulle, the head of the Free French forces. After Donovan was in France in May and June, and following the Normandy invasion, he had returned to Washington to attempt to heal the breach between FDR and DeGaulle. Later in July, Donovan returned to Europe and met with OSS personnel in Caserta and Algiers. There he learned "We are no longer welcome by the French."[14] Later, relations with French would deteriorate to the point where DeGaulle's government would ask the OSS people to leave Paris.

Poland, meanwhile, had an oblique impact on plans for Slovakia. Donovan was dismayed by the Soviet reaction to the Warsaw Uprising. The

Uprising began on August 1, and Donovan immediately pressured both Washington and London to support the desperate Poles. But, Roosevelt was in no frame of mind to allow the Polish question to dislodge Allied unity and imperil the chances of getting the USSR to join the proposed United Nations Organization.[15]

As Donovan steamed about the failure to give aid to the Poles, Lt. Colonel H.B. Perkins of the SOE in London met with Frank Roberts of the British Foreign Office. "We pointed out to Roberts that it was necessary to exercise care to prevent British aid to the Slovaks from injuring Polish feelings," Perkins wrote. Roberts replied that conversely the Slovaks could say the same thing about Polish aid.[16] This paralysis in the decision making process often was typical, sadly, of Allied decision making.

The Russians, meanwhile, now knew clearly where Donovan and the OSS stood and that he had been pushing policies and operations inimical to their interests.[17] As a result, the Russians ceased to cooperate fully with the OSS, a fact noted by OSS officer Robert Joyce in Caserta.[18] And the State Department, seeking to maintain good relations with Moscow, was troubled with Donovan's aggressive stance vis-à-vis the Russians.[19]

July, Italian Peninsula.

The indefatigable Baranski, meanwhile, began checking in Algiers among OSS personnel for individuals who could join the reconstituted FALCON mission. Czech linguists were in short supply. Also, Baranski suggested changing the name of the mission "to another bird" and therefore circumvent British censure. He wanted to go forward without Czech involvement. Throughout July, Baranski stewed over FALCON, seeking potential team members and continuing to lobby his superiors for support. But FALCON was dead, and Baranski subsequently had to find another mission. Frustrated, he later joined the ill-fated TOLEDO mission into Yugoslavia.[20]

Awaiting transport for Yugoslavia, Lt. Colonel Glavin authorized Baranski to make an eight-day trip to visit prisoner of war camps in Italy to find recruits for a Slovak mission. Slovaks who had defected to the *Wehrmacht* were held by the U.S, Army, and Glavin believed some would volunteer to work with the OSS. The trip was unproductive.

Undaunted by the failure of FALCON and other problems, meanwhile, Charles Katek left London for a swing through the Mediterranean to test the waters for other potential Czech and Slovak missions. He conferred with the SOE and also with Colonel Moravec before he left London.[21]

Katek wanted to organize missions into Yugoslavia, the Balkans and Slovakia. The dynamics of the region provided both the OSS and the SOE with a theater of operations where special forces could be successful. The Germans had occupied Greece, Yugoslavia and Romania in 1942. Civil Wars erupted in both Greece and Yugoslavia by 1943 where rival factions fought each other as vigorously as they did the Germans.

The Soviets, backing Communist organizations in both countries, were the wild cards in Yugoslavia and Greece. The left-wing EAM-ELAS insurgent group in Greece was threatening that country. In Yugoslavia, the Partisans were weak in 1943, but with the assistance of the Soviets, gained strength the following year. The British made the decision to back Tito, causing consternation among the OSS staff in Bari which was divided over whom to support.[22] To the north in Slovakia, Partisan groups were led by Soviet officers, although with less success than those directed by Tito in Yugoslavia. Tito and his rivals, the *Chetniks* continued meanwhile to seek both British and American aid. In the end, OSS Bari was forbidden to give any aid to the *Chetniks* which infuriated many of the OSS staff.[23]

August, 1944, Bucharest, Romania.

The OSS in Bari began to focus on retrieving American POW's in Romania. The Romanians under King Michael broke with the Third *Reich* on August 23 just as the Red Army was rolling into the country. Over 1300 American airmen had been detained in Romania, and the task of bringing them back to Italy was the type of mission close to the hearts of the 15th Air

Force. There had developed a strong bond between the 15th and the OSS over the retrieval operations in Yugoslavia where hundreds of airmen had been returned through the cooperation of both the Partisans and Chetniks. Some had been flown out on C-47's from the island of Vis and others had been ferried across the Adriatic on small boats. Now, the operation to Bucharest loomed as another spectacular success.

The 15th Air Force, meanwhile, was shifting its strategic bombing operations north to the synthetic oil refineries located in Silesia. Stiff *Luftwaffe* resistance knocked down numerous planes forcing Allied air crews to parachute out over the Czech Protectorate and Slovakia. The CIS was filtering reports of downed Allied airmen to London, and the OSS passed them on to the 15th Air Force headquarters.

Major Walter Ross, an administrative officer in the operations office in Bari, led the initial flight to Romania, and the mission went off smoothly. Bari concluded that a similar type mission to Slovakia, if done right, could be equally successful. Additionally, the OSS would be able to insert intelligence teams there to collect information for the Allied forces.

Hence, both the British and the Americans in London, Caserta, and Bari took another look at expanding intelligence operations in Slovakia where Partisans already were waging limited war against small Wehrmacht units and the Slovak National Uprising was beginning.

This was all taking place without the knowledge of the American airmen on the ground in Slovakia. Behind the wire at Grinava prisoner of war camp, Lieutenants George Fernandes and Neal Cobb and Sergeants Richard Moulton, John Schianca, Norton Skinner and others would soon benefit from clandestine events about to happen. The drama was about to begin.

---

1 OSS Against the Reich, *The World War II Diaries of Colonel David K.E. Bruce* (The Kent State University Press, Kent, Ohio, 1991), p. 11.

2 Chapman Pincher, *Their Trade is Treachery* (Sidgwick and Jackson, London, 1981). See Pincher's general discussion.

3 National Archives II (hereinafter NARA), RG 226, Entry 190, Box 171.

4 Edward Baranski, Report, July, 1944, NARA, RG 226, Entry 190, Box 171.

5 Ibid.
6 Ibid.
7 Edward Hymoff, *The OSS in World War II: The True Story of American Agents Behind American Lines* (New York: Richardson and Steirman, 1986), p. 246.
8 OSS Against the Reich, pp. 21, 25, 79.
9 Ibid.
10 NARA. Baranski, Report, July, 1944.
11 Edwin Putzell, a close aide to Donovan, recalled the General's chagrin 56 years later. Putzell, Letter to the author, December 9, 2000.
12 Anthony Cave Brown, *The Last Hero, Will Bill Donovan* (Times Books, New York City, 1982).
13 Ibid.
14 Ibid.
15 Author's MA thesis, *American-British-Soviet Relations Relative to the Soviet Union, March to August, 1945* (San Jose State University, 1959).
16 British Public Records Office (PRO), HS 4/40.
17 Donovan believed that the OSS could have success in central Europe where the British could not. Edwin Putzell, Telephone conversation with the author, December 19, 2000.
18 Brown, pp. 622-23. The OSS sent in the TOLEDO mission in late August to Yugoslavia. The Yugoslavs suddenly became uncooperative. Heretofore, they had been friendly, but abruptly changed their stance.
19 Ibid. p. 623.
20 NARA, Baranski, RG 226, Entry 190, Box 171.
21 Ibid.
22 George Vujnovich, E mail to the author, May 15, 2001; See Chapter 6 for a discussion of Lt. Holt Green's view of Tito's Partisans.
23 George Vujnovich, E mail to the author.

Chapter 3

Slovak Uprising Breaks Out

1939, Slovakia.

Adolf Hitler held all Slavs in contempt, and he also hated democracy. For the *Führer*, Czechoslovakia was anathema on both counts, prompting Hitler to devise a plan to control both the Czechs and the Slovaks. He concluded that the Slovaks would tolerate an alliance with the Third *Reich* in exchange for a measure of independence. In Josef Tiso, Hitler found a Slovak premier willing to go along. Then, he created the Czech Protectorate under tight German control. The latent tensions between Slovaks and Czechs would be rekindled in a way to serve Hitler's purposes.[1]

Tiso, a former Catholic Monsignor, proceeded in 1939 to create a police state, utilizing the black-uniformed *Hlinka* Guardists as the enforcers to suppress "the enemies of the state." Slovaks accepted the Tiso government because it was their first taste of independence in 1000 years.[2] Alas, it also appealed to a fascist, anti-Semitic element in Slovak society.

Tiso's deal with Hitler stipulated that Slovakia would be free of foreign troops, convincing the Slovaks they would escape the ravages of war with only small *Wehrmacht* detachments stationed in Bratislava and other cities. On the negative side, Tiso's willingness to send Slovak men – two divisions — to the Russian front to fight and die for the Third Reich produced simmering discontent.

In a mostly Roman Catholic nation of 5.5 million people, some Slovaks even today are hesitant to be overly critical of Tiso, reasoning that he did the best he could at the time to prevent the Germans from destroying their country. Others regard Tiso as a traitor and a willing accomplice of Hitler. After the war, the Czechoslovak government drew the same conclusion, trying him as a war criminal and sending him to the gallows.

Most Slovaks despised the Germans, and also harbored old grievances against the Czechs. When the fortunes of war began to turn in late 1943, a group of Slovaks began to plot a break from the Third *Reich*. By the Spring of 1944, as the Red Army advanced through Poland and into central Europe, the Slovak conspirators stepped up their activity. Thanks to a number of Communists in key positions in the underground, the Russians were keenly aware of the political climate in Slovakia.

The Underground Organizes.

By the end of 1943 The Slovaks' secret organization, the Military Revolutionary Command (*Vojenske revoucne velitelstvo — VRV*), was a functioning organization headed by Lt. Colonel Mirko Vesel. The Slovak National Council (SNC) was secretly in place by December in Banska Bystrica, working in tandem with the military group.[3]

> The *VRV*, which later merged with the military, had five goals:
>
> Re-establish Czechoslovakia with two equivalent nationalities.
> Assist the Allies in defeating Germany.
> Attempt to avoid the physical destruction of Slovakia.
> Bring about a democratic government.
> Position *VRV* units to aid the Red Army in crossing the Carpathian Mountains and sweep westward to Vienna.[4]

The OSS in London, meanwhile, was receiving from its CIS sources in Slovakia regular reports about the *VRV* and the SNC. Captain Charles Katek directed Blahoslav Hruby, an OSS analyst, to prepare a report on the leading Slovak political personalities. Katek wanted to know exactly with whom he might be dealing if the OSS sent teams into the country. Hruby concluded the SNC was dominated by the Agrarians, Communists, and a few Social Democrats.

Hruby identified several of the leaders: Vavro Srobar, Jan Ursiny, Josef Lettrich, Karol Smidke, a Communist deputy in the Czechoslovak parliament who had fled to the Soviet Union; Gustav Husak, a Communist; and Laco Novomesky, a well-known poet and Communist.[5]

July, 1944.

In late July, British agents interviewed a Slovak defector in Italy. This man (un-identified in the SOE records) believed that Srobar was a democrat who spoke for the middle class, and that Ursiny, in his role as leader of the Peasant Party, was an ally of the Communists. The defector maintained that the Communists were attempting to control the Partisans. The latter were guerrilla forces, a few organized by Slovaks but most organized and led by Russians. Hence, some of the Partisan units adhered to Slovak army discipline; most did not.

As early as April, the Ukrainian Communist Party, with Moscow's blessing, began organizing partisan groups for action in Slovakia. In July, an eleven-man team led by Red Army Captain P.A. Velichko parachuted into the Ruzomberok area. Several more Russian groups jumped into Slovakia in August. They all reported to Marshall Koniev in Kiev.[6]

The Soviets also had been organizing a Czech Parachute Brigade made up of mostly Slovaks. Moscow was determined to play a major role in the liberation of Slovakia, but on their terms. The Soviet officers who had parachuted into Slovakia had no intention of submitting to the discipline of the Slovak commanders, and immediately began attacks on German army and Hlinka Guard outposts. These attacks concerned the *VRV*. They regarded them as undisciplined actions. The Slovaks worried about precipitating the Uprising prematurely.[7]

July 26, London.

The CIS reported to Katek that a Partisan attack on German troops in a train station on July 26 took place with high loss of life on both sides. That same day an *SS* armored division arrived in eastern Slovakia from Hungary. A *Gestapo* group of 26 men, plus a large transport of *Luftwaffe* personnel and equipment, had arrived five days later at Nitra, southwest of Banska Bystrica.[8] The German representatives in Bratislava became alarmed and requested that Berlin institute plans to crush the Partisans immediately.[9]

The Germans, now aware of what was happening, stepped up their defensive operations. By July they established several supply depots in the country. Additionally, they inserted 250 intelligence personnel in Banska Bystrica alone.[10] This concerned the Slovaks who requested the Benes government to contact the Partisans to ask them to stop provoking the Germans. London replied that they had no direct lines of communication with the Partisans.[11] This was an indication of the state of affairs in Slovakia: a mixture of separate commands, coupled with an entangled and inadequate communication system.

On August 16 in London, Katek met with Colonel Moravec, seeking recommendations about possible OSS operations in Slovakia. Moravec replied that his sources of information reported that the "Czech Forces of the Interior (CFI)", as the British called them, and the Partisans needed medical supplies, arms and ammunition. The colonel had asked the British for the same aid. Moravec reported he was receiving several radio communications daily from four different locations from within Slovakia.[12]

OSS, SOE Both Promise Aid.

Katek told Moravec, the Czech intelligence officer, that aid would be forthcoming. But he went further and informed Moravec that the Americans hoped to "have their own people in place" inside Czechoslovakia after the war.[13] Katek clearly was reflecting the direction of General Donovan's thinking. In this context, Moravec informed Katek that the British ambassador in

Moscow had been told by the Russians "to go slow" in Czechoslovakia.[14] The Soviets wanted no Allied interference, now or later.

Moravec's request of aid surprised Lt. Colonel Perkins of the SOE. He informed the British War Office, observing, "It is strange that they should ask us for this assistance when it would presumably be easier for them to obtain it from the East."[15] This statement betrayed an appalling innocence about Russian intentions and total ignorance of the Soviet-backed Partisan movement.

Across Europe, the Allied successes began to affect Slovak public opinion. Despite the press blackout, the news of the German defeat at Stalingrad, the rout of Rommel's Afrika Korps, the invasion of Italy, the Normandy invasion and the successful campaign in Southern France reverberated throughout the country. Those Slovaks, who had been luke warm about supporting the Germans, now believed that political disaster awaited them if they didn't make a clean break from Hitler.

Slovak troops under Wehrmacht command in Russia had been deserting to the Red Army, and now in Slovakia, men were slipping away to join Partisan units. Meanwhile, the Red Army had reached the Baltic states and were advancing into Poland. The fluid military situation in eastern Europe led the OSS to conclude that conditions were ripe for inserting a mission into Slovakia.

The Slovak military leader, Colonel Jan Golian, and the *VRV*, meanwhile, had not yet picked a date for the Uprising to begin because they hoped to coordinate their campaign with the advance from Poland of the Red Army through the Carpathians. At the beginning of August, the *VRV* sent Lt. Colonels Mikulas Ferjencik and Karol Smidke to the Soviet Union to coordinate a strategy for joint operations.

In Moscow, the delegation had difficulty reaching agreement with their hosts. The issue was political not military. Simply put, Moscow wanted a "revolutionary struggle" to break out in Slovakia and eastern Europe. The Kremlin was concerned that a "bourgeois state" system would emerge from the war, and in Czechoslovakia, it would be led by the Benes government. That, of course, was exactly what the *VRV* intended. Moscow was counting on the Partisan groups in Slovakia, which they planned to control, to initiate the "revolutionary struggle" in a way the "progressives" (Communists) would triumph.[16]

Nevertheless, the Slovaks and Soviets reached an agreement that the uprising would begin when the Russians broke through the Carpathians in eastern Slovakia. Hopefully, that would occur by the end of August.

But the Partisans didn't wait. They began ambushing German columns, attacking police stations, and blowing up bridges. Was it because they were undisciplined, or were they simply following orders from Marshall Koniev in Kiev who was adhering to Moscow's directions?

German reaction, although restrained, was immediate. Nevertheless, the arrival of additional troops further exacerbated the revolutionary situation.[17] Following his meeting with the German ambassador in Bratislava on August 24, Tiso urged Berlin to expedite the arrival of larger units.[18]

The British again promised additional military aid to the *VRV*. The Soviets astonished the Slovaks by appearing to drag their feet, leaving them angered and dismayed. Stalin was not interested in assisting any military force in Slovakia he could not control.

August 27-29, 1944.

The Tiso government's state-controlled radio began broadcasting accounts of Partisan activity: the murder of six policemen in one town and the plundering of shops and stores in several other villages and towns. The most sensational incident occurred when Soviet Captain P.A. Velichko's Partisan group stopped the Budapest-to-Berlin train in the Turcansky Sv. Martin station, removed a German colonel and 16 members of his staff, and murdered them the next day. Partisans also were alleged to have murdered a group of ethnic German Slovaks in the town of Turany on the Vah River.[19]

The incident in Martin infuriated the Germans, and Berlin ordered stepped up military operations to crush the Uprising. Two days later, Slovak Army leaders arrived at their headquarters building in Banska Bystrica only to find the building controlled by pro-German Slovak officers. After a short fight, the *VRV* group seized the building.

There was no turning back now. Colonel Golian and his staff nominated Lt. Colonel Mirko Vesel to prepare a political statement proclaiming the Uprising. Golian was promoted to the rank of general as excitement rose as units of the Slovak Army began defecting to the rebel cause. Soon, a large area of central Slovakia was in rebel hands.

That night, Mirko Vesel and his two brothers, Milos and Milan, drove north to Donovaly where they joined Vavro Srobar and their uncle, Ludvik Nabelek, MD. The next day, Mirko Vesel and another member of the committee sat down to produce an agenda for the Slovak nation. After working through the night, they broadcast the statements to the nation, announcing the re-establishment of a united Czechoslovakia and proclaiming war against the Germans. Also, they made an emotional appeal to the nation to resist the enemy invasion.[20]

In Moscow, the announcement produced no response. The Kremlin was not pleased. The promise of a united, democratic – hence, a "bourgeois" — Czechoslovakia was not part of their plans.

Slovak Military Hit by Confusion.

In the wake of these events, confusion gripped several Slovak unit commanders. One Slovak colonel, the deputy corps commander, left his troops –two divisions —to travel alone without notice to Kiev to confer with Marshall Koniev. The bulk of the Slovak army was in eastern Slovakia, and it was here General Golian anticipated his troops would make a vigorous attack and link up with the Red Army. However, a German panzer division attacked the Slovaks and disarmed them within 24 hours. Some troops escaped to join the Partisans, while some of the officers went over to the Germans. The fiasco cost the Slovaks hundreds of lives.[21]

There were other Slovak military disasters. Garrisons in Bratislava, Nitra, and Trencin refused to join the Uprising. The London Czech government frantically asked Moscow to rush in the Czech Parachute Brigade. The Soviets hesitated, although on September 2, Moscow ordered Koniev to initiate an attack on German lines. The Russians immediately attempted to drive through the narrow Dukla Pass.

General Golian and his Slovak army, the "CFI," as they were referred to by the Allies, were plunging into a heroic, although desperate, rebellion. Although they didn't realize it, their destiny was in the hands of forces they could neither influence nor control. Eager to forge a postwar democratic state and hopeful that the Great Powers would support them, the Slovaks failed to anticipate the furious German military response. The Germans rushed troops into the Dukla Pass, surrounded Koniev's spearhead, and scored a crushing victory. The Russians suffered horrendous casualties.[22]

The Slovak populace, already holding divided views of the war, greeted the news of the Uprising with less than universal approval. Catholic communities generally supported the Tiso regime, and Catholic civilians occasionally reported evading Allied airmen to the authorities. The Partisans, and also downed Allied airmen, tended to find more support in the Lutheran communities, some allege. There were many instances, however, where Catholic churches and communities gave substantial aid to the airmen.[23]

The U.S. 15th Air Force, meanwhile, flying roundtrips through Slovak airspace, stepped up its relentless bombing attacks on the synthetic oil refineries in Silesia. With increasing frequency, the Slovaks watched American and British bombing fleets flying round-the-clock missions. Often the people would see lone, burning planes heading south. They frequently saw *Luftwaffe* fighters attack the bombers. Civilians – and Partisans — often watched the descent of the parachutes, and whenever possible, aided and subsequently hid the airmen. Because of German reprisals, it was a risky business.

Another factor in the political mix were the so-called *Karpatendeutsche*,

Slovak Uprising Breaks Out 31

the 150,000 ethnic Germans, in Slovakia. They occupied clusters of villages near Bratislava and also in the Handlova region west of Banska Bystrica. Other communities were in the northeast near the Polish border. A number of these towns and villages had been German since the 14th Century. Although the people all spoke Slovak, the German language was used exclusively in these German regions, which the Germans called "*Sprachinseln*" (language islands). Ethnic Slovaks had lived peacefully in the German communities for hundreds of years.

Hence, enthusiasm for independence might be soaring in one village, while a few miles away in another village, pro-Tiso Slovaks were feeling anger and chagrin. Idealism and cynicism existed side by side, producing a troubling national chemistry which simultaneously provoked patriotism and betrayal.[24]

Ethnic German Civilians Murdered.

The potential for internecine warfare was strong, and according to some German and Austrian observers today, the Soviets and left wing Slovaks eagerly exploited it. The Russian and Ukrainians leaders of the Partisan groups had a special hatred for all Germans.

The few *Karpatendeutsche* survivors in the postwar period (and some still alive today) later described the mass murder of German civilians, mostly older men and boys. In Slovakia, Germans discovered they were doomed by their national origin rather than their alleged or established sympathies for the Reich.[25] The hatred sewn by the brutal treatment of the Russian people by the Nazis on the eastern front now was inflicted upon the innocent Karpatendeutsche.

Examples of murder abounded. In the German communities in the so-called Hauerland area west of Banska Bystrica, the Partisans killed 30 civilians in Deutsch-Proben (Nitrianski Pravno today), 72 in Hochwies-Paulisch (Velke Pole-Pila), 130 in Krickerhau (Handlova), 187 in Glaserhau (Sklene), and 143 in Rosenberg (Ruzomberok).[26] In Glaserhau, the men were shot after being forced to dig their own graves.[27]

After the war, the Czechoslovak government blamed the atrocities on German *SS* units, but by the 1990's, 176 mass graves had been identified in the Hauerland and elsewhere in Slovakia which clouded the issue. These crimes probably had been committed by persons other than Germans. Altogether, nearly 4,000 human remains have been recovered from these mass graves.[28]

One atrocity in September, 1944, came to the attention of Major John Sehmer who notified his British SOE superiors in Bari.[29] A Partisan group reportedly had executed 150 *Volksdeutsche* working on a Slovak army defense line, a senseless act, Sehmer reported, and the Slovak military promptly had executed those Partisans responsible.[30]

In Bratislava, the German authorities reacted to the atrocities. The commander of *Einsatzgruppe H*, *SS* Colonel Josef Witiska, warned publicly he would take "an eye for an eye and a tooth for a tooth," which guaranteed there later would be bloodshed on both sides.[31] No one doubts the crimes Witiska's troops committed.

The German army, meanwhile, continued to pour troops into Slovakia. The Slovak landscape was dotted with *Wehrmacht* columns of horse-drawn artillery and infantry. In Banska Bystrica, General Golian and his staff marshaled their ill-prepared troops into a defensive perimeter, armed more with hope than fire power. Battles soon raged in different locales as the Slovaks fought desperately. Men and civilians died, first by the dozens, later by the hundreds, and before the Uprising concluded, by the thousands. The innocent, as in all wars, were caught in the crossfire. Advancing on Banska Bystrica, the Germans left a trail of mayhem and burning villages.

---

1 Igor Nabelek has pointed out to the author that prior to the 20th Century, the Slovaks suffered under Hungarian control and looked to the Czechs as "brothers." Igor Nabelek, E mail to the author, July, 2001.

2 Charles Kliment and Bretislav Nakladal, *Germany's First Ally* (Schiffer Publishing Ltd., Atglen, PA., 1997), p. 109.

3 Igor Nabelek, E mail to the author, 1999.

4 Nabelek. E Mail.
5 NARA, RG 226, Entry 190, Box 575, Folder 372; Although the above-mentioned political figures played key roles in the politics of the Uprising and later in the post-war government, they had only a minimal relationship with the Anglo-American intelligence personnel subsequently sent into Slovakia.
6 John Erickson, *Road To Berlin* (New Haven: Yale University Press, 1999), pp. 292-293.
7 Ibid.; The Soviets installed 230 Partisan instructors and political officers into Slovakia in 1944, Paul Strassmann, Lecture.
8 NARA, RG 226, Entry 190, Box 575, Folder 372.
9 Kliment and Nakladal, p. 92.
10 Kliment and Nakladal, pp. 92-93.
11 John Erickson, Road to Berlin, P. 295.
12 NARA, RG 226, Entry 190, Box 575, Folder 372.
13 Ibid.
14 Ibid.
15 Later, as the problems of the on-coming Cold War arose, Perkins would learn why.
16 John Erickson, Road To Berlin, p. 295. See Erickson's discussion of the Slovak National Uprising, pp. 291-307.
17 Kliment and Nakladal p. 92.
18 Ibid.
19 British Public Record Office (PRO), Major John Sehmer to SOE, Bari, HS4/27; Kliment and Nakladal, p. 93; The Germans may have been coming from Romania through Budapest. Also, the actual murders may have been committed by a Slovak army officer who was taking orders from Velichko.
20 Ibid.
21 Nabelek, E Mail to the author.
22 John Erickson, Road To Berlin, pp. 300-301.
23 A former Partisan, who wishes to remain anonymous, reported this in detail to the author in 1999. Other Slovaks challenge this view, insisting that there was widespread support of the Americans and the Partisans by Catholics.
24 Maria Gulovich recalls in 1939 through 1944 in her Slovak home town of Stara L'Ubovna that a few Germans proudly wore *Swastika* armbands around the town, much to the chagrin of most Slovaks. Telephone interview with the author, November 15, 2000.
25 Paul Brosz, *Das letzte Jahrhundert der Karpatendeutschen in der Slowakei* (Stuttgart: *Arbetitsgemeinschaft der Karpatendeutschen*, 1992); Rudolf Melzer, *Erlebte Geschichte, Vol. II* (Vienna: *Karpatendeutsche Landsmannschaft Oesterreich*, 1996. Brosz's book is titled The Last Century of the Carpathian Germans in Slovakia, and Melzer's book is Lived History. According to Dr. Thomas Reimer, Empire State University, some former Partisans such as Anton Rasla in *Civilista 5. Armada* (1967), wrote that "every German was seen as a spy and the enemy."
26 Broz, pp. 62-63; Melzer, pp. 491-495. These authors describe the account of two young Slovak-Germans who, although shot, survived mass murders by Slovak Partisans. Josef Poess was shot on September 21, 1944 in Glaserhau (Sklene) where nearly 200 died. Anton Prokein survived, although badly wounded, the mass murder of 72 people in Liptovska Luzna. Information and translation of Brosz and Melzer courtesy of Dr. Reimer.
27 Gypsies, according to one account, who lived on the fringes of the German communities, now found the Germans "fair game" and joined in the looting of German properties. They would, of course, later suffer the retribution of the *SS. Rudolf Melzer, Erlebte Geschichte* (Vienna: *Karpatendeutsche Landsmannschaft in Österrich*, 1996) p. 503.
28 Ibid. In 1984, the newspaper Praca blamed the Glaserhau massacre on Germans. Some intellectuals supported this view. Melzer has taken strong objection to this interpretation. In the early 1990's the

government of Prime Minister Carnogursky was willing to consider the controversy surrounding the 1944-45 deaths of the Germans. Later, Slovak public pressure ended the debate, especially after 1993 when August 29, the anniversary of the start of the Uprising, was declared a national holiday. Some Slovak intellectuals still challenge this view in Slovakia, however. Dr. Ondrej Poess in Bratislava, where he heads the Carpathian German section of the Slovak National Museum, has asserted that the only real guilt of the German victims in 1944-45 was "that they were born Germans."

29 PRO, HS 4/40; Kliment and Nakladal, p. 93.
30 PRO, HS 4/40.
31 Rudolf Melzer, *Erlebte Geschichte* (Vienna: *Karpatendeutsche Landsmannschaft in Österrich*, 1996) p. 494; Witiska was under the direct command of the RSHA in Berlin, and took no orders from the General Höefle who commanded the SS units crushing the Uprising.

Chapter 4

On The Loose

June, 1944.

Things had not turned out the way Sergeant Richard Moulton expected. His crew had flown their shiny new B-24 all the way from Florida to South America, across the Atlantic to Dakar and then up to Algiers. When they arrived at their base in Italy, a veteran crew took their plane, leaving them with one of the squadron's "dogs." The crew noted ruefully the several hundred patches on their new plane where German flak and machine gun fire had found their mark. They wondered, how would this Liberator fly?[1]

On their second mission, June 26, Moulton's B-24 was positioned in the rear element of a 650-plane raid. Inbound toward the target, an oil refinery east of Vienna, their number three engine began to backfire as the pilot and the flight engineer struggled to keep it running.

A few minutes later, a second engine began coughing. They began losing power precipitously, and soon were stragglers in a hostile environment. Almost immediately four *Messerschmitt* 109's jumped them, and shot up the right wing. With one of his gas tanks burning, pilot Lincoln Artz ordered the crew to bail out.

Richard Moulton hit the ground hard, still groggy after striking his head when he left the plane. They were near the Slovak-Hungarian border, and Hungarian militia captured him a few minutes later. One of the soldiers ripped off Moulton's dog tags. This would cause him problems later.

But in the midst of disaster, Artz' crew got lucky. Slovak troops rushed on the scene and, insisting the prisoners were theirs, carted them off to Bratislava, the Slovak capital, a few miles away.

The prisoners were treated so well in their Bratislava prison that the local pro-German mayor insisted they be moved out of the city to another camp. George Fernandes, the B-24 bombardier, recalls his surprise when civilians smuggled him bottles of beer and ice cream through the bars of the jail. The Americans soon realized that not all Slovaks were their enemies.

July, Grinava.

A month later, the prisoners were transferred 18 miles north to a camp at Grinava. Here, life was still beautiful. The prisoners were allowed to swim at a nearby quarry where they mingled with the local people. Other days they were allowed to venture outside the fence to play volleyball. This was hardly *Stalag 17*.

A trip to a wine cellar in Modra, eight miles away, was a treat the prisoners would never forget. They were transported in a bakery truck that made several runs to get them all to the party. Fernandes remembers being served bread, cheese and cold cuts—and lots of wine poured from oak barrels. There had been talk of escape, but no one was in condition to make a break for it. Some wondered, "why?"

On another evening the Slovak camp officials threw a party for the prisoners where the men consumed generous portions of Slivovica, a local favorite made from plum brandy. There were "noisy and frequent toasts." The men were not required to go on work details. Moulton and Lincoln Artz played bridge daily in a foursome including Nick Yezdich.

Among the prisoners at Grinava were a feisty New Zealander and a Brit who was a member of the Scots Guards.

Gordon Follas might have stepped off some Hollywood set when he arrived at Grinava. He and his buddy, David McSorley, the Scots Guardsman, charmed their new "Bloody Yank" friends with wild, colorful stories. Follas admitted to a spotty military record and to being twice reduced in rank for insubordination. He was a free-spirited, fiercely independent Aucklander. Follas had fought in North Africa, Greece, and Crete. He had killed German paratroopers in Crete and participated on a mission to assassinate Field Marshal Erwin Rommel in North Africa. The mission ended in failure when Follas and others were captured near Tobruk in June, 1942.

As a prisoner, Follas had been an instant and constant problem for his captors. His first escape attempt failed when he was shot and wounded. After a short stay in an Italian POW camp, the Germans sent him to *Stalag VIIIA* in Germany where he met McSorley. They immediately set to work hatching an escape plan. Transferred to *Stalag VIIIB*, they and two other men volunteered for a work detail in a mine, *Arbeits Kommando 768* at Kumau. On June 28, they gained access to the Red Cross stores and broke through two locked doors. Outside, they broke through a hole in a high masonry wall which they previously had weakened by removing several bricks.

They struck out for Hungary, going through Slovakia. Two weeks later, they made contact with Slovaks who promised a guide to lead them to Yugoslavia. After three weeks of impatient waiting, Follas and McSorley started out on their own and almost immediately were captured by Slovak police. They claimed to be downed airmen and wound up in Grinava. Their account illustrated that many Slovaks were ready to support the Allies, but some weren't.

George Fernandes, Neal Cobb, Richard Moulton and several others became fast friends with both Follas and "Scotty" McSorley. They traded stories and laughs, and at the famous and unbelievable wine party, they celebrated until they could barely stand.

By prisoner of war standards, life at Grinava was idyllic and incredible. As the days wore on, most of the men were content to wait out the war, enjoy the Slavic hospitality and greet the Russian Army when it arrived. The card sharks, meanwhile, honed their skills. But, Gordon Follas, unlike the Americans, became increasingly restless.

Lt. Frank Soltesz, a P-51 pilot who spoke Slovak, meanwhile, was friendly with Major Jan Savel, the Slovak camp commandant. Each night Soltesz would join Savel in his quarters for a drink or two and listen to the BBC from London. Good news prevailed and morale was high for both the Americans and the Slovaks. Paris and Rome had been liberated, and the Wehrmacht was in retreat on all fronts.[2]

Alas, as Moulton lamented years later, fate interceded. Unknown to the prisoners, the Czech government-in-exile in London was supporting plans for the Slovak National Uprising to begin. Renegade Partisan groups were causing havoc, and Tiso and the Germans became aware of the plans for an uprising and began securing government buildings and transportation facilities. Small German units and outposts became targets for opportunity for the Partisans.

September 1, Americans Are Freed.

Two nights after the revolt began, September 1, Major Savel informed Grinava's 28 prisoners at their evening meal that German SS troops were on the way from Bratislava, and they were free to leave. He advised them to strike out for the rebel headquarters at Banska Bystrica 120 miles to the east.

Savel's announcement left the prisoners stunned. Soon, the camp was in an uproar. Norton Skinner, the B-17 flight engineer, recalls a discussion about the wisdom of fleeing and getting caught and possibly shot by the Germans. A few men thought it might be wise to turn themselves over to the Germans to be sent to German POW camps. In the end, however, the prisoners scattered into the night, with only a vague notion of where to go or how to get there. A few Slovak Partisans were ready to lead some of them to the rebel headquarters.[3]

That same night, the Slovak army garrison in Bratislava had been disarmed by units of *Kampfgruppe Schill* which was a SS unit consisting of three infantry battalions, some artillery and several tanks and half-tracks.[4] The Germans had about 2,200 men. German troops were dispatched to Grinava to seize the Americans.

The Americans, forewarned, organized into groups of two to four men in order to slip safely through the country side. Excitedly, they said their farewells and fled into the night, unaware of the Uprising starting to rage through central Slovakia.

Sam Strode, the B-17 tail gunner, teamed up with David McSorley, who for some reason opted not to walk with Gordon Follas. It was a wild scene as ecstatic men prepared to hike out of the camp in the middle of the night. George Fernandes remembers the scene.

> Bob Hede and Howard Coleman and I chose to leave together. The guards deserted the gate just after midnight, and at 1:50 we left with our blankets made up in a bed roll. Just outside the gate a German army truck drove up, and we broke into a run toward the woods. When the sun came up the next morning, we could hear German patrols with dogs looking for us. We got some food and water from a Slovak farmer as we headed through the foothills of the *Male Karpathy*.[5]

This low-lying range of mountains eight miles wide stretched in a narrow range forty miles from north of Bratislava in the direction north by north-east to Brezova pod Bradlom. Jack Kellogg had made his way through these mountains two months earlier, heading the opposite direction which led him into the clutches of the Hungarian militia.[6]

Richard Moulton and Lincoln Artz and two others left Grinava at midnight. Another airman joined them several hours later after first visiting his Slovak girlfriend whom he'd met at the quarry. He wanted to sit out the war with her and her family, but fearful of German reprisals, she sent him on his way.[7]

Early September, A Few Miles North of Grinava.

Moulton and his group were assisted the next morning by a local forest ranger in the mountain village of Pila, north of Grinava. He convinced the

Americans to stay in the hills, dig a cave and wait a few days for a Partisan group to lead them to Banska Bystrica. It seemed like a good idea. The forest ranger and other Slovak families supplied the Americans with three meals a day. Soon after, another two flyers, recently shot down, joined them. The seven men suffered through an uncomfortable existence, sleeping in the cave and fitfully trying to keep a fire going at night. Over the weeks, Moulton and three others fought off boredom by playing bridge with breaks for walks through the woods when the weather was good.

Moulton has poignant memories of his strolls near the cave. The underbrush had been cleared out by local villagers by years of wood foraging in the hills, giving the woods a park-like appearance. He often saw deer. As fall approached and the leaves turned color, the beauty of the area seemed an eternity away from the war. And home. The exception, of course, was the frequent sight of vapor trails of the bomber fleets and the low hum of massed engines. The men gazed wistfully through the clouds at the formations high in the sky. Most of their buddies who had recently escaped from Grinava, meanwhile, struck out for Banska Bystrica, slipping through the Slovak countryside with the help of Partisans here and there and a few occasional farmers.

---

1 Courtesy of Richard Moulton, Unpublished manuscript.
2 Frank Soltesz, Telephone conversation with the author, 1997.
3 Norton Skinner, Telephone conversation with the author, 1995.
4 Kliment and Nakladal, p. 93.
5 Courtesy of George Fernandes, Unpublished Manuscript.
6 Ibid.
7 Moulton, Unpublished manuscript.

Chapter 5

Dodging Germans

September 1, 1944.

Most of the men who left Grinava headed into the *Male Karpaty* (Lessor Carpathian) mountains. Nick Yezdich and his group had difficulty finding enough food. Gripped by desperation and sinking morale, they knocked on the door of a farm house. Yezdich greeted the woman in Serbo Croatian, and although startled, she understood him. The men spent the night with the family who told them they were lucky as most of the farmers in the region were pro-German. Yezdich and his group left the next morning, and immediately ran into the Fernandes group. They spent the afternoon talking, but decided to split up that night and go their separate ways. They never saw each other again.

Yezdich's group hitchhiked a ride on an oxcart with an older Slovak couple, but because the oxen moved so slowly, they graciously thanked the couple and took off on their own. Later, they ran into six Jews on the run. "After they found out we were Americans, we sat around and drank toasts to all the heads of state. Then we said our good byes and went our separate ways. To this day," Yezdich says, "my thoughts still are in the forest with those desperate Jewish people."[1]

John Schianca and his five-man group, meanwhile, reached Modra the first day where they stumbled into a Partisan group of ten soldiers who arranged to drive them to Banska Bystrica. Traveling at night without lights, dodging German patrols and checkpoints, the Slovak drivers miraculously made it to Banska Bystrica.

Sam Strode and "Scotty" McSorley got to Ruzindol, only ten miles from Grinava and ran into a group of Partisans. Their leader also arranged for the men to be driven to Banska Bystrica.

A week out of Grinava, Neal Cobb and his group walked into another Partisan camp in the foothills south of Brezova pod Bradlom. They were surprised to find Gordon Follas and several Americans there.

This Partisan group, led by Captain Jan Repta, had captured Jack Wilson, a British intelligence agent, who had a complete set of German identification papers. The Partisans, thinking he was a German, were about to shoot him. The Americans and Gordon Follas convinced Repta that their prisoner actually was British. Wilson, 55 years old, had swallowed a cyanide pellet when he was captured. He thought he had been captured by pro-German Slovaks. The pill only made him ill. Wilson originally was from Vienna. A Jew, his real name was Wanndorfer. Wilson related that he was supposed to have been dropped near Vienna, forty miles west. Before Cobb's group left, the group posed for a photograph.[2]

The American airmen had begun realize that outside the fence, the comfortable life at Grinava no longer existed. German units were on the move, ready to attack and destroy Slovak opposition of any kind. Also, they were looking for the Americans. At the same time, Partisans were in the woods, intent on killing Germans at every opportunity. Although the Partisans enjoyed the support and loyalty of a large element of the populace, many Slovaks were loyal to the Germans and the pro-German Slovak army units.[3]

The Germans threatened that anyone aiding airmen would be shot. Understandably, people were frightened. The Americans didn't know whom to trust. Nick Yezdich's group had gone in one direction. George Fernandes and his group took a different route, and Neal Cobb's group still another. No one was sure where they were going.

Dodging Germans

September 13, Grinava POW Camp.

The 15th Air Force, meanwhile, continued to pound the synthetic oil plants in Blechhammer and Odertal to the north. Inevitably, more American aircraft were shot down. On September 13th, Lieutenant Manley Fliger's B-24 crashed in the foothills not far from Grinava. A villager hid him for several days and then arranged for him to be taken to Bratislava.

Fliger had fractured a vertebra in his back when he parachuted. He stayed a week with three women, one an "attractive ballet dancer," he recalls. They arranged for him to be taken to Trencin by train. The women wrapped his head and hands in heavy bandages and gave him a Slovak uniform to wear enabling his guide to describe Fliger as a disabled soldier on leave. They arrived in Banska Bystrica around the first of October.[4]

Those airmen walking to Banska Bystrica, meanwhile, had not only German patrols to worry about, but also the problem of finding water. Neal Cobb recalls they could deal with going hungry, but water was a problem. They barely survived by finding occasional streams. Sometimes they sneaked onto farms at night and used the farmers' wells.

Cobb's group decided to head northeast toward the Polish border. One day, his group ran into a Jew who spoke excellent English and claimed he had been hiding for two years.[5]

They also ran into a Partisan group commanded by a Russian, who fed them a meal and tried to recruit them into his band. They politely refused, and the Russian, being the "good ally," Cobb remembers with a laugh, ordered them out of camp at daybreak.

"We decided to stay out of the valleys," Cobb says. "Most days we didn't encounter anybody. We just kept walking, walking, walking. It was miserable when it rained. Luckily, Frank Soltesz could communicate with the farmers and usually was given bread, sometimes fruit and a glass of milk."[6]

One night Cobb, Soltesz, and Winberg stayed in a village, only to be awakened at 4:30 AM and told to leave before sunrise. The farmer gave each man a sack of food.

"His wife had fried each of us a chicken and also put in some white bread. I often thought about that family. We ate the whole chicken on our first break. Only a few Slovak people refused to help us. The usual reason, of course, was a valid one: The Germans shot civilians caught aiding the enemy."[7]

Approximately forty young airmen were now scrambling through Slovakia in those hectic days. In Italy, Major General Nathan Twining and his staff of the 15th Air Force knew the flyers were there, but neither where nor how many. The confusion was similar to the situation as it had been in Yugoslavia. Reports out of Slovakia by Czech CIS agents reached Bari via Banska Bystrica and the Czech government in London. How to effect the rescue was the problem. Some of the airmen were making it to Banska Bystrica.

August 29, Near Trencin.

First Lieutenant Thayne Thomas, a B-17 pilot from the 20th Squadron of the Second Bomb Group, was shot down near Trencin. His aircraft had exploded in midair, throwing him clear. When he regained consciousness, he was startled to find himself falling through space and seeing pieces of his plane falling by him. A flaming gas tank nearly struck him. Hesitating a few moments, he pulled his D ring (rip cord), and then drifted safely to the ground. Thomas hid his chute and headed southwest, only to run into the Vah River which was too wide to cross.

Thomas met two boys who summoned some men who took him to the local police who were anti-German. Later, they were taken to a nearby Slovak Army outpost where he met Private Jan Surovec, the young soldier who spoke English and who earlier had befriended John Schianca and Neal Cobb in Trencin. The following day Thomas was taken to another town.[8]

Sergeant Robert Donahue, a waist gunner in a different crew, was shot down the same day as Thomas. For Donahue, events unfolded differently.

He spent the first night hiding under a haystack. The next day he met several Slovaks, including one who astonished Donahue by claiming he lived once in Pittsburgh only twenty minutes from Donahue's home address.

Donahue subsequently was turned over to Private Surovec, who seemed to be everywhere. He took Donahue to a small town with a Slovak military building where they met members of another crew. The next day a German patrol arrived suddenly and took possession of the prisoners. Luckily, Donahue was in the latrine. Hearing the commotion, he looked out the window to see the flyers being marched off.[9]

Surovec later dressed Donahue in a Slovak army uniform and took him out of town. Had they been detected by the Germans, both would have been shot. Surovec told Donahue to salute the same men in uniform whom he saluted. Surovec and Donahue met Thayne Thomas that evening in the neighboring village. They spent the night in a country estate, enjoying an exquisite meal. The following day, they were driven to Banska Bystrica. The day after, John Schianca arrived there with three other airmen. Counting two Aussies, there were soon be a total of 12 men in the rebel capital.

An officer of the Czech Forces of the Interior (CFI) assumed control over the Americans. He gave them spending money, and they gorged themselves on local bakery products and ice cream.

The word began to spread in Banska Bystrica that the Germans were advancing on the city. The town was bustling with Partisans. But for the airmen, the atmosphere was relaxed. Suddenly, it was Grinava all over again. At a barber shop, they met Cleveland-born Nick Tomes who had been brought back to Slovakia by his parents when he was twelve. Tomes was eager to get out of the country and back to the States.

Donahue recalls some of their group being dinner guests of an aristocratic Hungarian. They also went to a lady's house for tea where several young girls eagerly practiced their English. Slovakia continued to be a pleasant place to spend the war. At least for the moment.[10]

Back in Italy, General Twining, acting on a request of Captain Charles

Katek, agreed to airlift an OSS air rescue team. This meant another landing behind German lines, flying into an airfield near the rebel capital in Banska Bystrica. Colonel John Ryan, the operations officer of the 5th Wing, selected two Lt. Colonels to fly B-17s to Slovakia, deliver the ordinance plus a five-man OSS team, and pick up an undetermined number of flyers.[11]

---

1 Nick Yezdick, Letter to the author, 1996.
2 Neal Cobb, Interview with the author, August, 1998; A British SOE agent talked to Captain Georges De Lannurian, leader of some French Partisans in Slovakia, who told him it was his group who originally found Wilson and turned him over to Repta's group, NARA, 226, Entry 196, Box 34, Folder 75.
3 Paul Brosz, *Das letzte Jahrhundert der Karpatendeutschen in der Slowakei* (Stuttgart: *Arbetitsgemeinschaft der Karpatendeutschen*, 1992); *Rudolf Melzer, Erlebte Geschichte, Vol. II*. (Vienna: *Karpatendeutsche Landsmannschaft Oesterreich*, 1996. The two authors have written that there was not widespread support for the Uprising.
4 Manley Fliger, Interview with the author, 1998.
5 Neal Cobb, Interview with the author, 1999.
6 Ibid.
7 Ibid.
8 Thayne Thomas, Letter to the author, July 20, 1995.
9 Robert Donahue, Letter to the author, 1995.
10 Robert Donahue, Telephone interview with the author, 1996
11 John Ryan later would become Chief of Staff of the U.S. Air Force.

Chapter 6

Holt Green

August, 1944, Bari, Italy.

When Captain Charles Katek visited Bari in August, he had started the ball rolling. He met with Lt. Colonel Howard Chapin, Major Walter Ross and Lt. Nelson Deranian, USNR, of the 2677th OSS regiment. He reviewed General Donovan's policy objectives and how to utilize the information from Colonel Moravec of the CIS. Katek endorsed Chapin's decision to insert a mission into Slovakia.[1]

Katek also updated the 15th Air Force in Bari on the number of downed American airmen in Slovakia. Meanwhile, preparations were set for "Operation Gunn" to Romania to pick up the American prisoners of war released by King Michael. Katek was eager to establish a solid relationship with the Air Force because of the need for airlift purposes.

On August 29, the same day the Slovak National Uprising broke out, Operation Gunn started with twelve flights of B-17's to Bucharest's Popesti Airfield. Colonel George Kraigher, USAF, led the mission. Walter Ross went along as second in command. Lt. Deranian went along on this mission. He was accompanied by Sergeant Joe Horvath and Photographers Mate Nelson Paris. Additionally, Joe Morton, a correspondent of the Associated Press went along.

Under the cover of this air rescue mission, the OSS established an operation code-named "Operation Bug House." Included in that group were damage assessment teams who headed for the Ploesti oil refinery complex to measure the effectiveness of the bombing. More significantly, the OSS brought in a "city team" to gather intelligence in Bucharest. Hence, General Donovan's dream of covert operations in the Soviet sphere of influence was underway as the OSS operations went far beyond the retrieval of downed American airmen.[2]

Staggered flights from Bucharest brought out 1,350 men. Another 350 flyers were retrieved later from Bulgaria. The OSS was careful to keep the Soviets apprised of the flights.[3]

Over 1900 airmen had been extracted from the Balkans by September 3. In the context of that success, Lieutenant Deranian submitted a plan the next day to fly a similar, smaller scale mission into Slovakia. It included the DAWES and HOUSEBOAT teams.[4] There was some question about how risky these missions would be. Operations into Yugoslavia were running efficiently and safely. Perhaps the same would be true in Slovakia.

Chapin and Otto Jakes, head of the Czech desk in Bari, recommended Lt. Holt Green, USNR, to lead the mission. Green had returned from Yugoslavia in June where he had headed up a small operation involving air rescue and intelligence gathering. In Slovakia, Green would have essentially the same mission. Instead of parachuting in, the Slovak mission would involve a daylight landing on a grass airfield only a few miles behind German army lines. The 15th Air Force would supply two B-17's.

Holt Green, the man Chapin and Jakes selected, was a socially prominent textile manufacturer from Charleston, South Carolina before the war. Eager to join the military, Green originally had been declared physically unfit. But he persisted and in 1943 talked his way into the Navy, thanks in part to well-connected friends and relatives. A graduate of the University of the South in Tennessee in 1930, he had also later did graduate work at the Harvard School of Business. Suave and intelligent, Green, a scion of prominent South Carolinians who had fought in both the Civil and Revolution wars, was successfully managing the family cotton mill business in

Burlington, North Carolina, when the war started.

Raised in the genteel atmosphere of Charleston, Green was polite and soft-spoken, and had the easy manner of a Southern gentleman. He was immensely popular with a large circle of friends.[5]

Once in the Navy, Green volunteered for the OSS and after special training was assigned to Cairo in March, 1943. Due to his business background and accounting skills, he was placed in charge of the Cairo station's financial affairs. John Toulmin, the station chief, later said that Green's handling of the Cairo finances was the most outstanding fiscal management of all the OSS worldwide operations.[6]

January, 1944, Yugoslavia.

Chafing at his desk assignment, Green begged his way into an operational status, and went through the mandatory parachute training course in Palestine. He later jumped into Montenegro in Yugoslavia on January 19, and was stationed near the Albanian border at Kolasin.

Green's mission was under British command. He attempted to convince the British it was an "Allied Mission," and he complained to Bari that his Anglo superiors had a strong "streak of empire in them."[7] Nevertheless, Green established close rapport with Major Anthony Hunter, the SOE commander in the region. Their main job was to coordinate the rescue of downed American airmen, although they also supplied Bari with German Order of Battle of information.

On February 20, Green forwarded a political report to Bari. The "locals are anti-communist and fear the Partisans, equating communism with atheism," he wrote. The people seemed to support the *Chetnik* faction, who always paid for the food they requisitioned. The Partisans were basically unorganized and unreliable. Green reported that he believed the locals would rather live under the Germans than the Partisans.[8]

Green and his radio operator operated in the ruggedly beautiful *Crna Gora* Mountains where the German units seldom dared venture. The

Partisans owned the high country. Green wore his Navy uniform around Kolasin, the standard operating procedure for the OSS agents.

Because of German pressure, Partisan commanders in the area moved Green and his radio operator to a remote 14th century monastery 8,000 feet elevation at Moracha. They remained there two months.

Green was able to assist dozens of downed American airmen who were brought to him by both the *Chetniks* and the Partisans. Captain Don Rider, who had similar successes in a northern region of Yugoslavia as head of the ASH mission, later compared his operational experiences with Green.[9]

June, Bari, Italy.

In the middle of June, Green was ordered back to Bari, keenly aware of the politics of the Partisan-*Chetnik* dispute as well as the dubious machinations of the Russians. He was put in charge of the Yugoslav desk at the 2677th OSS Regiment by Lt. Colonel Howard Chapin.[10]

Captain Rider, awaiting reassignment, complained to Holt Green that he was bored. Green told him there was a plan to put a combined team of nine British and six Americans into Slovakia where there were "2,000 guerrillas operating against the Germans."[11] This was the result of Katek's meeting the Lt. Colonel Glavin and other Bari staff members about implementing General Donovan's desire to penetrate Eastern Europe.

Green offered the mission to Rider who accepted. Rider immediately talked to Tibor Keszthelyi about going along as his second in command. Rider began boning up on Slovakia and interviewing candidates for the team. Then in early August, Tito approved of another American mission into Yugoslavia in the northern part of the country where the Soviets were expected to enter Yugoslavia. Rider opted to take his ASH team back to Yugoslavia where he already had considerable area knowledge and insight into the Partisans.[12]

Green obviously met with Lt. Nelson Deranian, Major Walter Ross, and Otto Jakes about going into Slovakia himself. When Katek arrived in

Holt Green

August, the decision was made to put Green in charge of the DAWES mission. Holt Green's superb leadership skills made him an easy choice to command the DAWES mission.[13]

Three days later, the Czech government in London forwarded another list of American airmen who were loose in Slovakia.

Holt Green began briefing his team.

---

1 NARA, RG 226, Entry 146, Box 36, Folder 485.
2 Brown, pp. 670-71.
3 Ibid.
4 The author has been unable to determine the origin of these names.
5 Frances Frost Hutson, Interview with the author, 1998.
6 John Toulmin, Letter to the Green family, July 12, 1946, courtesy of Frances Frost Hutson.
7 Holt Green, Memorandum to Paul West, NARA, RG 226, Entry 136, Box 34, Folder 375.
8 Ibid.
9 Don Rider, Telephone interview with the author, November 30, 1999.
10 NARA, RG 226, Entry 136, Box 34, Folder 375.
11 Don Rider, Telephone interview.
12 Ibid.
13 NARA, RG 226, Entry 136, Box 34, Folder 375.

Chapter 7

Rendezvous on a Grass Field

August, 1944, Bari, Italy.

Holt Green and Lt. Nelson Deranian selected five men for the Dawes mission. One was a school teacher, born in Prague. Two were born in central Slovakia, one of whom was a former member of the French Foreign Legion. The other was a rugged sergeant from Cleveland, eager to visit the land of his birth. Another was a native-born American who had learned to speak Czech from his immigrant parents. The fifth was a handsome, young radio operator who already had worked in Yugoslavia with Green.

Jan Schwartz was a student in a teachers college in Banska Stiavnica before the war when he was drafted into the *Hlinka Guard*. He hated the fascists and joined the underground before escaping to France to join the Foreign Legion. When the Germans invaded France, Schwarz was transferred to a quickly-organized Czech brigade. He was captured a few weeks later by the Germans and spent eight months in a POW camp before escaping to the south of France. He subsequently made it to the United States and joined the Army.

Schwartz, an Army private wearing a First Lieutenant's uniform, was an intelligent, glib individual. He adopted the cover name of Jan Kryzan, a common Slovak name, and was assigned to head the two-man HOUSEBOAT mission, a sub unit of the DAWES operation. Charles Heller, born in Chicago, spoke fair Czech and was young and enthusiastic. A Navy Specialist

Second Class, he was Schwartz' radio man.[1]

Army Private First Class Robert Brown was the radio operator for the DAWES team and a good one. He had worked in Kolasin, Yugoslavia, on another mission – Operation Redwood — where he met Holt Green. A native of Chicago, Brown trained as a radioman at Illinois Tech for the Army. His team in Yugoslavia, led by Lt. Rex Dean, sent weather reports back to Bari for the 15th Air Force.[2]

Army Sergeant Joe Horvath immigrated to the United States as a teenager with his family in 1928. He joined the Army when the U.S. entered the war, and because of his ability to speak perfect Slovak, wound up in the OSS. He also was trained as a radio operator. Physically strong, he was active and resourceful. He had accompanied Lt. Nelson Deranian to Bucharest on operation Gunn. Now, he hoped to visit his birthplace in Polomka, a few miles east of Banska Bystrica. Fate would give him a tragic opportunity.

Jerry Mican Appointed Green's Key Assistant.

Holt Green's key assistant, however, was Army Master Sergeant Jaroslav "Jerry" Mican. A native of Prague and a graduate of Charles University, he had immigrated to the United States in the 1920's. He earned a Masters Degree at Creighton University where he taught Czech for one year, and became a naturalized citizen. Mican later taught languages at Farragut High School in Chicago for 12 years.

When the war broke out, Mican was eager to get involved. He had been active in émigré groups in the Chicago area and was a good friend of Vojta Benes, brother of Eduard Benes, president of Czechoslovakia, who lived in Chicago. Vojta Benes remembered Mican's calming influence on the dissident groups among the Czech and Slovak communities in Chicago. He also recalled Mican's passionate love of his European roots.[3] Mican's elderly parents, whom he hoped to visit, resided in Karlin in the Czech Protectorate.

With Mican's language skills and his area knowledge of Czechoslovakia, it was only natural that he wanted to join the OSS. He knew

Charles Katek before the war and sought his help for acceptance into the organization. Mican, 42 years old, also listed Adlai Stevenson, the prominent Illinois politician, as a character reference.

Mican and the others were the classic type of OSS volunteers, stereotypical examples of what the OSS liked to advertise as "America's shadow warriors of World War II." Their focus was on the malevolent Third Reich which inspired them to enter the dangerous world working behind enemy lines. They were neither visionary idealists nor wild patriots. But, they did not hesitate to cloak their powerful emotions with a romantic spirit in this humanitarian war. Although they were unaware of what lay ahead, there was no hesitation. The Nazis represented evil. Simple folk across Europe were suffering and yearned for peace and stability. For Mican, Schwartz and Horvath, it would be a homecoming without drum rolls, only quiet exhilaration – and, hopefully, minimum anxiety. They were upbeat with no sense of foreboding.

Holt Green, Lieutenant United States Naval Reserve, the Tidewater aristocrat from the traditional south, typified the Naval officer-and-a-gentleman image. He could have stayed out of the war. Although he chose without hesitation to thrust himself into the war.

Jerry Mican, perhaps more than the others, had the maturity to appreciate what they were fighting for. He was a proud Czech, and deeply committed. He had relatives living under German domination. Mican penned a note to Captain Charles Katek on March 11, 1944, thanking him for getting him into the OSS. "Things are going to move fast," Mican wrote Katek. They were prophetic words.[4] Mican rounded out the six-man DAWES team, which included the two HOUSEBOAT men, Schwartz and Heller.

The 15th Air Force, meanwhile, prepared to deliver the DAWES team into Slovakia on two Flying Fortresses, aircraft normally reserved for dropping bomb loads on oil refineries or *Messerschmitt* factories. Two Lt. Colonels, Williard Sperry and Gil Pritchard, both veteran pilots, were selected to fly the mission. The next day they flew their B-17's from their

Italian base to Bari.

Pritchard had asked young Lt. Howard Dallman if he wanted to be his co-pilot "on a secret mission." Dallman blinked at the West Pointer, and immediately said yes, although with no idea what the mission entailed.[5]

The two Flying Fortresses carried partial crews because the planes were specially rigged for the heavy cargo load going in and the number of passengers coming back. The cargo consisted of Marlin machine guns and bazookas, ammunition, medical supplies, and radio equipment for the OSS team and the Partisans. During the briefing, Dallman learned their destination, shocked that they would land so close to the German army lines. And on a grass field![6]

September 17.

The ground crews and OSS personnel loaded the two B-17's the night before the mission. At 6:15 AM on September 17 they were airborne. The OSS men manned the waist gunner positions and the bombardier's gun position in the nose.

The two planes were escorted by 41 P-51's from the 52nd Fighter Group. Some of the planes escorted the Fortresses to Tri Duby, and others provided protective cover while they were on the ground, while another group covered the withdrawal from Tri Duby back to Italy.

The aircraft joined a large task force over the Adriatic heading to Budapest on a routine bombing run, and then peeled off near Kaposvar, Hungary. Dallman had never seen so many escort fighters. When the flight passed by Vienna, normally an active *Luftwaffe* area, Dallman was especially relieved.[7]

In Banska Bystrica, the Slovak command advanced money to the men and allowed them the run of the city. The day after Lt. Thomas and Robert Donahue arrived, they were invited to an estate outside the city for lunch. Their hostess, an elderly lady, reputedly a Hungarian countess, was disappointed they were not English, informing the Americans they didn't speak "proper English." Despite this amusing insult, which they ignored with a laugh, the Yanks found life pleasant in Banska Bystrica. The countess, although disappointed by her American guests, served them an elegant dinner. But, they were eager to get home, and help was on the way.

After three hours in the air out of Bari, the two B-17's and their P-51 escort flew over the Tri Duby ("Three Oaks") airfield at 9:40 AM. The airfield was six miles south of Banska Bystrica, situated in a broad valley surrounded by low hills. Firing two flares as planned, Pritchard saw no response. He made a second pass, and finally saw a flare at north end of the field. He looked for the expected green flare, signaling it was safe to land, but he didn't see it until the third fly-over. The grass field landing went smoothly.

While Lt. Dallman sat at the controls, Pritchard left the plane to talk to the men in charge of unloading the cargoes. Both planes kept their engines running the entire time they were on the ground, ready for a fast takeoff if necessary. Pritchard looked around at the large throng of people ringing the field. He was astonished at the reception.[8]

"We were surprised that the first people who greeted us were Russian personnel. The airfield began to assume the appearance of a carnival. Cars lined the highway, and civilians and Partisans crowded about," Pritchard wrote later. "We were warmly welcomed. Considering the number of vehicles, gasoline . . . shortages apparently were not acute. [Only a few of the] evacuees were at the field. We planned to wait for 40 minutes." A Czech officer sped back to Banska Bystrica to pick up the missing airmen.[9]

Dallman had observed the scene from his cockpit window. He watched a U.S. Naval Officer in a khaki uniform depart the aircraft. It was Lt. Holt Green. Prior to taking off, Dallman had not seen any of the passengers board the aircraft. Nevertheless, he was surprised by the sight of a naval officer disembarking here in the middle of central Europe. He had no idea so many Naval personnel were in the OSS. Partisan troops and the American airmen quickly unloaded the planes.

The OSS team unloaded their gear after greetings from General

Golian and his staff. Several British agents, according to one account also landed.[10] One was Chaviva Reik, a Palestine Jew, one of the few female agents in the Balkans. She was a member of the AMSTERDAM team under the cover name of Ada Robinson.

Two P-51 Mustangs Crash Land on Tri Duby Air Field.

While this was going on, the P-51's were controlling the sky above the field. Some planes flew only 500 feet above the parked B-17's while others were high in the sky looking for German fighters. The 41-plane escort, which had flown without incident, suddenly developed problems. Two Mustangs were forced to land.

Lt. Alexander Watkins was forced to land when a mal-functioning fuel system caused his plane, the "Swamp Angel," to lose power. He couldn't restart the engine after he landed, and jogged over to board Pritchard's aircraft. Watkins, a Louisiana native, had flown "Swamp Angel" on numerous missions and hated to leave it behind.[11]

The second problem involved Second Lieutenant Ethan Allan Smith who was flying only his second mission. His problems were similar to those of Watkins. Smith's engine stalled over the airfield. He came down for a dead-stick landing and hit the ground smoothly, but then struck a dirt revetment. Smith's face hit the gun sight above the instrument panel, breaking his nose and giving him a mild concussion. The plane was a total loss. The Slovaks gingerly removed Smith from the plane and took him ten miles south to a hospital in Zvolen where he remained for a week.[12]

Lt. Colonel Pritchard had watched in dismay when the two Mustangs landed. He later broke radio silence and informed the fighter commander, Colonel Charles Boedecker, that two of his planes were down, and he would bring one of the pilots back, although they were "leaving the other."[13]

The airmen, meanwhile, helped unload the B-17's. Other men were still in Banska Bystrica. Lt. Thayne Thomas had been walking down the main square of the city when he initially heard Mustangs fly over. Thomas thought they were Russian fighters until he was startled to see they were P-51's. Two Mustangs made a pass over the city at 500 feet as the Americans on the square cheered. Frantically, Thomas and the others began looking for transportation to the airport.[14]

"We found a military truck," Thomas remembered, "and drove up and down the square collecting Americans and our two Australians. Two of the Americans were missing, but we took off for the airfield anyway. The [road] to the airfield was over rolling country, and the truck seemed to be crawling. We could see the Mustangs continuing to buzz over the city and circle around. Finally we got to the airport just as the two Forts were beginning to taxi up the field. We drove the truck right in front of them to stop them, leaped out of the trucks, and quickly boarded."

The airmen now were all on board as the bombers headed down the grass runway and became airborne. John Schianca recalled his excitement. One of the Slovak officers had told him that morning, "General Twining is going to take you back to Italy." Schianca had been skeptical, but thirteen American airmen, two Australian airmen, and an American civilian, Emil Tomes, made the trip back to Italy.

The flight was uneventful. There were no flak attacks or sightings of German fighters. Upon arrival at 1:15 PM, Schianca and the others were startled to see General Twining on the runway apron waiting to greet them. "Boys, you made history today," Schianca recalls Twining saying. It seemed a little melodramatic. Schianca, the Harvard graduate, shook his head in amazement. Much of the OSS brass in Bari was on hand, Major Walter Ross, Lt. Nelson Deranian, Lt. Colonel Howard Chapin, Robert Joyce, General Born and other high ranking officers.

The OSS had scored a triumph with this mission, sending in agents and bring out airmen. For others, it had been a routing day. Fighter pilot Lt. Bill Coloney didn't learn until after returning that two pilots in the 52,nd Alex Watkins and Ethan Allen Smith, had been forced down at Tri Duby. One of Coloney's buddies told him that Smith had "cracked up pretty badly."

Another pilot recorded those facts in his diary, but noted also that they "had a good supper – ice cream, and then meatballs."[15] Here was another case of the Air Force having it over the infantry.

That night in Banska Bystrica, a pleased General Golian entertained Holt Green and his team. The impact of their arrival was both real and symbolic. The Allies had embraced the Slovak National Uprising.

---

1 The author was unable to locate any of Heller's relatives.
2 Edward Papierski, Telephone interview with the author, April 19, 2000.
3 Eduard Benes' Letter, NARA, RG 226, Entry 196, Box 34, Folder 75.
4 Jerry Mican, Letter to Charles Katek. Ibid.
5 Howard Dallman, Telephone interview with the author, September, 1997.
6 Ibid.
7 Ibid.
8 Gil Pritchard statement, 483rd Bomb Group newsletter.
9 Ibid.
10 Jan Schwartz, Interview with William Miller, 1984, Courtesy of Marilyn Miller.
11 Mrs. Alexander Watkins, Letter to the author, 1997.
12 Ethan Allen Smith, Letter to the author, April 6, 1998.
13 Ibid.
14 Thayne Thomas, Letter to the author, July 20. 1995.
15 Diary, Elvin Olaf Erickson, Courtesy of Bill Coloney.

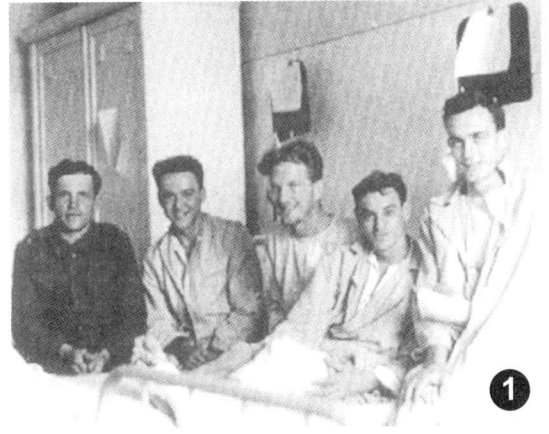

1. Sergeants Bob Hede, third from left, and John Schianca, fourth from left, recuperate in a Catholic hospital in Trencin, Slovakia, with two other American airmen and a Slovak guard. (courtesy of John Schianca) **2.** 2nd Lt. George Winberg, a B-24 navigator, was shot down on July 7, 1944, and later was flown back to Italy by the OSS. (courtesy of Jeane Vais). **3.** 1st Lt. Thayne Thomas was rescued by Slovaks and also flown back to Italy by the OSS. (courtesy of Henrietta Thomas). **4.** 2nd Lt. Neal Cobb was a 19-year-old bombardier shot down on the same plane as Schianca and Winberg. (courtesy of Neal Cobb). **5.** Sergeant Sam Strode, a B-17 tailgunner, was also rescued by Slovaks and the OSS. (courtesy of Don Strode).

1. Slovaks unload LTC Gil Pritchard's B-17, Tri Duby Airfield, October 7, 1944. (courtesy of SNU Museum, Banska Bystrica, Slovakia). **2.** 2nd Lt. Frank Soltesz, a P-51 pilot who spoke Slovak, was shot down on July 7, 1944. (courtesy of Mrs. Frank Soltesz). **3.** Sergeant Nick Yezdich could speak Serbo-Croatian and was able to communicate with the Slovaks. He and Soltesz were rescued by the Slovaks and the OSS and flown back to Italy on October 7, 1944. (courtesy of Nick Yezdich). **4.** 2nd Lt. George Fernandes was the bombardier on the same B-24 with Sergeants Bob Hede and Nick Yezdich. He missed the October 7 flight back to Italy and was forced to flee into the mountains with the OSS. Fernandes was captured by the *Abwehr* on November 11, 1944. (courtesy of George Fernandes).

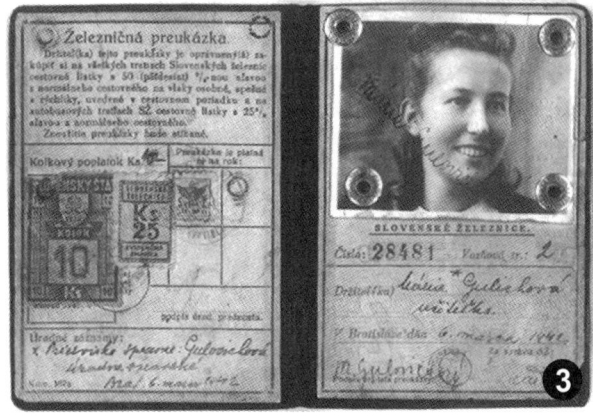

1. This photo was taken by Captain Edward Baranski in August or early September, 1944, at Bari, Italy. 1st Lt. Lane Miller is sitting at the left foreground. Lt. Nelson Deranian is seated next to him. At the end of the table on the left appears to be Lt. Jim Gaul. Lt. Holt Green is sitting on the right side of the second man from the front, looking away from the camera. Green, Gaul Miller, and Baranski lost their lives five months later. Deranian was the organizer of the DAWES mission. (courtesy of Kathy Baranski Lund). **2.** 1st Lt. Lane Miller was a student at the University of California at Berkeley when the war started. He had been a star athlete and a top student in high school at Coronado, CA. After being shot down over Yugoslavia in 1944, he was rescued by the OSS and later joined the organization. (courtesy of Buck Miller). **3.** Maria Gulovich's Slovak identification card, March 6, 1942. (courtesy of Maria Gulovich Liu).

1. B-24 crew, 1943. Later shot down in Slovakia, July 7, 1944 (with different crew members). Standing, Karl Reinerth; fourth from the left, George Fernandes, sixth from the left, Bob Hede; on the right, Nick Yezdich. Kneeling, Bob Fleharty. Reinerth, Yezdich, and Fleharty were flown back to Italy on October 7, 1944. Fernandes and Hede were captured on November 11. (courtesy of George Fernandes). 2. Palestinian Jewish SOE agents, Tri Duby Airfield, October 7, standing in front of 2nd Lt. Jim Street's B-17. Left to right, Chaim Chermesh, Chaviva Reik, Rafi Reiss, Aba Berdichev, and Zvi Ben-Yaakov. Reik and Reiss were captured in October, 1944, and later executed in Slovakia by the Germans. Berdichev and Ben Yaakov were captured with the OSS and SOE at Polomka and were executed at Mauthausen. (Courtesy of the SNU Museum). 3. Left to right, 1st Lt. Thayne Thomas, Jan Surovec, Sergeant Robert Donahue. Thomas and Donahue were flown back to Italy on September 17. Surovec was a Slovak army interpreter who rescued Thomas and Donahue. (courtesy of the SNU museum).

1. Captain P.A. Velichko, Soviet commander of Slovak partisan groups who ordered the murder of German prisoners which touched off the Slovak National Uprising. (courtesy of the SNU museum). **2.** At Captain Jan Repta's partisan camp, Brezova, circa September 5, 1944. Left to right, 2nd Lt. Frank Soltesz, Gordon Follas, a New Zealander escaped POW who decided to stay with Repta and fight the Germans; 2nd Lt. George Winberg, Sergeant Jesse Houston, 2nd Lt. Neal Cobb, British SOE agent Jack Wilson who was later captured with the DAWES mission at Polomka, and Sergeant Claude Davis. (courtesy of SNU museum). **3.** Captain Jack Gorman's B-17 at Tri Duby, October 7, a few minutes after being freed from the mud on the field. The other five B-17's had left for Italy an hour earlier. Here Gorman has just accepted several wounded French partisans to return to Italy. (courtesy of SNU museum).

1. Fred Ascani piloted a B-17 from the 483rd Bomb Group on October 7, 1944, to Tri Duby Airfield. He subsequently retired as a major general. (courtesy of Fred Ascani). 2. 2nd Lt. Manley Fliger, shot down near Bratislava, was flown back to Italy on October 7. (courtesy of Manley Fliger). 3. Bill Newton, radioman on LTC Pritchard's B-17, October 7, recalls talking with Associated Press correspondent Joe Morton in his radio room for three hours on the way to Tri Duby. (courtesy of Bill Newton). 4. Jewish volunteers with the British SOE. Second row, fourth from the left, Aba Berdichev; extreme right, Chaim Chermesh. Standing, fourth from the left, Chaviva Reik, sixth from the right, Rafi Reiss. Reik, Berdichev, and Reiss lost their lives after being captured in Slovakia. (courtesy of the Ghetto House, Israel). 5. Bill Coloney, a P-51 pilot, flew protective cover with the 52nd Fighter Group for the two B-17's on September 17, 1944. He returned on the six-plane October 7 flight aboard Jack Gorman's B-17 to attempt to fly back Lt. Alex Watkins' disabled P-51 from Tri Duby, but was unable to start the engine. (courtesy of Bill Coloney).

Chapter 8

"Unbelievable Environment"

September, 1944, Banska Bystrica, Slovakia.

Holt Green was ecstatic. Conditions in Banska Bystrica were "almost unbelievable." General Jan Golian and his CFI staff were cooperating on "any and all matters," and as for the "Balkan intrigue complex," a continual annoyance in Yugoslavia, it didn't exist here.

The biggest problem the CFI faced, Green reported, was the "pitiful" shortage of military equipment, guns, ammunition and medical supplies. Green concluded also that the Partisans were another serious concern for Golian. They appeared to be under the control of Moscow, and many units were unruly and undisciplined. On the other hand, he was pleased to find Golian and the higher echelons of Slovak society and the military staff expressing pro-democracy sentiments.[1]

Golian provided Green and his men office space in the headquarters building, a large edifice four stories high. They had dial telephones, maps on the walls, carpets, easy chairs and "all the trimmings," Green reported, a far cry from the primitive conditions in Yugoslavia.

General Golian received dozens of intelligence reports daily, most of which he shared with Holt Green and his team. Jerry Mican and Bob Brown were swamped with work, Mican translating and Brown encoding and sending on to Bari. They were putting in 18-hour days and at least one American was on duty 24 hours a day.

Green was amazed that there was so little indication of the war in the town except for the presence of military personnel, night patrols, restricted areas and the checking of passes. To be sure, there were constant air raid alerts, but the *Luftwaffe* did little damage. The markets were full of food. General Golian entertained lavishly, and Green and the others found Slovak cuisine special.

The Americans enjoyed *Kapustnica*, the hearty cabbage soup laced with smoked pork sausage and mushrooms. Their hosts introduced them to ham appetizers stuffed with creamed horseradish. They also had *Bryndza* cheese starters, seasoned with paprika. The Americans enjoyed pork chops and pork roasts, usually stuffed with cheese. They had a variety of sauerkraut dishes and potato pancakes or dumplings. On other occasions, beef steaks served with Slovak-style with a fried egg were served. The Americans had arrived in the middle of duck season and enjoyed several dinners of duck and goose, always served with steamed cabbage. Occasionally they had venison. Trout was plentiful, and was served stuffed with almonds, ham and cheese. Crepes were the most popular dessert, often flambed with liqueur. Dinner always started with Slivovice, the powerful plum brandy to which the Americans had trouble adjusting. For Holt Green, who had existed on a meager diet in Yugoslavia, Slovakia was indeed a totally different environment.

At the dinner table over these sumptuous meals, the hopes and dreams of Slovakia were laid out to the Americans. Golian always spoke of "Czechoslovakia," but there was never any mistaking his Slovak roots and orientation.[2] Nevertheless, the loyalty of the Army was to Benes and the London Government.

At first, Holt Green did not see the military situation as precarious. He radioed Lt. Deranian, "My visits to the fronts have been great fun. Drive up in a car and go where you please and see and freely talk with anyone. The whole thing takes only several hours. The people are most friendly and courteous, including the officers."[3] Green was impressed with the CFI underground intelligence contacts.

"*Unbelievable Environment*" 63

The British surprised Green by showing up in Banska Bystrica three days after the Americans. A four-man SOE team had parachuted in at night only 20 miles from Banska Bystrica. The team leader, Major John Sehmer, was upset that the British pilots missed the landing point by 18 miles, dropping them only five miles from a German army unit.

Sehmer was mainly irritated, however, that the Americans were already there – "They beat us to it – damn them" he radioed back to SOE headquarters.[4] His WINDPROOF team included Lieutenant Stefan Zeponian, Lieutenant Allan Daniels, a Canadian of Hungarian origin; and Corporal Bill Davies, a radio operator.

September 21.

That evening, General Golian had a dinner party for Holt Green, Jerry Mican, Sehmer, Zenopian, and Daniels. Green and Sehmer became fast friends.

Sehmer, 31, had a German-born father and an English mother. He had entered the British army in 1938 and subsequently attended special SOE courses at Bovington and Cambridge University. In 1943, he had taken a paratroop course and in April had dropped into Yugoslavia where he was attached to Mihavilovic's *Chetnik* headquarters in the Prestina area. He had left Yugoslavia in June, 1944, and returned to Cairo. He was then assigned to jump into Slovakia with SOE Force 399 with orders to work his way with his team into Hungary. Daniels and Zenopian both were fluent in Hungarian.[5]

Green, who was only 80 miles away from Prestina at Kolasin, and Sehmer had much to talk about as they were in Yugoslavia during the same time.

When Green and his men arrived, there were two flyers in Banska Bystrica. The men should have flown back to Bari that day, but they had been trying to get spending money from the Slovaks and missed the flight. One of them, Lt. Henry Tennyson, was a bright, energetic young officer, and Holt Green put him to work.

Three days later Norton Skinner and his group arrived from the Grinava POW camp. Green notified Bari, and asked if Tennyson could remain in Banska Bystrica to work with the mission. Later that day, Green informed Bari that there were now eight airmen in Banska Bystrica, and another fourteen were "on the way." That probably was the single group of men including Neal Cobb and George Winberg. Green also asked for a shipment of bazookas (anti-tank weapons).[6] In Bari, Lt. Deranian notified the OSS supply officer of another Tri Duby flight carrying five tons of supplies to be ready not later than September 22.

Again on September 20, Green radioed that the Germans were advancing toward the rebel capital and asked for that the 15th Air Force bomb two targets selected by General Golian's staff because Golian and his staff were struggling to mount an effective defense against the Germans.

The next day, Lt. Colonel Chapin and Major Walter Ross radioed Green that "two Fortresses" would arrive on September 24, but that Lt. Tennyson must be on the return flight. Also, Chapin and Ross said Joe Morton of the Associated Press would be with the mission to "cover the evacuation, but his material to be censored your end (sic) and this end." This reference to Morton would have significance later.[7]

On September 22, Green radioed Bari that 18 flyers "arrived today," making the total 25 men. He asked for the 15th Air Force to strafe German units at Turcianske Sv. Martin only 28 miles north of Banska Bystrica where heavy fighting was occurring.

Neal Cobb, Frank Soltesz, George Winberg and probably a dozen other airmen (nobody in that group remembers the exact number) had reached Turcianske Sv. Martin a few days before. Cobb remembers that they were invited to a wild party hosted by the Russian officer (perhaps Captain Velichko) in the city.[8]

The Germans were advancing upon the city from all directions. Green's message on September 22 added a note of urgency. "Believe situation likely become critical. Urge immediate evacuation flyers also urge military supp (sic) which are badly needed. Make every effort to prevail Fifteenth to send more planes with supplies. Please do not send planes loaded only with personnel."[9]

That same day Green radioed that the CFI had 15,000 recruits but had no arms for them. He said the Partisans were equipped to conduct raids only and could not resist a German advance from a static position. He mentioned that the residents of the city and the military both were concerned about the number of pro-German civilians in the area.[10] There loomed the foreboding possibility of reprisals if the Germans overran the city. In another message Green reported that the CFI wanted a shipment of propaganda leaflets.

September 24, Bari Cancels Second Flight.

Bad weather caused the cancellation of the flight on the 24th. Chapin and Otto Jakes directed Green to keep them informed on the number of airmen there. Clearly, the OSS was leaning on the 15th Air Force. The 15th was indifferent to airlift intelligence operations, but the motivation to rescue downed airmen was strong.

Major Sehmer notified SOE headquarters on September 25 that 2500 Russian Partisans had passed through the area on the way to Bohemia. He said Golian's headquarters had a number of Partisan leaders there, but Golian was doing his best to project the image of CFI, rather than Partisan, control of the country. Sehmer said the Germans were attacking from all directions and the situation was now "grave." The Slovaks, he emphasized, were begging for arms and ammunition.[11]

Lt. George Winberg, who had just arrived with Neal Cobb and Frank Soltesz, met with Holt Green and explained the circumstances of Jack Wilson, the British agent, who was on his way with George Fernandes and his group. Green reported this to Bari and reiterated that his over-worked radio man, Robert Brown, needed relief.

The flyers, meanwhile, were enjoying Banska Bystrica. Holt Green advanced them money, and the men liked to hang around a local bakery during the day. "As trays came out of the back," Neal Cobb remembers, "we would buy the whole tray. They called us the 'crazy Americans.'" At night the men went to the *Narodny Dom Hotel* on the main square to drink at the bar. Cobb recalls a "scroungy guy" who came by their table one night, and suddenly said, "Jesus Christ – a Camel! Can I have one? He had just arrived. I don't even remember his name.[12]

Norton Skinner and Nick Yezdich were among the Americans who had some contact with Holt Green.[13] Neal Cobb met Green the morning after his group arrived in the city. He, like all the other Americans, also was astonished to see the Navy uniform.[14]

Major Sehmer radioed his headquarters that the Soviet mission in Banska Bystrica had six officers. He said he needed a Czech-speaking officer and an additional radio operator. He noted that the Russian refugees were fearful of the arrival of the Red Army.[15]

Holt Green and Sehmer visited the front together. Sehmer sent details of the CFI defense zones back to the SOE along with reports of the strength of the Gemans and their positions. He detailed how the CFI was frustrated with the Partisans because they refused to follow orders, often retreated rather than fight, and routinely took food and provisions from the populace at gunpoint without paying. Sehmer criticized the Russian commanders whom he heard were Russian privates promoted to officers. He informed his superiors that if the Germans captured Zvolen, both Tri Duby and Banska Bystrica were "doomed." The CFI staff was speculating that the Slovaks perhaps would suffer the same fate as the Poles in the Warsaw Uprising, due to the apparent indifference of the Soviets in sending in troops and supplies.[16]

October 4 German Troops Reinforced.

John Sehmer received word that General Rudolf Viest would arrive from the Soviet Union and would replace Golian who would be a local commander only. Viest had commanded the Czech units in France in 1940.

Green notified Bari that day that 15,000 German troops had arrived in Trnava, and "more coming." He also reported that Slovak Jews in Trnava were being rounded up.[17]

As the situation became more ominous, Sehmer radioed out that "Huns" were attacking near Banska Bystrica. "If no supplies come will soon be in woods." Sehmer described a "tenseness in the air . . . a feeling of worry and hopelessness which is expressed by nearly everyone you talk with . . . many civilians are evacuation the town." [18]

The German occupation of Slovakia was brutal. Sehmer forwarded reports of civilians being shot for aiding downed flyers. In fact, he reported, anyone accused of aiding the Allies is "immediately shot." Despite this, local authorities were still aiding the CFI, the British and the Americans. Sehmer again informed Bari that the new recruits had inadequate arms.[19]

The Slovaks impatiently awaited Russian support. Their anger and dismay against the Russians mounted. Holt Green prepared a report for Bari, noting that there was a definite and general feeling that the Slovaks had been let down. "An analogy to Warsaw is frequently drawn." Sehmer said officials reported that the Russians apparently had perceived that the rebel leaders were oriented towards democracy rather than Communism, and this opinion is "probably the answer" why more Russian aid was not forthcoming. The conclusion was correct.

The Russians continued making nightly flights into Tri Duby bringing in more Russian partisans in civilian clothes but "very few supplies." Sehmer reported to Bari that the CFI has almost no control over the Partisans who "frequently plunder, and generally do as they please." The Russian officers are a "tough bunch," and Slovak officials reported that in January when the Russians arrived there was much enthusiasm but that support had receded.[20]

Green's lengthy report concluded that the current German offensive "probably will be successful. I consider it a tragedy that aid was not forthcoming, both from the point of view of the movement and people here and from the military point of view. . . the situation here is considered hopeless

... many will go underground again and the troops will return to their homes."[21]

Lt. Colonel Threlfall Urges More Aid To The Slovaks.

Lt. Colonel Henry Threlfall of the British SOE in Bari did his best to motivate his superiors in London to authorize more aid to the Slovaks. Threlfall had been notified by the OSS that another flight to Tri Duby was imminent. Threlfall arranged to go along. On September 30, he was told by London that he would be bringing out three Slovaks. He was given their names. Also, a Colonel Souhadra from London would accompany him to Tri Duby and remain there.

Threlfall radioed Major Sehmer and addressed the issue of the OSS delivering supplies to the Slovaks in defiance of Allied directives. He mentioned that the British Foreign Office and the Allied commands were sympathetic to the plight of the Slovaks, but that the issue was in limbo.[22]

When the Germans moved troops into Hungary in March, 1944, the German occupation of Slovakia had loomed as a possibility. By July, when the Slovak Partisans began isolated attacks on German troops, the German military commander in Bratislava notified Berlin that the populace supported the Partisans. The Partisans were estimated by one source to be between 18,000 and 26,000 while another believed the number to be no more than 6,800.[23] When the uprising began on August 29, the Germans in Bratislava were not surprised but not excessively alarmed.

Berlin responded with two regiments on August 29. President Tiso went on the radio to announce the imminent arrival of the German troops.[24]

On September 1, *Kampfgruppe Shill* disarmed the Slovak garrison in Bratislava. The *SS Kampfgruppe Schaefer* arrived from Poland the next day. On September 5, the 178th *Panzer Grenadier Division Tatra* was formed when 6,000 additional German troops arrived from Poland. On September 11, *Kampfgruppe Schill* overwhelmed a CFI force 30 miles west of Banska

Bystrica.

The *Wehrmacht*, well-trained and well-equipped, began a vigorous campaign in which the Germans consistently defeated larger, but poorly armed, forces.[25] Nevertheless, Berlin was displeased with the slow progress of the counterinsurgency operations, and installed *SS* General Hermann Hoefle in command. Hoefle met with Heinrich Himmler in Vienna on October 5 and asked for reinforcements. Himmler promised him the notorious *Dirlewanger Brigade* and the 18th *SS Horst Wessel Panzer Grenadier Division*.

Colonel Oskar Dirlewanger, known as the "Butcher of Warsaw," commanded a brigade made up of convicts and criminals which did not bode well for the CFI and the Slovaks.[26] The Soviets, meanwhile, had been flying in the Second Independent Czech Paratroop brigade to Tri Duby airfield between September 25 until October 15. But, it would be too little too late.

Banska Bystrica, an old mining town that lay at the foot of the Lower Tatra Mountains and was the jumping off point for skiers during the winter season in normal times, was facing disaster. Desperate refugees had swollen the pre-war population of about 8,000 to double that. The populace was aware German divisions were advancing. Many expected the city to fall before the end of the month. Panic was beginning to set in. Holt Green had been correct. The German offensive "probably would be successful."

---

1 NARA, RG 226, Entry 136, Box 34, Folder 375.
2 Ibid.
3 Ibid.
4 PRO, HS4/40.
5 James Sehmer, Letter to the author, August 21, 1997.
6 Messages 10, 11, Ibid.
7 Message 8, Bari to Green, Ibid.
8 Neal Cobb, Telephone interview with the author, May 19, 2001.
9 Message 18, Green to Bari. This message later would have much significant (See Chapter 35). Ibid.
10 Message 19, Green to Bari. Ibid.
11 PRO, HS4/40
12 Neal Cobb, Interview with the author, August, 1998.
13 Norton Skinner and Nick Yezdich, Telephone interviews with the author, September, 1996.

14 Neal Cobb, Interview with the author, August, 1998.
15 PRO, Ibid.
16 Ibid.; This observation that the Russian Partisan officers were low caliber probably illustrates that Koniev's staff and the Ukrainian Communist Party who organized the groups gave low priority to the Partisans.
17 Messages 69, 70, NARA, RG 226, Entry 136, Box 34, Folder 376.
18 PRO, HS4/40.
19 Ibid.
20 Holt Green message, October 6, 1944, NARA, RG 226, Entry 136, Box 34, Folder 376.
21 Ibid.
22 PRO, HS4/54.
23 Kliment and Nakladal, p. 94.
24 Ibid., p. 93.
25 Ibid., p. 99.
26 Ibid., pp. 90-94.

Chapter 9

Krajne

September, 1944, Western Slovakia.

Eleven American airmen had made it to Banska Bystrica in time to catch the September 17th flight back to Italy, but others were not so fortunate. George Fernandes and his group, for example, had been moving cautiously through the German lines.

"We had been warned that some Slovak families were German sympathizers," Fernandes remembers. One woman answered the door of her farmhouse and asked them if they were "from Grinava." Fernandes realized the Germans had been spreading the alarm. "This woman was frightened about our being at her house—not afraid of us but of the possibility of German reprisals. We moved on."[1]

Fernandes' group ran into four Partisans who took them to the same Partisan camp that Neal Cobb's group had just left two days before. They were reunited with "Scotty" McSorley, who had become separated from his buddy, New Zealander Gordon Follas. McSorley was traveling with Sam Strode, the tail gunner from Ira Corpening's crew.

Jack Wilson, the British agent, was there, still recovering from ingesting the cyanide pill. Meanwhile, Cobb's group was moving faster, perhaps because of their confidence that Frank Soltesz could speak Slovak and get clear directions and information on the location of German troops. Soltesz also was able to get food from the farmers.[2]

Fernandes had several long talks with Jack Wilson who claimed he was from Scotland. Actually, he was a Viennese who had migrated to Scotland. His native tongue was German, and his real name was Wanndorfer. Wilson also spoke fluent French. Fernandes persuaded him to join their group as preparations were made to move on. Wanndorfer never told Fernandes his real name.[3]

The following day a German patrol attacked the Partisan camp, and the men split into two groups and sprinted into the woods. Fernandes' group now included Wilson, Frank Bulfin, Bob Hede, and Howard Coleman.

They walked six miles through the hills to a small village, and two days later, they went to Krajne, a larger town where they would remain for two weeks. One of the Partisans took them to Michal Knap who operated the town bakery. Fernandes was surprised to discover that several people in this small village spoke English. Michal's brother, Martin, operated a tavern.

Michal Knap arranged to hide the men in three different households at great risk to the families. German vehicular patrols came through the village regularly. A few days later, a German patrol appeared suddenly, driving slowly down the street. The locals spread the alarm enabling Wilson, Bulfin, and Hede to dive out of windows or dash out rear doors and sprint into the woods.[4]

Coleman and Fernandes were in another house across town. Alerted, they also ran into the woods. Later, the Knap family moved the men to a farm owned by Jan and Katarina Galik on the edge of town. Katarina was Michal Knap's sister. Hede and Wilson already were there. The men slept in the loft for ten days, working on the *"Lashteki"* farm, as the Galiks called it. They shucked corn and weeded vegetable fields. Coleman, a farm boy from Virginia, tried to teach the farmers some improved methods of farming, but his hosts smiled and ignored him.[5] Nevertheless, the threat of discovery by the Germans was constant.

At night Fernandes would slip into town and listen to the BBC with Michal Knap. During the day, the men worked around the farm and killed time amusing themselves teasing Galiks' flock of domestic geese. Katarina Galik, who had lived in France for a time before the war, enjoyed speaking French with Jack Wilson.

At *Lashteki*, the Fernandes group ate well. Also hiding with the Galiks was Dr. Eugem Kulka, a Jewish physician from Prague, and more recently, Piestany. He was a pediatrician and cared for many of the people in the Krajne area. The Galiks had constructed a hiding place in their home behind a double partition where Kulka hid when the Germans visited the village.[6]

One day nearly two weeks later, Frank Bulfin was picking apples at *Leshteki*. The other four men were a half-mile away at another farm called "*Spotzky*" where they were shucking corn when a patrol of Germans entered the village. Bulfin hid in a ditch while the Germans carefully searched the farm. Katarina Galik ran to the Spotzky farm to warn the others.

The Knaps and Galiks finally decided it was time for the men to move on and Fernandes agreed. The Slovaks lived with the threat of German reprisals hanging over their heads. A Partisan led the group back to Jan Repta's camp at Brezova. Fifty-four years later, George Fernandes would visit Krajne for an emotional reunion with Michal and Anna Knap.

September, Brezova.

Here they met Repta and were reunited with Gordon Follas, their popular buddy from Grinava. There also was a group of four American airmen there who had been shot down on September 13, Richard Rippon, Guy LaFata, John Kacaja, and Ben Raczka. A Russian fighter pilot who had been flying an American P-39 Bell Aircobra also was at the camp. Ben Raczka and his B-24 crew had been shot down about 10 miles northwest of the camp. He escaped the Germans with the aid of two young Slovaks who later were betrayed by villagers sympathetic to the Germans. The *SS* shot the two boys.[7]

Fernandes and the others were surprised to meet an attractive female Partisan, Sonya, in Repta's brigade who had grown up in Ohio and spoke excellent English. It was a strange war.

Follas had been eager to show Repta his skills as a fighter, and went on his first raid while Fernandes and his group were at the camp. The Partisans set an ambush on a mountain road. A German motor column had been driving slowly up the winding route when Follas, waiting in the bushes by the side of the road, jumped up on the running board and shot both the officer and the driver. He took off running and the German soldiers chose not to give chase. Follas indeed had impressed Repta and the Partisans.[8]

The next day and that night, Fernandes talked with Follas about coming with them to Banska Bystrica, but the fiery New Zealander was adamant. Follas said he was staying with Repta so he could "kill Germans."[9]

Some of the men who had fled the camp at Grinava already had reached Banska Bystrica. Others were walking there. Richard Moulton and his buddies, meanwhile, were back at Modra counting the days. Jack Kellogg, who had endured half of July and most of August in solitary confinement in a Budapest prison was settling down in the British compound in *Stalag Luft III*. His new roommates included tunnelers in the Great Escape which occurred the previous March. Kellogg had been grilled by his interrogator in Budapest because he was captured in civilian clothes. The *Luftwaffe* officer repeatedly accused Kellogg of being an intelligent agent. Kellogg learned years later that the OSS used the "I'm an airman" cover story to attempt to fool the Germans if they were captured. John Schianca, Thayne Thomas, and Robert Donahue, meanwhile, already had arrived back in the States and were enjoying family reunions.

---

1 George Fernandes, Unpublished manuscript.
2 Neal Cobb, Interview with the author, August, 1998.
3 George Fernandes, Unpublished manuscript.
4 Ibid.
5 Ibid.

6 Vladimir Galik, Letter to the author, 1998.
7 Juraj Rajninec, Monograph, presented to the author, 1996.
8 George Fernandes, Unpublished manuscript.
9 George Fernandes, Telephone interview with the author, August, 1998.

Chapter 10

Return to Tri Duby

October, 1944, Bari, Italy.

The anxiety in Banska Bystrica did not extend to Bari. Spurred on by Captain Charles Katek's recent visit from London to implement General Donovan's ambitious policies, Major Walter Ross and Lt. Nelson Deranian decided to expand the DAWES mission. Donovan's objective for increased intelligence operations into central Europe was underway.

In retrospect, Holt Green's reports to Bari in the previous 20 days did not reflect the grave situation confronting the rebels. His accounts of the cooperation of General Golian and the Czech Army staff and his trips to the front failed to convey the possibility, or probability, of an impending tragedy.

Green traveled about freely on the Slovak-German front. Soon, however, the German *SS* brigades began relentlessly to pound the Slovak Army. Although the Slovaks did throw the Germans out of Telgart, east of Brezno, it was a momentary success. The Partisans, ill prepared for static defensive operations, were of little help to the Slovak army. The latter in turn was no match for the better-armed and disciplined Germans. The Slovaks had no effective armor, little artillery and no anti-tank weapons. Their rifles were World War I vintage, and they were short of automatic weapons.

The Germans began to advance up the Vah River Valley. On October 3, they had just captured Ziar nad Hronom, 16 miles southwest of Banska Bystrica. The day before, they had occupied Kremnica, only 14 miles west of the rebel capital, and fierce fighting was underway around Biely Potok, 28 miles north. On October 5 in Vienna, Heinrich Himmler had ordered General Hoefle on October 5 to step up his offensive.[1]

Although Holt Green noted in his messages to Bari the slim odds of the Slovak uprising succeeding, his level of concern did not match that of General Golian and his staff. Green's messages simply lacked a sense or urgency.

Was Green cautious, and even a bit cavalier, because to suggest excessive concern might have demonstrated a lack of nerve? Intelligence personnel operated behind enemy lines with daring and dash. They were expected to perform their deadly and dangerous work in a routine fashion, always holding themselves to a high standard. Could valor have exceeded good judgment in this instance?

Holt Green Advises Against Additional Personnel.

Green did advise against sending in any more OSS personnel, but Ross and Deranian took little notice. Green mentioned that in a worst case development, they could slip into the mountains and evade the enemy. This had worked in Yugoslavia, and both Green and his superiors in Bari believed, if necessary, it could work in Slovakia.[2]

Lt. Jim Gaul, USNR, was selected as Holt Green's second in command. He had impressive credentials. A young boy of some privilege, he had grown up in Pittsburgh. His father was a well-known organist and composer. The family spent their summers in Provincetown, Massachusetts where they were active in the community theater. His parents sent him to the St. Albans School for boys in Washington DC where he prepared to enter Harvard. In Cambridge, he later earned his BA and MA, receiving his PhD in archaeology in 1940.

One summer in college Gaul sailed on a freighter to Europe, and visited Carthage, Greece, Egypt, and Istanbul. After receiving his bachelor's degree, he had taught in a private boys school in Paris for a year. Later, he spent two more years of travel in Europe during which he visited Czechoslovakia.

As a graduate student, Gaul worked on some archaeological digs in Slovakia. In 1935, he lived in Persia for a while and later spent time in Bulgaria. He had familiarity with 14 languages. When the war started, he quit his teaching job at Brooklyn College and entered the Navy. He ultimately wound up in Cairo where he joined the OSS. Six feet two inches tall, he was strong and active, the perfect OSS agent.[3]

Lt. Nelson Deranian responded to the Slovak requests for ordinance and weapons experts. He picked two Army infantry lieutenants, Bill McGregor and Kenneth Lain, to accompany Gaul. McGregor recalled later that Holt Green had informed Deranian that "the situation was ripe."[4] McGregor was not privy to Green's communications with Bari, but after arriving in Banska Bystrica, he believed he had a sense of what had transpired. He recalled years later that the OSS team rehashed daily the purpose of the mission.[5]

McGregor had landed at Salerno, Italy, with the 36th Division in September, 1943. He had been severely wounded in December, and spent the next six months recuperating in an Army hospital in Oran, Morocco.

McGregor's parents contacted an old family friend, Betty Lussier, who visited him in the hospital. An X-2 OSS agent in Algiers, Lussier subsequently recruited him into the OSS. Released from medical care, McGregor was sent to a special British mine and booby-trap school in the Sahara Desert.[6] One of his new OSS friends was Jack Hemingway, son of the famous author. McGregor was impatient to get into action, and was elated when he was sent to Bari and put on the DAWES team.

McGregor, self confident and a natural leader, had been captain of the lacrosse team at the University of Maryland. Outgoing, he was popular among the men. He laughed years later when he recalled that the affable Nelson Deranian gave him a bottle of whiskey when they left the Bari airport.[7]

Army Sergeant Kenneth Dunlevy, one of the four OSS survivors of the DAWES mission, in his official report written jointly with Army Sergeant Steve Catlos in the Spring of 1945, was generally critical of the mission. "We had no briefing in Bari on the Army of Liberation. We were selected to go in last week of September. There was no briefing on topography, weather, political situation or economic conditions, and we actually had no idea of the purpose of the mission." Dunlevy's comments must have shaken both Major Ross and Lt. Deranian when they were apprised near the end of the war of the his criticism. Dunlevy, being an enlisted man, undoubtedly was not briefed on the information known to the officers, Green, Gaul, and Edward Baranski.[8]

Jan Schwartz, leader of the two-man HOUSEBOAT mission, also spoke critically of the purposes of the mission to writer William Miller in May , 1984. He told Miller he had suppressed his feelings for forty years because he did not want to criticize members of the mission, all of whom he considered to be courageous men.[9]

Bari Adds Outstanding Personnel to Dawes Mission.

Ross and Deranian's other selections for the mission were all top notch. The OSS team was large, but it was designed to be split into small teams. Francis Moly (cover name), Steve Cora (cover name), Stvev Catlos, and Tibor Keszthelyi were to be sent into Hungary. Captain Edward Baranski, Dunlevy, Emil Tomes (the Slovak civilian brought out of Tri Duby on September 17), Daniel Pavletich (a Yugoslav civilian), Lt. Lane Miller and Anton Novak (a Slovak civilian) were to go into lower Slovakia. Green was overall chief of DAWES, HOUSEBOAT, DAY and the other group. Jim Gaul had volunteered for the mission when he had learned they would be rounding up downed airmen, and he was to be out in the field.

Baranski was to lead the DAY mission. Lt. Lane Miller, Daniel Pavletich, and Anton "Tony" Novak were assigned to him. McGregor and Lain and were prepared to train the Partisans how to use Bazookas. Miller had been a B-24 pilot in the 376th Bomb Group, the famed "Liberandos" who participated in the famous low-level raid on Ploesti in 1943. He flew only a few missions when he was shot down on July 30, 1944, over Yugoslavia. He was rescued by either *Chetniks* or Partisans and delivered to the OSS who brought him back to Italy on August 14.

Army Lt. Tibor Keszthelyi, Army Lt. Francis Perry, Army Sergeant Steve Catlos had special assignments. Keszthelyi and Catlos spoke Hungarian and hoped to travel south from Slovakia into Hungary. Perry was Austrian and was prepared to get into Vienna, his home before immigrating before the war to the United States. Although Croatian, Pavletich was able to communicate in Slovak. Tomes, who had come out of Banska Bystrica on September 17, was fluent, of course. First Lieutenant Lane Miller was an air combat veteran.

The 483rd Bomb Group was selected again for the airlift to Tri Duby. Lt. Colonel Gil Pritchard, the mission commander who flew the September 17 mission, wanted experienced pilots who were captains or above to fly the other five aircraft. Major Fred Ascani led the flight of the six B-17's from their Italian base to Bari on October 6 where he was greeted by Pritchard. Colonel Jack Ryan, later to become Chief of Staff of the Air Force, briefed the crews that night. Captain Hugh Rowe remembers the huge 10x20 feet wall map which had a ribbon stretching from Bari to Slovakia, the type used in major headquarters installations and familiar later in Hollywood movies. Jim Cinnamon, Pritchard's co-pilot, recalls that all the crewmen, officers and enlisted men, slept in the same large room with an armed guard.[10]

The B-17's flew with reduced crews, two pilots, a navigator, a radio operator, and a tail gunner in order to carry the supplies and ordinance. The nose gun and the waist guns were manned by the passengers. Fighters from the 52nd Fighter Group would be their protection.

Captain Jack Gorman, a squadron commander in the 483rd, had recruited his friends Glen McSparran, Hugh Rowe, and Jim Loughner, all captains. Gorman and Loughner had finished their 50 missions, but young, adventuresome pilots, they volunteered for this secret mission without knowing what it entailed. Gorman selected the squadron's newest B-17's to fly.[11]

The aircraft were loaded in the evening of October 6. Ordinance was the first priority, but there also were medical supplies, gasoline and personal gear, as well as clothing for the rescued airmen.[12] The ordinance included 18 tons of 150 bazookas, 3000 rockets, 100 Marlin (similar to a Tommy gun) 9mm machine guns, 100,000 rounds of 9mm ammo, 75,000 rounds of rifle ammo, 99 Bren guns, plus other items.[13] Fred Ascani remembers that he had a two-wheeled bicycle on board. The planes were specially rigged. Each bomb bay had flooring installed, and the area was filled to the ceiling with five-gallon gas cans.[14]

October 7.

They took off at 10:15 the next morning and joined a large mission headed for Vienna. An escort of 32 P-51 Mustangs from the 52nd Fighter Group accompanied them again. Cinnamon recalls being introduced to Colonel Charles Bodecker, commanding officer of the fighter group, at the briefing.

Lieutenant Bill Coloney of the 52nd rode as a passenger on Jack Gorman's plane. His instructions were to leave the aircraft after landing and get to Alex Watkins' Mustang, the "Swamp Fox," parked on the Tri Duby field. Colony hoped to start the plane and fly it back to Italy. Sergeant Jim Pittman, one of the airmen who had made it to Banska Bystrica from the Grinava POW camp, had inspected the fighter on October 1 and informed Holt Green that it appeared to be in perfect condition.[15]

Pritchard told the group during the briefing that German troops were in the vicinity of the Tri Duby airfield, and that before landing, personnel on the ground would signal an all-clear with flares. Pritchard told them that the airfield could be controlled by the Germans. The field was not easy to find, Pritchard warned. It was located in one of three parallel valleys among low-lying hill systems.[16]

Because of the last minute selections, one B-17 pilot was a 19-year-old second lieutenant, Jim Street. A "real fuss" was made in Bari when the operations officers learned second lieutenants were piloting one of the planes, Eugene Kennedy, Street's co-pilot, recalled years later.[17]

Colonel Jack Ryan and Major Walter Ross, who was going along on the flight, impressed upon the group that the mission was top secret and that important OSS and SOE intelligence personnel would be on board. Colony was excited about the trip. He learned that among the passengers on Gorman's plane were two colonels, Henry Threlfall, an English SOE officer; and the other a Slovak, Jindrich Souhadra.[18] Threlfall explained the significance of the cargo and its importance to the Slovaks in the uprising to Coloney, the young lieutenant.[19]

Joe Morton of the Associated Press Comes Along.

There was another passenger waiting in the wings, Joe Morton, an Associated Press war correspondent. The next morning, Morton showed up at the airport and boarded Pritchard's lead plane with Major Ross, Lt. Deranian, and Lt. Jim Gaul and another OSS officer. Radio man Bill Newton remembers the flight. The four officers played backgammon for most of the trip while Morton sat in the radio room with Newton.[20]

Joe Morton's permission to accompany the team later became an issue of some dispute. Morton had flown into Yugoslavia on OSS missions, and also had accompanied the OSS team into Bucharest in August. He was a popular and energetic reporter, and the OSS Bari command was not unmindful of the public relations benefit of an eye-witness account.

For American newspapermen, World War II was the opportunity they had been waiting for. Eager reporters hustled off to every corner of the world where GI's were fighting. Morton, a native of St. Joseph, Missouri, joined this legion of news hounds, knowing the war would spawn an endless number of great stories.

Morton was remembered by some as "gentle, ever-smiling Joe," although his charming and friendly demeanor disguised an aggressive reporter who would go anywhere and do nearly anything to get a story. In 1942 Morton was sent to Dakar in West Africa and later to Algiers where he covered the air war in Tunisia. After that, he reported on the invasion of Sicily, and repeatedly found himself drawn into the most difficult, dangerous places. When Morton wrote to his boss at AP headquarters in New York that he and his wife, Letty, his wife of seven years, were expecting a child, he was cautioned not to "risk your neck in any stunts."[21]

But Morton continued to chase the big story. He had flown over Monte Cassino when the 15th Air Force bombed the historic abbey, and on a later mission, he looked down on Rome from a B-26 medium bomber in the first Allied raid over the city. Later, when the Fifth Army entered Rome, Morton, recorded the sights and sounds of the historic city. For Morton, the war was an adventure.

Hanging around the 15th Air Force headquarters in Bari, Italy, Morton became intrigued with the Balkans, especially Yugoslavia and Joseph Tito, the legendary Partisan leader. Morton made three flights into Yugoslavia where the OSS, the 15th Air Force and the Yugoslavs cooperated to rescue downed airmen. Morton was fascinated by the secrecy of these missions and loved to hang around the "cloak and dagger boys." He attempted to interview Tito, and was rewarded with a 1600-word memo from the Partisan guerrilla leaders which took the AP weeks to get past the censors. It was a sensational scoop for Morton.[22]

Morton's contacts with the OSS continued to pay off. He learned that the 15th Air Force was transporting an OSS operating into Romania. His friend, Walter Ross, allowed Morton to accompany the flight to Bucharest where Ross was formulating the final rescue plans. Morton chanced to be there when the Red Army entered Bucharest, and his vivid accounts caught the attention of his bosses in New York.

In August Morton joined Ross and the OSS team for a second trip to

Return to Tri Duby

Bucharest with Operation REUNION, the airlift to bring out the airmen. The OSS team stayed at the Ambassador Hotel, recently vacated by the German *Luftwaffe*. It was a heady atmosphere with colorful personalities going and coming at all hours. Morton was able to interview King Michael and the Queen Mother at their castle. The *New York Times* subsequently complimented Morton on his dramatic account of the young monarch racing around Bucharest in his convertible.

Later, Morton learned of the September flight to Slovakia. How could he have made the trip without getting permission from Ross?[23] Bari had earlier noted Holt Green that Morton was coming. Before sunrise on October 7, Morton was at the Bari airfield.

Jim Street and one of his crew, Clyde Feemster, years later recalled one of the SOE agents who rode on their plane, Aba Berdichev, a Romanian Jew. He wore the uniform of a British Army lieutenant, using the cover name Robert Willis. The SOE AMSTERDAM team which earlier had parachuted into Slovakia had lost their radio sets, and Berdichev was bringing them replacements. The radios were not on the cargo manifest, and Berdichev asked Street for permission to load them. The young pilot agreed, and Berdichev gratefully gave him a bottle of whiskey.[24]

The OSS and British SOE men manned some of the .50 caliber machine guns on the B-17's. Although they saw no enemy planes, they found the slight exhilarating. McGregor manned a gun in the nose gunner's position on one of the planes.

Bill McGregor Thrilled To Be a Gunner.

"Can you imagine?" McGregor joked in 1996. "A bullshit soldier like me flying in a plane, manning a machine gun. You gotta be kidding! I watched the P-51s flying around. It was a real thrill for a doughfoot like me."[25]

Lt. Colonel Henry Threlfall, a British SOE officer, and Colonel Jindrich Souhrada manned waist guns. Like McGregor, Threlfall found it an exhilarating experience. "I had a superb view of the blue waters of the Adriatic or the fleecy white clouds or the long straight roads of the central European landscape," He reported later. ". . . and with the escort of Mustangs skidding about the skies above us in the most extraordinary fashion, the effect was a dramatic as any flying film or propaganda leaflet which you have seen could make it."[26]

The flight was routine until they neared Tri Duby. A cloud cover made it difficult for the lead navigator to locate the field, so Lt. Colonel Pritchard led the six-plane formation down through a hole in the clouds and began skimming over the hills. They had to double back. Fred Ascani recalls the group making 45 to 60 degree banking turns. In a tight formation, that was a spectacular feat for Flying Fortresses. Ascani recalls Pritchard (Both later became major generals.) as a "helluva pilot," always smiling and fearless.[27] Jack Gorman agreed that it was "pretty wild getting though the clouds in formation."[28]

Pritchard saw the green flares signaling it was safe to land after making one pass over the field, and he landed with the other pilots following him in, one after the other. It had been raining and the field was soft and soggy. Hugh Rowe was the last to land and noticed that Jack Gorman, just ahead of him, had to turn wide to avoid Major Ascani's plane which had landed to Gorman's front.

"Our right gear sank in – broke the surface" Gorman remembers. "Fortunately the plane's right props cleared the ground so we could use the engine power to attempt to free the aircraft."[29]

The five other planes taxied over in front of a large row of hangars, wing tip to wing tip. Slovak soldiers rushed out and unloaded the planes, including Gorman's. Bill Coloney leaped out and raced across the field to Alex Watkins' Mustang. Jack Gorman's plane, meanwhile, was stuck in the mud at the south end of the field.

---

1 Kliment and Nakladal, pp. 103-104

2 NARA, RG 226, Entry 136, Box 34, Folder 375.
3 NARA, RG 226, Entry 196, Box 34, Folder 407.
4 Bill McGregor, Tape recording made in 1960's, courtesy of his daughter, Sandy Woods.
5 Bill McGregor, Telephone conversation with the author, February, 1996.
6 Bill McGregor, Unpublished notes, courtesy of Sandy Woods.
7 Ibid.
8 Kenneth Dunlevy, Interview with William Miller, May, 1984, courtesy of his daughter, Marilyn Miller.
9 Ibid.
10 James Cinnaman and Hugh Rowe, Letters to the author, 1996.
11 Jack Gorman, Telephone conversation with the author, 1996.
12 Kenneth Dunlevy, NARA, RG 226, Entry 108B84F691, Box 84, Folder 691 (Hereinafter cited as OSS Report).
13 Nelson Deranian, OSS report, NARA, RG 226, Entry 141A, Box 12, Folder 89.
14 Fred Ascani, Telephone interview with the author, 1996.
15 Bill Coloney, Telephone interview with the author, March, 1996.
16 James Cinnaman, Letter to the author, 1996.
17 Eugene Kennedy, Letter to the author, 1996.
18 Bill Coloney, Telephone interview with the author, March 1996.
19 Bill Coloney, E mail to the author, June 14, 2000.
20 Bill Newton, Letter to the author, 1996.
21 Larry Heinzerling, Unpublished manuscript.
22 Ibid.
23 Ibid.
24 Jim Street, Telephone interview with the author, 1997. The British officer may have been Captain R.B.H. Page, Threlfall's aide. Street recalls that the officer spoke with an educated British accent.
25 Bill McGregor, Telephone interview with the author, April, 1999.
26 Henry Threlfall, O.B.E., was a 37-year-old who had worked for Lever Brothers in Berlin from 1936 until 1939. His German was excellent, and he also had some fluency in French. He had previous postings to Stockholm and had worked in the London SOE headquarters where he was responsible for liaison with the Czech and Polish governments in exile. In April, 1944, he was sent to Bari to command Force 139, Central Mediterranean Forces, in Bari, Italy. He was highly regarded by his SOE superior in London, Lt. Colonel H.B. Perkins. Letter to author from Duncan Stuart, SOE Records, October 9,2000.
27 Fred Ascani, Letter to the author, 1996.
28 Jack Gorman, Telephone interview with the author, 1997.
29 Ibid.

Chapter 11

"Carnival Atmosphere"

October 7, Banska Bystrica.

Holt Green spread the good news to the airmen. The 15th Air Force was coming! The 28 American and two Australian airmen hustled aboard trucks headed for Tri Duby. Spirits were high, and although the stay in the city had been pleasant, the airmen were eager to get to Italy. At the airport, some men wandered around impatiently, and others lay around in small groups on the grass.

A few men examined Lt. Ethan Allen Smith's dismantled Mustang which was stacked along the wall of one of the hangars. Several *Swastika* decals adorned the fuselage, and Smith explained that he had been flying another pilot's plane.

Lt. Manley Fliger remembers Smith lamenting that he had been flying a veteran pilot's plane, and now Smith had to return and explain what happened. Smith had been lucky to escape with minor injuries. After he had been released from the hospital at Zvolen, he was taken to Banska Bystrica where he stayed at the OSS headquarters.[1]

The weather began to turn bad and the planes were late. Depressed, the men mulled around, fretting and preparing to get back on the trucks and return to Banska Bystrica. The situation looked grim. "We could hear shelling in the distance, and we were afraid we would have to take off for the hills," Neal Cobb remembers.[2]

Suddenly, P-51 Mustangs came through the clouds, their engines roaring. One buzzed the airfield at 500 feet, and the airmen burst into cheers. Moments later six "beautiful" B-17's flew over, and then made two more passes over the field. The Slovaks fired green flares into the sky, signaling the all clear and the planes touched down at 1:55 PM.

Holt Green had assigned five airmen to each plane. The planes taxied up to the hangar area and parked wing tip to wing tip as the flyers rushed over to their assigned aircraft to assist Slovak soldiers in unloading the cargoes. Five flyers, including Manley Fliger, ran to the south end of the field where Jack Gorman's plane was stuck.[3]

Slovak and Russian Officers In Dress Uniforms.

Lt. Colonel Henry Threlfall recorded the scene. "There was the most motley crew you can imagine watching the arrival. Lots of Slovak troops in light khaki uniforms with blue facings, elegant Slovak officers with red and gold collars, British in battledress, Americans in everything conceivable, including the stranded airmen whom one would hardly expect to be dressed strictly according to military regulations, gaily uniformed Russians with huge gold epaulettes, and heaven knows what!"

Bill McGregor recalled the "great mob of people there to greet us." Everyone was excited about our arrival. Steve Catlos remembered a "battery of cameras." He wondered to himself about the likelihood of German agents in the crowd. Ken Dunlevy estimated the photographers at 200.[4] He wondered, would this represent a problem later?

In the midst of this colorful scene, a Slovak bi-plane landed on the field. Piloted by Julius Goralik, the Praga E-39 resembled an American Stearman trainer. Aboard was Charlie Muller, a B-17 tail gunner, who had been shot down on August 27 near the target, Blechhammer. Muller had bailed out over Swidnica, 40 miles northwest of the target. His B-17, on automatic pilot, later crashed at Makov, 50 miles southeast.[5] Muller's pilot, Jack Wilson, was found by a Slovak partisan unit led by Alexander Dubcek.[6]

Sergeant Charlie Muller Is Flown To Banska Bystrica.

Muller was captured a few days after he was shot down. The Germans took him to *Stalag Luft VII*, located in the village of Bunkau near Kreuzburg and only a few miles from Blechhammer.[7] He stayed to himself in the camp and carefully planned his escape, studying the German supply trucks which came almost daily into the camp. Most of the German guards were diligent, but two of the guards only casually inspected the undersides of the trucks. Muller concluded if those guards were on duty, he would crawl into the undercarriage of the truck and ride out of the camp. Muller volunteered as a regular worker, unloading the trucks. When the opportunity came, he executed his plan and out of the camp he went![8]

A few miles later at a stop, Muller dropped from the truck, and rolled into the bushes by the side of the road. He subsequently evaded for four weeks, traveling 35 miles to the Czech border. He later wound up with a Slovak Partisan group near Parnica, 13 miles northwest of Ruzomberok. He recalls that he became a "problem" there for the Partisans who were constantly on the move, and they arranged to fly him out. The *Praga* biplane had a Jerry-rigged oxygen tank strapped to the belly of the aircraft with rubber hoses leading to the cockpits so the plane could fly at high altitudes.

On the 50-mile flight to Tri Duby, however, the pilot Goralik hedge-hopped all the way to Tri Duby, flying right over the *Wehrmacht* front lines which were advancing on Banska Bystrica from the west. Muller arrived just in time to see the crowd of Slovaks around Jack Gorman's B-17. That night, he was back in Italy.[9]

At Tri Duby, the sight of these six B-17's sitting on the landing field was intoxicating to the Slovaks. The air was filled with hope and excitement as they saw what they imagined as the United States, the great champion of democracy, coming to their aid on a dramatic scale. The euphoria convinced the Slovaks that the Uprising now would succeed. They had seen these four engine bombers overhead in fleets of hundreds flying north to punish the *Reich*. Now they were here on the ground among desperate people, bringing aid to them to assist in throwing off the German strangle hold. The symbolic impact of the Flying Fortresses was powerful.

Lieutenant Bill Coloney, meanwhile, was the first out of Gorman's plane and sprinted across the field to where Alex Watkins' Mustang was parked. Colony couldn't start the engine. The battery was low. It turned over a few times, coughed and sputtered and died. Colony realized he could hear the artillery in the distance. He noted that the people around the airport looked prosperous and happy, and a number of them were driving shiny new Packards. Colony was puzzled by the fact that Slovaks were setting fire to several vintage bi-planes on the edge of the field.

Frustrated, Coloney gave up and ran back to Gorman's plane. "I got the scare of my life when Colonel Charles Boedecker, the Group commander, and Huston "Blanch" Blanchard buzzed the field right above me." Colony thought at first they were German planes on a strafing run. Later, Colony regretted he had not been properly briefed about the Mustang. He felt had he brought along a spare battery, a new fuel pump and some tools, he might have been able to start it.

Bodecker and Blanchard made two or three runs over the field no more than 20 feet above the grass runway, "noisy but reassuring," Fred Ascani remembers.[10]

Years later, Ascani wrote an account of the incident involving Jack Gorman's plane. Ascani saw that the plane was stuck in the mud and left his aircraft to ask Pritchard what to do. Pritchard told him to run over to Gorman to tell him to set the plane afire and get on Major Ascani's B-17 with his crew. Ascani took off on the run.[11]

Jack Gorman and Ascani have different versions of the conversation that followed. Major Ascani thought he was giving Captain Gorman an order. Gorman heard it as a suggestion and declined. Ascani was flabbergasted, but didn't argue. Gorman told his crew they could get on another plane if they chose. They elected to stay. During all of this, the Mustang pilots continually buzzed the field. Slovak troops continued to arrive on the run with ropes. There were soon over 100 men working to free the plane. The scene was hectic.

Sergeant Bill Newton Gets To Know Joe Morton.
Sergeant Bill Newton had been intrigued by Morton, who rode to Tri Duby in the radio compartment with Newton. He later remembered:

> Joe was a friendly, outgoing person. He had an interview technique which made me ready and willing to give him all the details of my life history. He provided a number of details about our mission which were not covered in our briefing. Also, when he learned I had never heard of the OSS, he gave me a short rundown. He also told me about where he was from and about some of the stories he had covered. We had been told that Joe would be returning with us, but it wasn't hard to figure out that he planned to stay with the OSS team. He mentioned plans to write a book about his experiences, and that this would make one helluva story. As for getting official permission to stay with the team, he said something to the effect that it would be much easier to get official forgiveness than permission. When we landed, he shook my hand, then flipped me a salute, and said, I'll send you a copy of my book. We also had four OSS men aboard [Major Ross, Lt. Deranian, Lt. Gaul, and another, and probably Captain Edward Baranski]. Pritchard had told me to stay with my radio, so all I saw on the ground was through the small window next to my table. I was able to see Maj. Gorman's plane stuck in the mud, and all the Partisans trying to help free it. There were many people milling about. Our engines were running the entire time we were on the ground. I remember being very impressed with Pritchard. He was a macho type, very confident, and obviously relishing the unusual mission.[12]

Neal Cobb and John Pittman were assigned to Lt. Colonel Pritchard's plane. Both remember Joe Morton leaving the plane to stand near them as they helped unload the aircraft. They watched Morton set up his portable typewriter on a box and begin typing.[13] A photograph in the Banska Bystrica museum of the Slovak National Museum shows Pritchard's olive drab plane with what appears to be Morton standing under the tail of the aircraft taking notes.

Meanwhile, Lt. Colonel Threlfall and Colonel Souhrada met with Major John Sehmer, Generals Golian, and Viest, while Major Ross and Lt. Deranian conferred with Holt Green.

General Golian picked up Threlfall and Colonel Souhrada at the plane in his Packard sedan and drove them to the hangar where they were introduced to General Viest. Viest had been flown into Tri Duby that morning from Moscow aboard a Soviet C-47 to take over as the commanding general of the Uprising. Golian was to command the Banska Bystrica garrison. Major John Sehmer also participated in this meeting.

Threlfall also was introduced to Lt. Colonel Mirko Vesel, Jan Ursiny, and Alco Novomesky, who were to return to Bari with Threlfall and proceed on to London to report to the Benes government.[14] Vesel represented the Slovak Army, Ursiny the Social Democrats and Novomesky the Slovak Communist Party.

General Golian Complains About Soviet Aid.

Golian "tactfully," Threlfall noted, complained about the lack of Soviet aid. He also requested bombing support from the 15th Air Force. As the men stood there in the hangar, they could hear the German guns. Threlfall concluded quickly that the situation indeed was serious and that the German offensive was on the verge of crushing the uprising.

Golian handed Threlfall a situation map and described the current fighting in the nearby densely wooded hills and valleys. Sehmer said he believed Tri Duby would fall within a week, an opinion which was not disputed by Golian. Golian pleaded again for bombing support, adding that a week's delay "might be too late."[15]

Back on the airfield, Major Ross listened to Lt. Deranian review the OSS mission with Holt Green, although Green was occupied with the unloading and loading of the planes much of the time. A number of Russian officers walked about the B-17's, obviously interested in these famous "Flying Fortresses."

Lt. Manley Fliger, one of the airmen assigned to return on Jack Gorman's plane, had run to the south end of the airfield to assist unloading the aircraft when they landed. "The pilot was outside the aircraft looking over the situation with the engines running. It didn't look good. My heart sank." Years later Fliger recalled "the other pilot" (Ascani) talking to Gorman, but did not hear the conversation.[16]

Slovak soldiers, meanwhile, lined up to pull on the ropes to drag the plane free. Gorman re-entered the plane and raced the engines. It wouldn't budge. Holt Green finally drove up and told the airmen standing outside to get on another plane. "'Get down there—you'll be left!' He shouted." I didn't hesitate," Fliger remembers.[17]

About the same time, Bill Coloney arrived on the run and was also told by Green to get on another plane. Pritchard had delayed their departure until Coloney either got the Mustang in the air or he was back on board one of the B-17's. Coloney, Lt. Colonel Threlfall, the three Slovak emissaries, and the others flew back on Hugh Rowe's aircraft as did Lt. Colonel Threlfall.

---

1 Manley Fliger, Interview with the author, September 15, 1997; Smith doesn't remember the conversation about his plane, but he told the author that he doesn't doubt it took place. Telephone interview with the author, September, 1997.
2 Neal Cobb, Telephone interview with the author, March 1996.
3 Fliger, Conversation with the author.
4 Kenneth Dunlevy, Interview with William Miller, 1984; Bill McGregor, Telephone interview with the author, 1996.
5 Viliam Klabnik, E mail to the author, March 7, 2001. Klabnik is a military historian in Martin, Slovakia; Charles Muller, Interview with the author, March 7, 2001.
6 Jack Wilson, Letter to the author, February, 2000.
7 *Stalag Luft VII* was 35 miles east of Breslau.
8 Charles Muller, Interview.
9 Ibid. Silas Crase was the ball turret gunner on Muller's plane. Crase evaded with another Partisan group. At the end of the war, he was liberated by Russian troops who occupied the area. Crase was uncomfortable with the Russians, and slipped away and took off for Prague where he found the American military mission. He was then sent to Pilsen and subsequently on to France, Telephone interview with the author, March, 2001.
10 Fred Ascani, Letter to the author, 1996; Bill Coloney, E mail to the author, June 14, 2000.
11 Ascani, Letter to the author.
12 Bill Newton, Letter to author, 1996.

13 Neal Cobb, Interview with the author; John Pittman, telephone interview with the author, 1996.
14 PRO, HS4/27.
15 Ibid.
16 Fliger, Interview with the author.
17 Ibid.

Chapter 12

Going Home

October 7, 1944, Flight Back to Bari.

Lieutenant Bill McGregor had watched the Partisans struggling to free the B-17. "I admired that crew, sticking with their pilot to save their plane. When it later took off, I watched it fly down the valley just above the trees and head home without fighter support. It was a long way back to Italy. That pilot and his crew had a lot of guts."[1]

Gorman had taxied his plane up to the hangar area before he took off. Holt Green entered the plane to ask him if he would take five wounded French partisans back to Bari. Gorman agreed but asked for a formal, written request. Major John Sehmer wrote it out, and both he and Green signed it.[2]

On the flight to Bari, Threlfall noted that his plane was filled with American airmen in "every available corner." He found it gratifying to be with these men who had "spent anything from a fortnight to three months in the wilds of Slovakia, and had never expected to emerge again."[3]

There were 28 American airmen, plus two New Zealand airmen, on board the five aircraft. They left Tri Duby at 2 PM and arrived back at Bari at 5:50.

Neal Cobb was troubled by the lack of sufficient parachutes. When the flight landed in Bari, "I grabbed the first guy I saw and gave him a hug—the only time I ever hugged a general. When we later got back to our base, we didn't know a soul. All our old friends had been shot down or rotated back to the States."4

Sergeants Norton Skinner, Nick Yezdich, Ralph Fuchs, and Lt. Manley Fliger plus the other airmen were elated that they were on their way home. Life had been comfortable in Banska Bystrica, but the ominous presence of the Germans in the surrounding hills had been unsettling.

Sergeant Bill Newton had read the situation right about Joe Morton—the Associated Press correspondent had no intention of returning on the flight. Morton, like any good newsman, had exploited his friendship with Major Ross to get on the flight, and now he was going a step further. He was convinced this was the biggest story of his career, and he wasn't going to let it slip away.

Regarding Joe Morton, he later wrote, "I didn't pay too much attention to Morton until our plane was ready to close up and take off. Morton was sitting there on a box with his typewriter in front of him, typing away. I thought he was coming right along to get on our plane, but when I asked him if he shouldn't be closing up, he said, 'Well, I think I'll wait and probably come out on the next airplane.' Which at that time was being dug out at the end of the field."5

Deranian and Threlfall Produce Different Reports.

Both Lt. Nelson Deranian and Lt. Colonel Threlfall wrote official reports of the Tri Duby mission to their respective headquarters in Washington and London. A half-century later, a comparison of these two documents sheds some light on the perception of the crisis in Banska Bystrica as seen by the two intelligence officers. Additionally, the reports highlight the different styles and insights of the Americans and the British.

Deranian's report contained ten enclosures, documents produced by Holt Green, his staff, and captured German documents. His report had 19 numbered paragraphs, summarizing Green's mission, its accomplishments, and the substance of his and Major Walter Ross' conversations with Green on the airfield. Deranian and Ross spoke only to the Americans. Indeed, the

Going Home

mission to date had been a tremendous success.[6]

On the other hand, Threlfall described the geography of the area that he observed from the air when they circled the field prior to landing. He noted that the hills were between three and four thousand feet high and covered with thick woods "impenetrable to vehicles and difficult for men on foot." He concluded that the terrain was suitable for guerrilla warfare but was not "wild and inaccessible enough to hold out there for good."[7] Threlfall reported that it appeared to him that General Golian was delighted to meet "an English officer"[8]

Threlfall pointed out that the Germans were only ten miles away from the airport, and he quoted Sehmer who emphasized that the situation was "grave." Golian gave Threlfall a detailed situation map showing the positions of the Germans. He quoted Golian as practically begging for additional arms. Golian was cautiously critical of the Russians for failure to deliver promised aid. Threlfall also made a point to note that Golian, who conversed with him in German, referred to "Czechoslovakia," rather than Slovakia.

In contrast, Lieutenant Deranian's report was more of the chest-thumping variety which praised Green's accomplishments. There was no reference to the perilous situation in Banska Bystrica until page five of the report. The report was tailored in such a way that Deranian knew would be favorably received by General Donovan back in Washington. Deranian reported Holt Green was "concerned" about the situation and the "possibility" that the airfield might soon be overrun by the Germans, an observation that appears as almost an after-thought. This was clearly an understatement. Yet, the assessment may have reflected Green more than Deranian.

Threlfall Is Drawn Emotionally To The Slovak Cause.

Lt. Colonel Henry Threlfall was drawn emotionally to the Slovak cause. He reported to London two days later that, "The experience was a moving one, and the visit to that small army, which is doing its best with the most slender resources imaginable, really did make one understand rather better the human element involved in the phrase 'Resistance Movement' which is such a common and everyday occurrence in the mass of paper we have to deal with. Golian and his officers were very dignified and reasonable, but there is no doubt they need help badly, and I feel it is up to us to do whatever we can."[9]

Baranski Named To Head DAY Mission.

One of the subgroups of the DAWES mission, code-named DAY, was led by Captain Edward Baranski. Since the collapse of the FALCON mission (see Chapter two), Baranski had joined the TOLEDO team. This mission to Yugoslavia had been rejected by the Yugoslav general staff, and the men returned to Bari.

Originally there were only three or four OSS and SOE missions in Yugoslavia, but soon there were over a dozen. General Donovan's expansive ideas had been taking hold. But, Tito's permission was required before infiltrating. Soon, friction developed between Tito and both the OSS and SOE. The TOLEDO mission was one of the casualties. In September, plans were put together for expanding the DAWES mission, and personnel were available. Baranski, eager to go on a mission after months of frustration jumped on board. He was especially excited since he was now going to the land of his mother's birth.[10]

Baranski, six feet tall and athletic, had been a high school football star in Chicago. Later, he attended the University of Illinois where he graduated in 1941. He had been in the ROTC, and in October, 1941, he entered the Army as a 2nd Lieutenant. When the war started six weeks later, he subsequently was assigned to Hill Air Force Base in Ogden, Utah. He inherited nondescript assignments (He was the mess officer.) but in May, 1943, he was sent overseas to the Mediterranean. He left behind a wife and little girl. In September he had volunteered for the OSS and went to Algiers. Baranski was 27 years old.

Daniel Pavletich was Baranski's radio operator on the DAY team. A native of Split, Yugoslavia, he had worked before the war as a radio operator for a number of shipping lines. His travels took him to American ports, and he eventually decided he wanted to become an American. He tried to enlist, but wound up as a civilian member of the OSS. His Italian mother was from Fiume who had taught Pavletich fluent Italian.[11]

Lt. Tibor Keszthelyi was well liked around the OSS headquarters in Bari. He also had been with Baranski on the TOLEDO mission and was picked by Holt Green to join the DAWES team. Captain Don Rider originally planned to make Tibor his second in command. A handsome Hungrian, Tibor was Jewish. He was born in Fiume, had immigrated to the United States and was living in New York city when the war started. Tibor was a typical OSS recruit, intelligent, multi-lingual and with a European background.

Lt. Lane Miller was a 15th Air Force B-24 pilot who had been shot down over Yugoslavia. missions. He volunteered to go on the DAY mission to assist in rounding up downed airmen. He himself had been rescued by the OSS earlier in Yugoslavia.

A handsome young officer, Miller had been a star football player and track athlete in his hometown of Coronado, California. A brilliant student, he attended the University of California at Berkeley, but when the war came, he enlisted in the Army Air Corps.[12]

Miller, whose father was a U.S. Naval officer, had been shot down over Yugoslavia, but while his crew all survived, they had been captured by the Germans. Miller was in the 379th Bomb Group, one of the groups which participated in the famous 1943 low-level raid on Ploesti. Miller only flew a few missions until he was shot down on July 30, 1944.

He free-fell for over 15,000 feet before pulling his D-ring, and hit the ground ahead of the pursuing Germans. Rescued by either the *Chetnik*s or Partisans, he was turned over to the OSS and who transported him back to Bari. Although he volunteered to work for the OSS, the details of his recruitment are unknown.[13]

Major Howard Chapin talked about increasing the DAWES mission, in his weekly report ending 16 September. Hence, the decision was made even before the first DAWES group entered Slovakia, a fatal error.

Promoted later to Lt. Colonel, Chapin had other missions besides the DAWES group on the drawing board. One notable mission involved Lt. Jack Taylor, USNR, head of the DUPONT mission. Taylor was collecting German uniforms from prisoners in northern Italy, making ready to drop into Vienna. This mission would not have a happy ending.

Chapin ultimately planned to insert Major Donald Suhling, Lt. Franklin Lindsay and Lt. Francis Perry into Vienna also. Another mission was planned for Munich. Tibor Keszthelyi was ticketed for Budapest. Otto Jakes, Holt Green, Charles Katek and Jan Schwartz were scheduled to go into Prague. The OSS was getting into high gear, confident and aggressive. That's the way Major General Bill Donovan liked it.

---

1 Bill McGregor, Telephone interview with the author.
2 The author found the original copy of the note in the National Archives in 1999 and in 1998 gave a photocopy to Gorman who had forgotten the incident. NARA, RG 226, Entry 190, Box 116, Folder 407.
3 PRO, HS4/27.
4 Neal Cobb, Interview by the author, 1999.
5 Walter Ross, Letter to William Miller, 1983.
6 Nelson Deranian, OSS Report, NARA, RG 226, entry 141A, Box 12, Folder 89.
7 PRO, HS4/27.
8 Ibid.
9 Ibid.
10 NARA, RG 226, Entry 124, Box 28, Folder 221.
11 NARA, RG 226, Entry 196, Box 34, Folder 75.
12 Buck Miller, Lane Miller's brother, Telephone interview, 2000, and interview, August 9, 2001.
13 The author could find little about Miller in the OSS records at NARA.

Chapter 13

Shaky Ground

Banska Bystrica, October 10.

Major John Sehmer shook his head at the contradictions. Five different local newspapers were being published daily, and the trains were running on time. The new government was collecting taxes and governing the city in all respects — all this in apparent indifference to the fact that the advancing Germans were only a few miles away.[1]

The members of the DAWES team, now in Banska Bystrica for three weeks, were busy carrying out their mission. The OSS personnel were housed in three places: the *Velitelsvo*, the large Army headquarters building by the river; the *Narodny Dom Hotel*, where the airmen reveled in a lively party every night in the bar; and the Slovak army barracks. Others were fanning out over central Slovakia. Some of the men noticed Lt. Holt Green obviously was upset about the number of men sent from Bari on the last flight. There was no bitterness, just frustration on Green's part, one survivor later declared.[2]

After their arrival on September 17, Holt Green, Jim Gaul, Jerry Mican, Steve Catlos, and Ken Dunlevy had left for Brezno accompanied by Bill Davies and Aba Berdichev from the SOE A Force. That night the first elements of the 2500 Slovak members of a Soviet-trained parachute brigade landed at Tri Duby. The Slovaks were happy to see them, but resented the long delay of their arrival.[3]

Some Slovaks harbored suspicions about the Soviets. In Warsaw, Poland, for example, the underground, loyal to the Polish government-in-exile, had seized control of the city on August 1. The Soviets immediately halted their forces on the east bank of the Vistula River in the eastern suburbs, giving no reason. Without hesitation, Hitler threw SS divisions into Warsaw and systematically devastated the city. The Soviets, who had raced 300 miles in the previous three weeks, now waited six weeks until the Germans had nearly stamped out the insurgents before they made a serious effort to cross the Vistula.

The SS troops in Warsaw, meanwhile, fought brutally and gave the Poles no quarter. The Germans brought Colonel Oskar Dirlewanger and his SS troops, fresh from a savage campaign in the Ukraine, into the fight. Dirlewanger would wage another war of extermination and would soon earn the opprobrium, "Butcher of Warsaw."

The cynical action by the Soviets in Poland was not lost on the Slovaks. Stalin clearly viewed nationalistic underground armies as a threat to his postwar plans. Frantisek Moravec, the Czech intelligence chief in London, watched events unfolding in Slovakia. He was convinced the Soviets were dragging their feet for the same reasons they failed to assist the Poles.[4] Other Slovaks also believed the same.[5]

McGregor and Lain Enjoy Life in Banska Bystrica.

In Slovakia, Lieutenants Bill McGregor and Ken Lain, when not in the field training Slovaks, were enjoying the good life at the *Narodny Dom Hotel*, drinking and socializing. Many of the airmen also were hanging out at the hotel bar.

"We thought we had died and gone to heaven—a couple of infantry officers sleeping in real beds," McGregor recalled years later. "I relished the freedom we had in Banska Bystrica to do things in our own way. This was a Sunday school operation. Hell, I landed at Salerno with the 36th Division where we crawled through the mud. The Slovaks were friendly, happy people living in a beautiful country."[6] Unfortunate, this scenario would not last.

Jan Schwartz (cover name, Kryzan.) did not share Bill McGregor's casual outlook. He had sharp words with Lt. Jim Gaul about the latter's eagerness to advertise the American presence in Slovakia by wearing American uniforms in public. Schwartz knew there were German spies everywhere, and refused to pose in a number of pictures taken of Americans taken in the city.[7]

The Americans watched the Slovaks round up the pro-German sympathizers to force them to build tank obstacles, clear roads and work patching the bomb craters at the Tri Duby airfield. The Slovaks, meanwhile, gave the Americans a warm welcome. The Yanks identified with the Slovaks' desperate need for Allied assistance. The symbolic arrival of the small OSS mission signaled that they had not been forgotten. America was so far away and Russia was so close, a fact not lost on the populace.[8]

Bill McGregor Trains the Partisans.

Bill McGregor recalled years later.

> The Hron Valley was totally controlled by the rebels. They had a domain all of their own. We were overwhelmed by their needs. Ken Lain and I immediately went to work, training the Slovak army how to operate the weapons we brought with us — primarily the bazookas. The Slovaks were spooked by the rumors that the bazookas often blew up. Some Partisan groups were good; some were not. The best ones were commanded by Russian officers. The camps were all high in the mountains, well hidden. Many of the Partisans had rags for uniforms. It was a mixed bag. My interpreter, Jan Survorec, earlier had saved nine American airmen. He was young, smart, brave, and spoke good English. We did this training for two and a half weeks.[9]

Joe Morton accompanied the two infantry lieutenants for two days, always adding to his journal. His U.S. Navy photographer, Nelson Paris, took movie film of the training sessions.[10] At times the experience in Slovakia seemed like a lark, but hardened German battalions led by capable officers were on the march, and some of the Americans sensed they were on shaky ground. Morton, meanwhile, interviewed every person he found. He requested an interpreter from Golian's headquarters.

Josef Piontek was ordered to report to the Velitelsvo, where Jerry Mican interviewed him, and immediately passed the charming young man off to Morton. Piontek' diary would later prove to be an excellent source of information a half-century later.[11]

Piontek moved into the *Narodny Dom Hotel* with Morton. "He gave me a great deal of work. He asked me to arrange for interviews with certain people. These people later told me they wanted all questions written out in advance." Piontek was totally reliable and formed a strong bond with the American correspondent.[12]

Another odd twist in the Banska Bystrica scene was the emergence of Cecilia Wojewoda, a Polish refugee journalist, who had fled Hungary in March with her husband when the Germans took over in March, 1944. When she learned Americans were in the city, she eagerly sought them out.

Wojewoda's husband had been a member of the Polish consulate in Budapest. "I got to know an American War correspondent, Joe Morton. It was like a heavenly message to me," she wrote after the war. "I was working for a Slovakian press agency in Banska Bystrica. Meeting someone who had never lived under the Nazis was an amazing experience, she later wrote, I was taken aback with joy. It meant freedom at last. I looked forward to a meeting with this war correspondent and was [introduced] to him in one of the two coffee houses in the town. It was Joseph Morton. . . . I saw him every day."[13]

Wojewoda was well educated and spoke several languages. She and her husband invited Holt Green and Jim Gaul to dinner and played bridge afterwards, a curious pastime, it seems now, for people literally living on the edge and facing the imminent arrival of German storm troopers.[14]

Wojewoda was one of those unique personalities who occasionally turn up in unlikely places. A sensitive, sophisticated intellectual in a hellish world, she remembered Jim Gaul. [He had] " handsome good looks," [and was] "a man full of energy. I loaned him my typewriter as he wanted to write something. [Once he] wanted some milk to drink and some fruit, and the following day I was able to get both for him. He subsequently visited me and my husband often, and we had one wonderful dinner party. He told me how much he enjoyed it and that it helped him forget our dreadful circumstances. He later came to us and gave us advice on where to flee when the Germans arrived. . . . We were such friends. I begged to go along with the Americans. Now it seems [Gaul] was right, that it would have put us in greater danger."[15]

Captain Edward Baranski, Daniel Pavletich, Emil Tomes, Tony Novak, and Lt. Lane Miller, members of the DAY team, headed south on October 10 and found housing in the small town of Zvolenska Slatina, 20 miles southeast of Banska Bystrica. Baranski and Novak began collecting information of German army movements immediately. Pavletich coded and sent the messages to Bari.

October 9, Banska Bystrica.

Holt Green radioed Bari that General Viest believed the Slovak situation was "very grave and only speedy and adequate aid with arms and ammunition can save the threatened airport."[16] The airport was vital to their survival.

Three days later, Major John Sehmer visited the front at Zvolen and notified SOE headquarters in Bari that the situation was again "grave. . . . Huns in great strength with many mortars."[17] That same day Holt Green sent word that Lt. Bill McGregor and Ken Lain were doing a "splendid job" instructing the Slovaks. He also praised Jim Gaul and others.[18]

On the 10th, Lt. Lane Miller checked out the P-51 which Lt. Bill Coloney had been unable to start at Tri Duby. Two days later Miller informed Bari that the Mustang was in "excellent mechanical condition with a few minor exceptions."[19]

Sehmer's and Green's messages to their respective headquarters indicate subtle differences – Sehmer's were anxious and pessimistic and Green's upbeat and positive. Green did report General Rudolf Viest's "grave" concern, but Green's choice of words did not indicate that he endorsed Viest's views. Green did make a strong plea for the shipment of more arms as the situation deteriorated.

The Slovaks desperately wanted more aid, but it was not forthcoming. General Gubbins headquarters at SOE clearly stated to all echelons that Allied aid was restricted to sabotage and guerrilla operations only, not for major uprisings.[20]

October 13, Resupply Becomes a Problem for Holt Green.
Major Walter Ross radioed Green that it appeared impossible to resupply the mission unless they would could count on night landings or parachute drops. He said the 15th Air Force cited a shortage of long range fighters for escort service. He asked Green to join with Major Sehmer to appeal to the Slovaks and Russians to share the field for night landings.[21] That same day Lt. Lane Miller notified Bari that he had located an alternate airfield.[22] Miller was surveying the area by air, flying with the Slovak pilots.[23]

That night 72 Russian planes flew into Tri Duby, bringing in troops and supplies, and taking out wounded and political figures. The Slovak army had recaptured Telgart earlier in the day (45 miles east of Banska Bystrica), and the situation was looking up.[24]

General Jan Golian opted to put his wife on one of the Russian planes. The young general clearly was worried about the prospects of protecting the city. She would never see him again. The emotional parting took place on the Tri Duby airfield as the C-47's landed in the dark, kept their engines roaring, and took off as soon as the planes were loaded.[25]

Lane Miller, meanwhile, was active. He had located several acceptable airfields and was advising the Slovaks on how to build new landing strips. The Germans were now bombing Tri Duby regularly.[26]

Bill McGregor and Ken Lain continued to train the Slovaks. They

Shaky Ground 109

traveled through the hills to the east and north of Banska Bystrica, but not without incident. One day they were caught in an open field and were strafed by two German Stukas.

"Man it was close," McGregor recalled. "We laughed at experiences like this which would make you a Christian real quick."[27]

The outgoing McGregor relished his experiences with the Partisans. One unit was commanded by a Russian, Alexei Sadjalenko. He nicknamed McGregor "Bazook," which amused the American. McGregor and Lain had trouble convincing the Partisans that the bazookas would not blow up when they fired them. Later, the Americans discovered that the Partisans had thrown away many of the weapons.[28]

Joe Morton also was busy and piled work on Josef Pioutek, his interpreter. Piontek had worked with Jerry Mican to prepare a specialized dictionary so he could better interpret newspapers and documents for Morton.[29]

Jan Schwartz who arrived with Lt. Holt Green was edgy about the security of the OSS in Banska Bystrica. Wearing uniforms still bothered him. One afternoon after the second group arrived, Schwartz recalled telling Lt. Jim Gaul his habit of wearing his all-weather jacket with US Navy printed on the back in large letters was reckless. Gaul disagreed, saying, "It's good propaganda," Schwartz was preparing to go underground if the Germans overran the city and believed that both Holt Green and Gaul were naïve about their security. Schwartz thought Gaul's views were "the biggest hang-up of the mission."[30]

Much of this was indicative of the poorly planned, by-guess-and-by-gosh nature of the mission. Disaster was about to descend on the Anglo-Americans.

---

1   PRO, HS4/27.
2   Kenneth Dunlevy, NARA. OSS Report, RG 226, Entry 108B84F691, Box 84, Folder 691. Hereafter identified as Kenneth Dunlevy, OSS Report.
3   Steve Catlos, Interview with William Miller, 1983; Many of the Czechs were "Volyn Czechs" who

had lived in Russia for generations. Some were Rusyns or Ukrainians, and others were Slovaks. Courtesy of Dr. Igor Nabelek Letter to the Author, February, 2001.
4 Frantisek Moravec, *Master of Spies, The Memoirs of General Frantisek Moravec* (Garden City, New York: Doubleday and Company, 1975, pp. 228-235.
5 Frantisek Moravec, *Master of Spies, The Memoirs of General Frantisek Moravec*, p. 231.
6 Bill McGregor, Telephone interview with the author, 1999.
7 Jan Schwartz, Interview with William Miller, 1984.
8 Dunlevy, OSS Report.
9 Bill McGregor, Telephone interview with author, 1998.
10 Dunlevy, OSS Report.
11 Josef Piontek, Diary, Courtesy of Hazel Frost Hutson, 1996.
12 Ibid.
13 Cecelia Wojewoda, Letter to Hazel Frost, Courtesy of Hazel Frost Hutson.
14 Ibid.
15 Ibid.
16 Dawes to Jakes, Message 77, 9 October, NARA., RG 226, Entry 136, Box 34, Folder 375.
17 PRO, HS4/27.
18 NARA, RG 226, Entry 136, Box 34, Folder 375.
19 NARA, RG 226, Entry 136, Box 26, Folder 263.
20 Gubbins message SOE, PRO, F3.
21 NARA, RG 226, Entry 136, Box 34, Folder 375.
22 NARA, RG 226, Entry 136, Box 26, Folder 263.
23 Dunlevy, OSS Report.
24 Messages 123, 124, 125, NARA, RG 226, Entry 136, Box 34, Folder 375.
25 Peter Scrien, *Slovak National Uprising*, Publisher Unknown, Courtesy of Zuzka Durisek.
26 Message 07, Baranski to Bari, NARA.
27 Bill McGregor, Telephone interview with the author, 1998.
28 Ibid. McGregor saw Sadjalenko in 1964 when he, Ken Lain, Steve Catlos and Jan Schwartz were invited back to Banska Bystrica for the 20th Anniversary of the Uprising. McGregor claims the KGB agents refused to allow Sadjalenko to talk with the Americans.
29 Piontek Diary.
30 Jan Schwartz, Interview with William Miller, 1983.

Chapter 14

More Airmen

October 1, 1944.

George Fernandes and his group – Sergeants Bob Hede, Ben Raczka, Richard Rippon, John Kacaja, and Guy LaFatta, the two British agents, Jack Wilson and Keith Hensen; and the Russian fighter pilot — had left Jan Repta's Partisan brigade. Led by two Partisan officers, Lt. Ladislav (Pavel) Rosina and Dr. Ivan (Jan) Lesak, they struck out for Banska Bystrica.

The roads were heavily patrolled by Germans, making it difficult for the Partisans to move quickly. They were forced to travel through the woods, across streams, up and down rugged ravines and steep hillsides. Fernandes and his group struggled through the trails. The Germans generally kept to the roads and in their vehicles. Around October 15, Fernandes' group reached a small house in the *Cierny Vrch* (The Black Mountain) woods. There were about two dozen Partisans there near Zavada pod Ciernym Vrchom. Years later, Fernandes wrote an account of the meeting.

> The Russian lieutenant who commanded this unit was inside the house having breakfast while his troops were in the cold rain. They were just returning from a raid. Our arrival was reported to the Russian officer. He sent word that he wanted to meet the American officer and invited Rosina and me in to join him. We took Jack Wilson along to help with the interpreting. The Russian and I sat at opposite ends of the table, with Rosina sitting on the Russian's right, and Wilson sitting to my left. We were served fried eggs, onions and tomatoes. The Russian had a bottle of Slivovica or

Borovica (I couldn't tell the difference.) and was drinking heavily. He had his Mongolian orderly pour drinks for all, not shot glasses, but tall, full water glasses. The Russian rose and praised Roosevelt and America as valuable allies, and we all drank a toast to that. Then I did the same for Stalin and Russia, followed by another toast. I think Jack Wilson even got a good word in for Churchill. One speech followed another, with a toast after each. The Russian would stand and speak, Rosina would translate into German, and Wilson would translate to English. When I spoke, the procedure was reversed. When my glass was empty, the Russian screamed at his orderly for neglecting an American officer. He filled my glass after every toast to the brim. Rosina and Wilson were smart, as they only took a little sip for each toast. I drank toe to toe with the Russian officer and paid dearly for it. You would think we were high level diplomats the way we were acting. I had a small pair of wings, the collar insignia for the Army Air Corps. It had been in my pocket since I got into civilian clothes. I presented the wings to the lieutenant, followed by another speech and a toast, of course. He was touched and wished he had something appropriate to give me. He pulled a small pocket knife from his pocket and following another speech and toast, he presented the knife to me. Living in the woods as we were, this was truly a magnificent gift, and I told him so, followed by another toast. Finally it was over and I staggered out into the rain to my friends who were thoroughly soaked by this time and had no sympathy for me or the terrible hangover that was on its way. I think the Russian was deliberately trying to drink me to death and what disturbs me is that he nearly succeeded. It took me three days to recover.[1]

Fernandes and his group walked to Zvolen, dodging patrols and avoiding roadblocks. German troops were on all the roads. Once through the German lines, they boarded a rebel-operated train and rode to Banska Bystrica, 20 miles north.

October 13, Jack Shafer Shot Down.

Another group of U.S. airmen were rounded up by the Partisans. Lt. Jack Shafer and his crew were flying their 13th mission over Blechhammer when their B-17 was bracketed by radar-directed flak and was hit in three engines, the radio shack, the waist area, and one of the fuel wing tanks. Shafer grimly tried to make it to Yugoslavia, but "we couldn't keep a reasonable altitude," and he gave the order to bail out about 35 miles southwest of Banska Bystrica.[2] There was no luck this Friday the 13th of October.

A teenage boy found Shafer and Sergeant Theron Arnett, the radio operator, and led them to a "post-card village in a beautiful valley," Shafer remembered. Edwin Zavisa, one of the waist gunners, was already there. Arnett spoke a little college German and Zavissa spoke Polish and could communicate with the Slovaks. Another crewmember, who later joined them, spoke Slovak. "We used to joke if we ever got shot down, we'd have a whole team of interpreters. We never dreamed it would come true."[3]

The boy took them to his home where the family and neighbors welcomed the Americans. One large lady spoke some English and told them she once lived in the States. They were fed a large, sumptuous dinner and then taken, one by one, a few miles to another farm on the back of a motorcycle. It was a wild ride at high speed without lights. They were fed again and then put to bed in a large feather bed. Shafer and Arnett reminisced frequently over the years about their experiences that day.[4]

They were moved again the next day to a large hunting lodge on the top of a hill where they were re-united with Zavissa. They had two large meals that day as Zavissa spoke Polish to his Slavic hosts and Arnett used his German as the multi-lingual group swapped stories.

October 17, Banska Bystrica.

Lt. John Brinser, Shafer's co-pilot, and four other members of the crew arrived in the rebel capital. The Partisans were rounding up airmen everywhere possible.

The following day, Shafer and his two crewmen went back to look for their parachutes, but didn't find them. On the way back, they stopped at another lodge with a large wine cellar. The group stayed there until after dark, drinking, eating cheese, and sampling delicious apples. They ultimately took off, singing. Arnett knew the words to a lot of songs, and he had drunk too much. The Slovaks told them to quiet down, and they got off the road to rest. They heard singing in the distance. A German patrol came marching toward them lustily singing marching songs. The group had difficulty keeping Arnett quiet.[5]

Shafer and Arnett, who remained close friends until Arnett's death in 1998, always marveled at the cordial hospitality they received from the Slovaks. They finally were smuggled into Banska Bystrica in mail sacks in a mail truck. They were driven up to the Czech Army headquarters and were greeted immediately by Lt. Holt Green. Arnett and Shafer often said they would never forget the sight of a Navy officer standing there behind enemy lines in Czechoslovakia. They had no idea the American military was even in the country.[6]

On October 23, two more airmen, Sergeants Howard Luzier and Wesley Raubolt, arrived in Banska Bystrica. Raubolt, a combat photographer with a B-17 crew, had gone down on August 27 and was badly scarred across the face by a rope burn suffered from the shrouds of his parachute when he bailed out. Luzier had been down since September 13.[7]

Both wound up in the hands of a six-man Russian group of sappers northwest of Zilina, approximately 70 miles from Banska Bystrica. Raubolt and Luzier were fed by a Slovak family which housed the Russians while the Americans slept in the barn. The two Americans offered to join the Russians on their sabotage missions, but they refused. Raubolt and Luzier enjoyed the relaxed life on the remote farm and never saw any German troops.[8]

Luzier recalls being shocked one day when the Russians executed a 13-year-old Slovak boy whom they believed was giving information to the Germans. The boy brought newspapers to the Russians daily, but one day, the Russian commander was furious at the boy. They walked him to an open grave and machine-gunned him to death.[9]

As the German forces closed in, the Russians decided to lead the two Americans to Banska Bystrica. The radio operator with the Russians was a woman whom Luzier recalls as a strong lady who never sought assistance in carrying her heavy radio. Raubolt and Luzier later would be involved in a unique incident with Holt Green.

---

1. George Fernandes, Unpublished manuscript; Paul Strassman, a 15-year-old Partisan at the time, remembers meeting Fernandes and Jack Wilson. Strassman recalls that the camp was at the north end of a long valley. He was from Trencin, and as a Jew, was trying to stay alive. He chose to join the Partisans and fight the Germans. Strassman later immigrated to the U.S in 1948, and subsequently rose to become Deputy Secretary of Defense at the Pentagon, Telephone interview with the author, 2000.
2. Jack Shafer, Interview with the author, Oceanside, California, 1999.
3. Jack Shafer, Telephone interview with the author, 1997.
4. Ibid.
5. Ibid.
6. Ibid.
7. Silas Crase, Telephone interview with the author, July 1, 2000. Crase and Raubolt were on the same B-17 with Charles Muller. (See Chapter 11).
8. Howard Luzier, Telephone interview with the author, July 31, 2000; Former Partisans have told the author of other incidents of murder and summary execution, but all refuse to be quoted in print.
9. Ibid.; Cecilia Wojewoda, in a letter to Laura Frost, Holt Green's sister, November 16, 1945, recounted how a Slovak, a close friend of Wojewoda's, was murdered in 1944 by "blood-thirsty Russian partisans." She described how she also expected to be murdered, but luckily escaped. The Slovak, according to Wojewoda, had helped organize the Slovak Uprising and had donated large sums of money to the cause but whose "only fault was that he was not a Communist." Letter given to the author, courtesy of Hazel Frost Hutson.

Chapter 15

The Situation Becomes Desperate

Banska Bystrica, October 18, 1944.

Anxiety engulfed the populace as the Germans, advancing from all directions, continued their relentless drive on the rebel capital. Wounded Slovak soldiers were retreating into the city in increasing numbers, soon filling the hospitals to overflowing. Soldiers rushed about, putting up tents to house the troops. Others feverishly constructed gun emplacements. The city rapidly evolved into an armed camp as the Slovaks prepared to make a last stand.

Of concern to the civilian populace was the fear of retribution by the German security and police units – the *SS*, the *Sicherheitsdienst* and the *Gestapo* — because of atrocities against the *Volksdeutsche* committed in August and September (See Chapter 3). Those Slovaks who had abused the ethnic German minority, especially those unsympathetic to the Tiso regime, would now face an uncertain future if the Germans triumphed. Both sides were guilty of committing summary executions as accounts of atrocities reached the city.

The Slovak Uprising was a civil war with all the bitterness and hatred that such conflicts inevitably produce. The Americans concluded that their fate was tied to that of the Slovaks as this ugly side of the war surfaced. A determined Holt Green had no intention of allowing his team to fall into the hands of the Germans.

One rumor, which Major John Sehmer reported back to Bari, had it that a Partisan group had executed 150 ethnic German civilians — Slovak citizens — working on a defense line for the Slovak army. It was a senseless act. The Army – CFI personnel — allegedly arrived at the murder scene and promptly executed those responsible.[1]

Holt Green sent word the same day, October 18, that Lt. Jack Shafer had arrived with two members of his crew.[2] Bari replied that weather had ruled out a flight that night but that they were planning to drop supplies at Brezno "as soon as possible."[3] German *JU-87 Stukas* bombed Tri Duby and Banska Bystrica that day. Slovak crews rushed to fill bomb craters on the runways.

Major Walter Ross and Lt. Nelson Deranian replied within hours that they were "pleased to find you have gathered some more flyers as this will permit us to lay something on with the 15th AF again—mostly likely soon."[4] General Twining would risk a flight to rescue airmen, but was not inclined to take chances solely to aid OSS personnel.

Later that day, there was good news from Bari. Ross and Deranian sent word that the 15th Air Force had agreed to send three B-17's with supplies on October 22, the "soonest" day of good weather. They asked for updates on the condition of the airfield and local weather.[5] This was the news Green had been waiting for.

October 19, Fernandes and His Group Arrive in Banska Bystrica.

Lt. George Fernandes and his group arrived just in time for dinner at the Narodny Dom Hotel. Afterwards, they were surprised to bump into two members of the DAWES team wearing American uniforms.

The men were taken to the *Velitelstvo*, the Slovak headquarters building, where they were photographed by Nelson Paris before being taken to the Army barracks and allowed to shower. Given new uniforms and boots, they were photographed again. "It felt like we were on U.S. soil" Bob Hede remembered. We had a great reception."[6] But for all of Hede's enthusiasm,

Situation Becomes Desperate 119

Kampfgruppe Schill was now only eight miles south of Zvolen and bearing down on Banska Bystrica.

The Fernandes group met Holt Green and other OSS personnel the next morning. Like others, they were astonished at the sight of a Navy officer in uniform so far behind German lines. Green lectured Fernandes about wearing civilian clothes, warning him they could be shot as spies. Fernandes didn't argue. He knew Green was right, but he knew also they could not have made the long distance from Grinava to Zvolen if they had not been wearing civilian clothes.[7]

Green informed Bari that day that the airfield was too soft, but would be "ready tomorrow." The Russians continued to fly the lighter DC-3 transports in and out every night. This contributed to the frustration and anxiety of the Americans.[8] What was keeping the 15th Air Force!

October 20.

As tension mounted in the city, Holt Green and Bari communicated several times daily. On the 20th Green said they were checking the condition of the airfield again to see if it was dry enough for landings. The *Luftwaffe* was bombing both the city and the airfield daily. Seven *Stukas* hit the city this day, but German ground forces were the greatest concern. Green informed Bari that the situation was "urgent" and warned that the airfield "may soon fall." Zvolen was expected to fall within hours.[9]

On the evening of the 21st, George Fernandes and his group posed for a photograph, a copy of which Dr. Lesak sent him after the war. The two British agents, Jack Wilson and Keith Hensen, posed with the Americans.

Ken Dunlevy later recalled that October 22 was a clear day. There were rumors that the Americans had bombed Bratislava. The Germans conducted several bombing runs over Banska Bystrica, and the flyers continued to wonder what happened to the 15th Air Force.[10] Meanwhile, the nightly Soviets flights continued.[11]

Holt Green intended to send most of the OSS personnel back to Bari.

But, he planned to keep Horvath, Brown, Schwartz, Mican, and Heller – the original DAWES and HOUSEBOAT teams — in Banska Bystrica. The rest would return with an accumulation of "pouch material" (documents).

Schwartz and Jerry Mican had concluded that the "days of the Uprising were over." The two men knew that ranking CFI personnel and civilians in the city felt the same way.[12]

Although most of the American personnel were anxious, Joe Morton calmly continued his work. He visited the airmen in the Slovak Army barracks one evening to interview the airmen at length, promising to devote an entire chapter to them in his book.[13]

October 22, Americans Prepare to Leave.

The OSS personnel and the flyers arrived at Tri Duby at 10 AM to await the flight of B-17's. Jack Shafer and some of the others helped the Czechs load bombs on Russian-built aircraft, all the time keeping an eye on the hills to the south. Shafer was amused that the Slovak pilots would warm up their engines inside the hangars and then roar out to take off without stopping. They ran continuous missions in almost a "traffic pattern." The planes would land and taxi over the bombs which then would be lifted into the bomb racks. The pilots then would take off immediately. The Germans were so close that it was just a short hop to the targets. "One of the planes crashed one day by the airport, and we went up to look at it. It was made out of plywood with a steel frame around the pilot's seat. The plane was totally smashed, but the pilot survived."[14]

Josef Piontek, Joe Morton's interpreter, described the situation in Banska Bystrica "[as] obviously bad now," . . . and "Mican seems downhearted." Mican, of course, had been informed by Holt Green that he was staying in Slovakia.[15] Clearly, Mican saw the handwriting on the wall and wanted out.

The flyers went back the next day on a truck. Cecilia Wojewoda remembered discussing it with Joe Morton. "Ten days he waited for the

Situation Becomes Desperate

planes to come – in vain."[16] During this period, Wojewoda wrote, "many planes from Russia landed at Tri Duby, but not to take Morton and the other men out of Slovakia."[17] That night, for example, the Russians evacuated a Russian general and several political officials plus approximately 300 wounded men.[18]

October 23, Bad Weather in Italy.

Major Ross explained to the men that on the 23rd bad weather in Italy had caused cancellation of all 15th AF operations, explaining the failure of the B-17's to arrive at Tri Duby on the 22nd. Ross and Deranian were now keenly aware of the urgency of the plight of Green and his men.[19]

Years later, Ross discussed the dilemma.

> [Regarding landing planes in Slovakia], . . . it wasn't like [Yugoslavia]. I don't think the trouble was anticipated at that time at all, but apparently just the mere fact that two B-17's had been able to land at Tri Duby and bring in supplies caused action on the part of the enemy to get rid of that group and to close off the Tri Duby airport for any such purpose in the future. We did have radio communication, and we knew the unit was in trouble. On October 22, I took over as commanding officer of Company B of the 2677th Regiment. At that time pressure was mounting every day to give out some information about the people who were members of that group in there. We just couldn't do anything. There wasn't anything known, except that they were in trouble, and that they were moving. There was absolutely no way we could get any help to them. I'm sure the people in there, as much as they wanted help, realized it was impossible to get in there with an airplane and pick anybody up, or do anything about it. It was just as simple as that, and we were just as disturbed as we could be about the whole thing.[20]

On the 23rd, Edward Baranski sent Tony Novak back to "Bystrica" (as it was called by locals) to obtain the latest news. When he returned two days later, the Germans had occupied Zvolenska Slatina and German patrols were everywhere. Baranski and Pavletich had left town. Baranski had left word he was going north east to Polana. With the German forces converging on Bystrica and the *Gestapo* operating aggressively, Baranski had to take care.

October 24, Airmen Wait In Vain.

After two days of wrenching disappointment, Holt Green trucked the airmen and some of the OSS group again to Tri Duby for a noon departure. Spirits were high and the weather was clear. The men listened again for the distant roar of B-17 engines. They watched the mountain passes to the south for Mustang P-51's to come slashing through the sky. The optimistic Yanks had been convinced there would be an eleventh hour rescue. Just like in the movies, when the ammunition ran low, the cavalry would always ride over the pass at the last minute to save the wagon train. But, anxious men now realized this was not going to be a Hollywood ending. Morale continued to sag.

The airmen remained at the field all day until after dark and watched the Russians fly out two C-47's loaded with men "packed like sardines." A Russian major (probably Studensky who was Marshall Koniev's liaison officer) told George Fernandes in broken English that 20 C-47's were returning that night and early the next morning the Americans would be flown out to Kiev.[21] Morale soared momentarily, but there was still bitterness over the 15th Air Force's failure to show up. The men didn't know there was bad weather over Italy.

Earlier that same day, Major Studensky informed Green that the Americans could fly out on the next available Russian flight, probably on the evening of the 25,th weather permitting. Green suggested to Bari that they accept the Russian offer.[22]

The Americans remained at Tri Duby until after dark, watching Russian-operated C-47's taking off filled with wounded men and other Russian personnel. They returned to the barracks at ten P.M., passing a burning Slovak tank along the road. The tank apparently had been destroyed by a German patrol. The sight unsettled them. "...I had never seen a more

Situation Becomes Desperate

dejected group in my life. I think all of us had at this time given up all hope of getting out." George Fernandes recalls.[23]

The indefatigable Joe Morton kept working. Late in the evening of the 24th, he interviewed Generals Viest and Golian as Josef Piontek interpreted. Morton was eager to get an updated report on the front. The news, of course, was "very bad," Piontek recorded. He and Morton studied the maps after the meeting until past midnight. The Germans were advancing steadily.[24]

That night after dark, the Czech Brigade, the 2000-man unit flown in by the Russians, began withdrawing into the mountains north of the city.[25] Holt Green also notified Bari that the Czechs were flying their fighter aircraft to Russian territory, and they would burn Lt. Alex Watkins' P-51. Green advised Bari that Tri Duby would fall to the Germans by the 27th or sooner.[26]

Late that night, Holt Green, Jim Gaul and Tibor Keszthelyi went to see Major Studensky. Tibor awakened the Russian interpreter, Maria Gulovich, to translate. She and Tibor always conversed in Hungarian as she did not speak English. Green asked Studensky to provide space on a Russian plane to take out the American group. He said planes were arriving the next day at 11 AM and he promised to try and get them on the flight.[27] The flight never materialized.

The next day, Major Walter Ross radioed Green that the 15th Air Force had approved the evacuation of the flyers by either the Russians or the CFI. Ross gave this his approval advising him to include those OSS personnel "not needed." Ross cautioned Green, "Play it safest, always." Ross added that weather had shut down air operations out of Italy for the next two days.[28] It was a little late to play it safe.

Green replied immediately. Another Russian flight was planned. Holt radioed, "Hoping to evacuate flyers, Tibor, Catlos, Dunlevy, Lain, McGregor, Perry, Miller, Paris, and Morton tonight on Russian planes. Other personnel and equipment evacuated. Brezno taken today." Green reported.[29]

Banska Bystrica was about to fall, and for the Americans, the cavalry was not going to make it. That the Russians had been conducting air operations in and out of Tri Duby — but on the 15th couldn't, or wouldn't — had enraged the airmen and some of the OSS personnel. Now, an escape into the hills was the only option left.

---

1. Report by British Major John Sehmer to SOE headquarters in Bari, Italy, PRO, HS4/27; NARA Message 55, NARA, RG 226, Entry 136, Box 36, Folder 375. Holt Green notified Bari that a Partisan assassination in Liptovsky Mikulas of a German soldier had provoked the Germans to announce that for each German killed, the Germans would shoot ten civilians and burn ten houses.
2. Message 52, Green to Bari, Ibid.
3. Ibid., Message 995, Bari to Green, NARA, RG 226, Entry 154, Box 42, Folder 642.
4. Ibid.
5. Ibid.
6. Bob Hede, Telephone interview with the author, 1997.
7. George Fernandes, Unpublished manuscript.
8. Kenneth Dunlevy, OSS Report.
9. NARA, RG 226, Entry 190, Box 116, Folder 407.
10. Kenneth Dunlevy, OSS Report; Author found no records of any 15th Air Force flights in the Bratislava area on October 22.
11. Kenneth Dunlevy, OSS Report. Dunlevy recalled it incorrectly as October 25.
12. Jan Schwartz, Interview with William Miller, 1983.
13. George Fernandes, Unpublished manuscript.
14. Jack Shafer, Interview with the author, April 10, 1999.
15. Josef Piontek, Diary.
16. Cecilia Wojewoda, Letter to the author, 2000.
17. Ibid.
18. NARA, Message 1102, Major Ross to Holt Green.
19. Walter Ross, Interview (on tape) with William Miller, 1984.
20. Ibid.
21. George Fernandes, Unpublished manuscript.
22. NARA, RG 226, Entry 154, Box 42, Folder 642.
23. George Fernandes, Unpublished manuscript.
24. Josef Piontek, Diary.
25. Most accounts refer to it as the "Czech brigade," although perhaps a more accurate name would be the Slovak brigade.
26. NARA, RG 226, Entry 190, Box 116, Folder 407.
27. Maria Gulovich, Interview with William Miller, 1984.
28. NARA, RG 226, Entry 136, Box 34, Folder 376.
29. Ibid.

Chapter 16

"Imminent Catastrophe"

October 25, Banska Bystrica.

"This is the last contact from here. The situation is most serious. Going into hills north of here. Flye (sic) is with us. Urge supplies by dropping. Will arrange for British reception elsewhere is believe Brezno lost." Holt Green's message, hurriedly and sloppily coded, informed Bari he had reached the end of his rope.[1]

The brutal truth was that the 15th Air Force would not risk landing on an airfield about to be overrun by the enemy. The Russians were their last hope to escape. Green reported, along with other bad news, that the *18th SS Panzer Grenadier Horst Wessel Division* had overrun Brezno earlier in the day.[2]

The grim CFI battle reports continued to come in. Green and Jim Gaul reviewed their options. Evacuation seemed the only choice. Green informed Bari that Tri Duby landings were no longer possible. He also reported that Captain Edward Baranski and his team had slipped out of the city and had made it through the German lines to Zvolenska Slatina, east of Zvolen.[3]

The Slovaks wasted no time. Generals Rudolf Viest and Jan Golian called in Holt Green and Jim Gaul and informed them they were moving their headquarters to Donovaly, 16 miles north, seemingly the only safe haven available. Viest said the Russians were evacuating their high ranking officers and certain political figures by air. "Tomorrow will be the last day to get out," Viest said.[4]

Gaul asked Viest whether the Russians would evacuate the Americans. Viest said he didn't know. He suggested that the Americans should get out on their own planes. He knew the Russians were unreliable. Green agreed to follow the Slovaks to Donovaly if they couldn't get a flight out.[5]

The air was filled with tension as the Germans tightened the ring around Bystrica. The situation deteriorated by the hour. A cold rain began falling intermittently as the temperature fell. The dreary overcast matched the depression now gripping the Americans.

The prospects of surviving would prove no better in Donovaly than in Bystrica. The 6,000-man *Kampfgruppe Schill Brigade* was driving up the Hron Valley from the south. The *SS Horst Wessel Division* with 8,000 men was advancing down the Hron Valley from Brezno in the east. The *Tatra Division*, with 6,000 men, was securing the mountainous areas northwest of the rebel capital. The 14,000-man *Kampfgruppe Wittenmeyer*, which included the *14th SS Galizien Brigade*, moved down the mountain road from Liptovsky Hradok, brutalizing the populace as it advanced. The Ukrainians overran Maluzina, just 13 miles northeast of Brezno. Under this pressure, demoralized CFI units broke up and fled into the hills.

Colonel Sergei Popov, the Russian political commissar with the Russian military mission was attempted to recruit Ukrainian defectors from the *Galizien Brigade* through propaganda leaflets. But, according to the German war diary, Popov had only snared 50 turncoats. The successful advance of the Ukrainians discouraged potential defectors.[6]

To the north, the *SS Dirlewanger Sturmbrigade* with a force of 4,000, mostly convicts, and was engaged in bitter and bloody fighting with three CFI infantry battalions three miles north of Liptovska Osada near Donovaly. The Slovaks put up stiff resistance, but finally cracked. The only unanswered questioned was which German unit would get to Bystrica first. And how close was Donovaly to getting caught in the German net?

Bystrica had been converted into a garrison city. The parks and the lawns around government buildings were covered with white tents. Soldiers, many apparently leaderless, wandered around. Blood-soaked bandages identified the steady stream of wounded coming into the city. German aircraft were in the air from dawn to sunset, and bombing continuously. Artillery barrages echoed in from the foothills and up the Hron Valley. At night, flares illuminated the sky, creating an incredible scene, Maria Gulovich remembered a half-century later.[7]

Americans Stunned By The Slovak Collapse.

In the midst of the pandemonium, the Americans were stunned by the deterioration of the military situation. The euphoria in the rebel capital, so wide spread only weeks before, had evaporated. Bystrica had assumed a Gone-With-the-Wind image of Atlanta reeling under the assault of the Union army. The high hopes of the Uprising had succumbed to dismay and despair, leaving Holt Green and his men in a situation they had neither expected nor bargained for.

The OSS team scurried about collecting their equipment and gear. The flyers aided where they could, but they selected only what they could carry. Green barked orders to destroy equipment and records, while Bill McGregor supervised the packing of weapons and ammunition. Jim Gaul frantically worked with a group of men collecting food supplies. Jerry Mican, Joe Horvath, and Robert Brown packed radio gear and batteries, their last means of contact with Bari. Green decided to stay one more night in the city with Joe Horvath, and Bob Brown, and send the others on their way.[8]

Joe Morton calmly immersed himself in recording the story that had lured him into this environment. No one—neither Morton nor anyone else—had anticipated the German counter-offensive.

Amid the scrambling to get organized to leave, Morton remained calm. He seemed to feast on the riotous disorder and turmoil that brought others to the verge of panic. Cecilia Wojewoda later remembered, ". . . as the Jerries drew nearer, there was no hope for support. The Russians, who promised help, were as far [away] as ever. . . The ghost of [an] imminent catastrophe haunted the city. We were all of us doomed. [Yet], I never saw Morton bothering about the hopelessness of the situation. He had a kind of recklessness about himself, a carelessness of a fine sort, that made only his work important for him."[9] The Wojewodas prepared to flee also to Donovaly.

Afternoon of October 25.

Green sent Jim Gaul, Jerry Mican, Charles Heller and Jan Schwartz to Donovaly to scout out living arrangements. The CFI had picked out a multistory hotel, a ski resort, as their command center and offered space to the OSS personnel. Gaul recommended to Green to accept the offer and billet the airmen in private homes in and around Donovaly. Because transport was a problem, Gaul commandeered an old bus which they drove back to Bystrica.[10]

The disconsolate flyers had just spent three frustrating days at Tri Duby airport. Now, they braced themselves for a 100-mile forced march through the rugged Carpathians to reach the Red Army lines. The weather still was reasonably mild, but the winter snows were on the way.

Lt. George Fernandes had sensed the oncoming freeze. He knew what they were facing. Fernandes had been eyeing a store in the town that sold cossack style fur caps, and received money from Holt Green to purchase 19 of them.[11]

In the late afternoon, some of the airmen and a few OSS personnel piled into the school bus, which reminded the Americans of an old school bus, with their gear. Powered by a charcoal-burning engine, the jury-rigged vehicle, was quickly filled to the ceiling with men and material. Some of their gear was piled on top of the bus. With a whoop and a holler, they lumbered out of town. It was a bizarre sight.[12]

The driver coaxed the vehicle, sputtering and coughing, through and around the endless line of refugees. Intermittent road blocks required fre-

Imminent Catastrophe 129

quent stops. Lt. Bill McGregor couldn't stop laughing at the comic opera situation as the Americans repeatedly piled out of the rickety bus to push it over the crests on the hilly road. The bus lacked the power to climb the steepest inclines. McGregor, the hard-charging Anzio veteran, who previously considered his OSS assignment as a lark, now found his outlook changing.[13]

When they got out of the bus to push it on the hills, McGregor noticed a *Fieseler-Storch*, a German Piper-Cub type observation plane with the awkwardly long landing gear, following them up the valley and circling overhead. The plane flew only about 70 miles an hour.[14]

Refugees continued to pour out of Bystrica. The Stare Hory Valley road to Donovaly, believed to be the only escape route, soon became a 16-mile-long logjam. The ragtag remnants of the Slovak military were led up the winding road by officers mounted on horseback. The officers, moving among the men, shouted orders and encouragement.[15]

The terrified populace mingled among the soldiers as many pulled small carts with their meager possessions. The elderly and ill sat along side the road, wondering how they would get up the hill. Hundreds of horses pulled wagons holding children and baggage. Women walked along side with bundles on their heads. Weary soldiers hung on to the sides of the wagons. A few Slovaks drove cars and trucks. Car horns blared constantly.[16]

It would take two trips and most of the night to get all the American personnel and their gear up the mountain. In the middle of this exodus, the American contingent, both intrigued and shocked, watched the spectacle from the windows of their rickety "school bus."[17]

Back in the city, there was still a shred of hope for evacuation by air. Green had learned in mid-afternoon that the Russians were flying a C-47 out at 9 PM. He rushed some of the remaining flyers and OSS personnel down to Tri Duby. The tumultuous scene at the airfield was wild. Dozens of desperate Russians fought to board the plane. One forced his way the door by brandishing a machine gun. The Americans watched in dismay and gave up. Depressed, they returned to the city. Later, they left for Donovaly on the bus which Jim Gaul had driven back to Bystrica.[18]

Dirlewanger Sturmbrigade Closes In.

Holt Green had spoken of retreating to the "hills" to find refuge. But what kind of refuge? Two days earlier the *Dirlewanger Sturmbrigade* had seized the high ground around Biely Potok, just 30 miles north of Bystrica (and six miles north of Liptovska Osada). Biely Potok was 16 miles north of Donovaly.

Another parallel column of Dirlewanger's troops captured Necpaly, 28 miles to the northwest of the rebel capital. The next day, besieged CFI forces laid down a fierce artillery barrage on the Germans. Nevertheless, Dirlewanger overran Biely Potok and occupied the high ground to the southeast. The fighting was intense. The CFI fought bitterly to prevent Dirlewanger from sweeping up the Necpaly Valley. The German army reported "tough" opposition by the Slovaks.[19] General Rudolf Viest sent reinforcements, and the CFI made a valiant, although hopeless, stand. In the mountains to the east of Donovaly, *SS Kampfgruppe Wittenmeyer* was sending patrols into the *Lower Tatras*, west of Maluzina.[20]

Josef Piontek, meanwhile, was ordered back to his Army unit. Joe Morton begged him to remain. Fond of the young Slovak, Morton needed Piontek to interpret for him. The boyish soldier recorded in his diary, "Okay. Maybe some plans. Italy!" He retrieved his luggage and joined the Americans.[21]

Probably no more than an hour later, Green contradicted his former position and reported to Bari that Tri Duby was "still available for safe landings." He was desperate. The Russians had "fully-loaded" C-47's taking off "with no difficulty." Green attributed the report to Lt. Lane Miller, the DAY team member who had stayed with the main party of the DAWES group.[22] In reality, the Germans were within four miles of Tri Duby.

Jan Schwartz, who had been wearing civilian clothes, was not surprised it had come to this. He went to Holt Green and said he had arranged for a place to hide. Schwartz offered to take several flyers with him. Green objected and told him he was needed because of his language skills. Grimly, Schwartz put on his uniform.[23]

Meanwhile, the German communiqués were describing the "stubborn resistance" of the Slovaks. Nevertheless, they soon collapsed in front of Dirlewanger's *SS* troops who seized the high ground north of Liptovska Osada, only eight miles north of Donovaly. To the west, Dirlewanger's troops advanced four miles southeast of Necpaly.[24]

Panic began to take over as German *SS* units of regimental and battalion strength approached the Bystrica city gates. For all practical purposes, the dispirited Slovak army had collapsed, melting into the countryside or fleeing into the mountains. After Generals Viest and Golian and their staffs had fled to Donovaly, rampaging Slovak soldiers began looting hotels and stores. Crazed men ran through the main square firing their weapons into the air. Civilians, packed in vehicles piled high with their possessions, moved slowly toward the Stare Valley Road to escape the city. Most of the frightened citizens moved out of the city on foot.[25]

Pro-fascist civilians behind curtains and window shades watched expectantly – some quietly ecstatic — as the desperate rebels and their supporters fled. In addition to the local pro-fascist Slovaks, there were over 50,000 ethnic Germans in the Handlova-Kremnica region west of the city, separated from Bystrica by a 3,000 feet mountain range.

Known to be apolitical before the war, the Slovak-Germans' loyalty now was solidly linked to the Third *Reich* in the eyes of many Slovaks. This was an unfair conclusion, many argue today.[26] Rumors and stories of murder and terror accompanied the troops of *Kampfgruppe Schill* and the *Horst Wessel Panzer Grenadiers*, although this was of little concern to the pro-Tiso sympathizers who prepared to cheer the imminent arrival of the *SS*.[27] One thing was certain: It was a complicated political scene in which all sides would pay a bitter price.

The *Dirlewanger Sturmbrigade*, newly arrived from Poland, rarely took prisoners. Stories of Oskar Dirlewanger burning prisoners alive with gasoline, bayoneting infants, and brutalizing Polish women now terrorized the Slovaks.[28] Dirlewanger preferred "Medieval methods," Heinrich Himmler once said approvingly. The Germans had now unleashed the Dogs of War on the Slovaks.[29]

One of the battalions serving under Dirlewanger was the *Osttuerkischen Waffen-Verbaende der SS* led by *SS-Standartenfuehrer* (Colonel) Harun-el-Raschid Bey. The commander was an ethnic German, 58-year-old Wilhelm Hintersatz, imagining himself a German version of Lawrence of Arabia. He had converted to Islam after World War I and assumed the name of Harun-el-Raschid Bey.[30]

This unit of Muslim volunteers had excelled in the Ukraine by crushing partisan units and slaughtering partisans as well as "suspected partisans." Difficult to control, one of the previous German commanders of the unit had ordered the execution of 78 suspected mutineers. The unit had been involved in the bloody suppression of the Poles in the Warsaw Uprising prior to being transferred to Slovakia.[31]

October 26, Germans Poised to Overrun Tri Duby.

Holt Green, Joe Horvath and Bob Brown left during the afternoon to join the others in Donovaly. The route was still packed with refugees, and intermittent road blocks slowed traffic to a crawl. *Kampfgruppe Schill* got an early morning start in Zvolen and martialled its troops for an assault on Tri Duby. The Germans had overcome mined roads and blown bridges to get into Zvolen earlier in the day, and the Slovak defenders were fading away.[32]

Major Studensky and Russian staff frantically burned records in the *Velitelstvo*. He finally gave an order to get his staff car, and with his aide, Tamara, and Maria Gulovich, one of his interpreters, in tow, he sprinted down the stairs out of the building. A driver was waiting to take them to Tri Duby. The traffic jam was maddening, and what was normally a 20-minute ride took over an hour.[33]

The airport was no safe haven because of the German artillery shelling. The Slovaks were answering with their own. In the middle of this exchange, a C-47 appeared out of the clouds. The courageous Russian pilot circled the field. Medics on the field were poised to hurry out to load the wounded men on the plane when it touched down. The pilot brought the plane in smoothly. As the last person was crowded aboard and the wounded loaded with the plane's engines running, the pilot hit full throttle and the plane roared down the runway. Crewmen wrestled to shut the door. Miraculously, the plane was airborne and circled east.

That was the last flight out of Tri Duby. Maria Gulovich, lying prone on the ground, watched the C-47 disappear over the hills, listening to the artillery fire which never once abated.[34]

Studensky, deeply frustrated, returned to the *Velitelsvo*. He then took his aide, Tamara, and her encoding equipment with him to Donovaly. He promised Maria he would return later for her and some of the equipment.[35]

October 27, *Kampfgruppe Schill* Captures Banska Bystrica.

At 1:00 AM, the First Battalion of the *Kampfgruppe Schill*, led by the dashing Hans Kettgen, a 27-year-old *SS-Obersturmführer*, fired up its armored vehicles and struck out for the rebel capital. Effectually, there was little opposition. Kettgen and his troops drove into the main square of Banska Bystrica at 6:30 AM. Three days later, the *Horst Wessel Brigade* and several *Hlinka* Guard units would join in a victory parade before Jozef Tiso and *SS* General Hermann Hoefle. Kettgen was awarded the Knight's Cross for taking the city. President Tiso also awarded Slovak decorations to the Germans.

Thus, the Slovak National Uprising was over. A peripheral and insignificant operation in the overall scope of military operations, the Uprising had been remote from the dramatic Allied advances in France, Italy, Poland, and Hungary. But while the Supreme Allied high command gave it little attention, the Uprising gave expression to those Slovak soldiers and citizens who attempted to break away from the Third *Reich*. At the same time in Bari, anxious officers in the 2677th OSS Regiment worried about the fate of their men. It was a time of anguish for all parties.

---

1 NARA, RG 226 Entry 190 Box 116 Folder 407, Message 208.
2 Ibid., Message 210.
3 NARA, RG 226, Entry 136, Box 34, Folder 381.
4 Maria Gulovich, Interview with the author, August, 2000.
5 Ibid.
6 *Wehrmacht* War Diary, Slovak Situation report, October 24, 1944, Courtesy of the State Archives, Prague, The Czech Republic, and Julian Hendy, Yorkshire Television Limited, Leeds, England; The 14th German division had fought in eastern Galicia (Poland) in July and had sustained a major defeat by the Red Army, losing 7,000 men. After rest and reinforcements, a battalion from the division, which had been sent to Slovakia, captured Brezno on October 25. Allen Milcic, E Mail to the author, March 29, 1999.
7 Maria Gulovich, Telephone interview with the author, August, 2000.
8 NARA, RG 226, Entry 190, Box 116, Folder 407,Message 211.
9 Cecelia Wojewoda, letter written from Brussels, Belgium, to the Associated Press November, 1945.
10 Kenneth Dunlevy, OSS Report; Slovaks who lived there in World War II say there were no public school buses. The Americans probably mistook a public bus for a school bus.
11 George Fernandes, Unpublished manuscript.
12 Bill McGregor, Telephone interview with the author, 1998.
13 Ibid.
14 Bill McGregor, Tape recording, courtesy of his daughter, Sandy Woods.
15 Jack Shafer, Interview with the author, April, 1998.
16 George Fernandes, Unpublished manuscript.; Maria Gulovich, interview with author, September, 1999.
17 George Fernandes, Unpublished manuscript; Jack Shafer, Interview with the author, April, 1998.
18 Kenneth Dunlevy, OSS Report.
19 *Wehrmacht* War Diary, October 25.
20 Ibid.
21 Josef Piontek, Diary.
22 NARA, RG 226, Entry 190, Box 116, Folder 407, Message 09.
23 Jan Schwartz, Interview with William Miller, 1984.
24 *Wehrmacht* War Diary, October 26.
25 Maria Gulovich, OSS Report.
26 Dr. Thomas Reimer has pointed out that the Slovak-Germans were no less divided than the Slovaks. Ferdinand Zimbauer, a German Communist, led a force of 250 German Partisans who supported the Uprising. He was captured and died at Mauthausen concentration camp. Reimer also points out that there was German Communist support of the Uprising in the communities of Muennichwies (Vricko), Zeche (Malinova), and Krickerhau (Handlova) until the Partisans began to "indiscriminately murder Germans." E Mail to the author, April 11, 2001.
27 Kliment and Nakladal, pp. 99-108.
28 French L. MacLean, *The Cruel Hunters* (Atglen, PA, Schiffer Military History, 1998) p. 177.
29 Ibid.
30 Courtesy of Glenn Jewison, May 31, 2001.

31 Ibid.
32 *Wehrmacht* War Diary, October 27.
33 Maria Gulovich, OSS Report.
34 Ibid.
35 Ibid.

Chapter 17

Maria Gulovich

October 26, Banska Bystrica.

Maria Gulovich was one of the few people remaining in the deserted *Velitelsvo* Slovak Army headquarters building when anarchy erupted in the streets of the doomed city. Maria's curiosity led her to walk over to see what was happening. The work in the Russian Intelligence Center was finished, and Major Studensky, Maria's boss, had left for Donovaly with most of his staff.

Entering the main square, she decided to look for a bottle of cognac in a liquor store which was being looted. Slovak soldiers were taking or smashing everything they could get their hands on. She pushed her way through the mob to get in the door. Raucous singing and shouting and the pungent smell of alcohol struck her as crazed and drunken men stumbled about.

Soldiers staggered against each other, cursing and yelling. Other men, unable to stand, lay on the floor among the debris. Liquor flowed out of barrels in the stockroom as men kneeled to drink the gushing wine and cognac. Others sloshed about on the floor which was covered with alcohol. Maria looked on incredulously. "In that moment, I lost my idealism," she would write later.[1]

Maria walked back to the *Velitelsvo* where there were two Russian lieutenants and four enlisted men remain in the building where she worked. She started up to the third floor where her office was located when a shot rang out. The bullet went through her hair, just missing her scalp. A crazed Slovak soldier ran up and down the halls, firing wildly. Maria was terrified, but tried to appear calm as she kept walking. A second soldier chased after the gunman, exchanging gunfire. Finally, the second man killed the assailant and then fled. Shaken, Maria continued into the intelligence office.

"So this is a revolution," she thought as she collapsed into a chair. She had been a good history student in college, and she was familiar with the bloody histories and random murder of the French and Russian revolutions. Simultaneously terrified and shocked by this wild scene, she nevertheless was intrigued by the chaos occurring around her.

The six Russian soldiers were destroying equipment and ripping out telephones. A short time later, and the last to leave, Maria joined the men and took off for Donovaly in a staff car. It was now dark.[2]

The mayhem on the Stare Valley road had not abated. German planes were still bombing at will along the route now lighted by burning vehicles. Stalled and damaged cars and trucks had been pushed off to the side of the road. The dead lay on the road and off to the side. In the shadows, women and children, some sobbing and wailing and others deathly silent, huddled in small groups. Maria was astonished when the planes began dropping flares in order to continue the bombing. She realized again how much she hated the Germans.[3]

Donovaly.

When Maria and the Russians arrived at Donovaly, there was no place to sleep. She met Lieutenants Tibor Keszthelyi, Ken Lain and Bill McGregor talking in a room in the resort hotel. She knew them from their contacts earlier in the headquarters building. Keszthelyi was Hungarian, and because Maria spoke no English, she had been able to converse with both him and Steve Catlos, who also spoke Hungarian. Also, Joe Horvath, Jan Schwartz or Jerry Mican who spoke Slovak or Czech, were able to communicate with Maria. Meanwhile, Tibor gave up his room to Maria, a gesture which surprised her.

Maria had first met Holt Green and Jerry Mican shortly after they had arrived in Slovakia in September at a reception given in honor of the minister of Slovakia. The Russian mission did not attend but asked Maria to represent them. Out of curiosity, she attended the function. She remembered Holt Green's stylish tan dress uniform with his lieutenant's rank on his shoulder boards.

She had seen Mican and Joe Horvath daily in the CFI communications center where they picked up reports for Holt Green. She did the same for Studensky and his staff. That Maria worked for Studensky and the Russians, however, raised the issue of her political views in the minds of the Americans. Was she a Communist? This was a concern because most of the Americans had developed anti-Russian views because of their contacts in both Yugoslavia. They would soon learn that Maria Gulovich was no Communist.

Who was this young woman who was to play such a unique role in the Uprising?

23 Year Old Carpatho-Rusyn.

Maria, who had just celebrated her 23rd birthday, was born in the mountain village of Jakubany, a few miles south of Stara L'Ubovna near the Polish border. Without electricity and existing on well water, Jakubany was in the heart of the Carpatho-Rusyn region of eastern Slovakia. Much of the lifestyle and social structure there was no more than a decade or two removed from feudalism. Maria's father, Edmund Gulovich, was a Greek Catholic priest, and her mother, Anastasia, was an elementary school teacher.

Her parents had middle class origins. Edmund Gulovich had received his gymnasium education in Presov and continued on there to receive his divinity degree. Later, he did graduate work in Budapest where his father once managed large estates for the Esterhazy family. When the Communist Revolution of 1919 led by Bela Kun broke out in Hungary, Edmund returned to Presov where he became a Greek Catholic priest. Under the doctrine of this church, he was allowed to marry and in 1920 he and Anatasia married. He subsequently was assigned to a church in Jakubany which was connected to Stara L'Ubovna, Anatasia's home, by a narrow dirt road rutted by wagon tracks. Sheep rearing was the main activity in such villages where the stolid farmers wore traditional peasant clothes.

Maria's early childhood education occurred in a one-room school where the teacher taught 100 students, ages six to fourteen. Edmund feared Maria, his eldest daughter, and his second daughter were receiving an inferior education. He attempted for a time to educate them at home. This proved difficult and he finally sent Maria to Stara L'Ubovna to live with an aunt where Maria was enrolled in a private school. The elderly lady had difficulty relating to her young, spirited niece, so Maria was moved again, this time to Presov to live in a Roman Catholic convent.

The convent, steeped in tradition, bore all the trappings and atmosphere of a church from the Middle Ages. The children were rousted out of bed at 5 AM daily and immediately went to the chapel for mass. So began the regimen each day. Obedience was among the highest virtues, and punishment by the nuns always was harsh. Little Maria wondered what she had done to deserve such a fate. Nevertheless, she studied German and Russian there and began to acquire a life-long interest in history as well as languages. Personally, however, she never was able to adjust to the constraints of such a doctrinaire lifestyle.

Sewing School in Vienna.

Later at 14, too young to enter the university, Maria was sent by her father to Vienna to live with another aunt where she attended a sewing school as an apprentice dressmaker. She lived in the suburb of Grinzing, 20 minutes by street car from downtown Vienna. Relieved not to have to worry about school, Maria became the close friend of another girl in the sewing school. They reveled in the old Hapsburg capital, drinking in the culture of the rich museums, strolling down Kaertnerstrasse to watch the well-dressed aristocrats and the middle class Viennese. They visited the St. Stephen's cathedral and took wistful walks by the Hofburg Palace. Maria loved the historic city.

Maria's stay in Vienna intensified her independent outlook which nurtured her self confidence, but which also led inevitably to conflict with her parents. Returning to the village of Jakubany always resulted in arguments provoked by Maria's expanding worldly ideas. Edmund and Anatasia wanted her to marry a young priest, for example. Maria was introduced to a number of prospects, but the thought of winding up in another Jakubany, living a life among peasants, was not acceptable to her. Vienna had changed her forever.[4]

Father Was an Intellectual.

Although staunchly conservative, Maria's father was an intellectual who had introduced her to the works of Pushkin, Gogol, and other literary giants. She began to dream of becoming a university history professor. But her dreams were quashed when her father enrolled her in the Greek Catholic Institute for Teachers in Presov in September, 1935. It was a four-year curriculum with all the rigor of a European university. The classes were taught in Carpatho-Rusyn. Gifted in the study of languages, Maria excelled in formal Russian and German. She also enjoyed her literature classes, and especially, her history classes. It was a happy time. But, World War II was just around the corner.

When the Third *Reich* occupied the balance of Czechoslovakia in March, 1939, the impact on Slovakia was dramatic. Most of the Czechs from all social classes were rounded up and deported to Moravia and Bohemia and their property confiscated. The Slovaks were awarded independence by Hitler, but the *Führer's* control of Josef Tiso, the former Monsignor, was total. The Catholic peasant class took little notice of this, but the intellectuals in the country were dejected.

Maria still recalls the general meeting in the auditorium at the school in 1939 when the policies of the new regime were announced. President Benes and democratic government were finished, Tiso's picture was suddenly everywhere, and it was clear the fascist state of the Hlinka Party would control all aspects of life. Maria was both depressed and outraged.[5]

Begins Teaching Career.

She graduated in 1940 and accepted a teaching position in Jarabina near Jakubany. She taught first grade. The school year was cut short when the school was taken over by the German army in June, 1941. The *Third Reich* was preparing for the invasion of the Soviet Union and Jarabina became a staging area for *Wehrmacht* troops. One of the main routes into Poland and points east ran by Jarabina.

Maria witnessed the round-the-clock troop movements once the invasion began. She recalled the well-fed horses, the shiny new harnesses, and the smartly dressed men. Enthusiasm was the hallmark of the Germans as seemingly endless battalions marched by, singing in full voice their traditional marching songs.

Later, Maria remembered that when she returned home to Jakubany during the summer of 1943, it was a different story. The bloody battles of Stalingrad and other fighting throughout the Caucasus sent the Germans back through Jarabina. It was a steady stream of hollow-faced soldiers in dirty, ragged uniforms riding in dilapidated trucks. "What a difference two years made!" she later wrote.[6]

In 1941, Maria was once reported to the police for not giving a Heil Hitler style salute to her students and superiors. One of her colleagues was arrested by the *Hlinka Gestapo* and sent to a labor camp. Because of this, Maria's anger against the regime and the influence of the Germans heightened.

She feared she might get into trouble, so she moved to the village of Hrinova in May, 1943. A village not unlike Jakubany, Hrinova was 22 miles east of Zvolen, a farm community with a strong pastoral peasant base. She had 40 students between the ages of nine and 12. This was not Vienna, but she loved the school and her children. The school principal taught the primary grades, and his wife taught the upper grades. Maria was content.

---

1 Maria Gulovich OSS Report.
2 Ibid.
3 Ibid.
4 Maria Gulovich, Interview with the author, September 17, 2000.
5 Maria Gulovich, Interview with the author, September 19, 2000.
6 Maria Gulovich, Fax to the author, September 22, 2000.

Chapter 18

Underground Courier

Hrinova, Slovakia, 1944.

Maria was shocked one day to see her sister, Marta, and Julius Goldberger, a friend of the family, arrive at the school in Hrinova. A Jew, Goldberger lived a precarious existence. Goldberger operated a lumber mill in Jakubany, and because of his skill and usefulness to the Germans, he was allowed to survive. It was a typical cynical practice of the Germans. Maria wondered immediately why her sister and Goldberger had come to Hrinova.

Goldberger explained that he had been hiding his sister and her small son from the Germans, and he had learned that he was under suspicion. His property had been searched once already by a German officer. Goldberger feared for his sister's life, her child's, and his own. He had persuaded Maria's family to help find her and her son a new hiding place. They went to Maria and she reluctantly agreed to take them.

Recruited Into The Underground.

The Jewish woman proved to be a difficult, temperamental person, and Maria found herself upset much of the time and concerned about being discovered. Maria's supervisor knew about the lady and her son. If arrested, the consequences of hiding Jews usually meant imprisonment, or worse. He wanted them gone.

A few weeks later, Captain Milan Pollack of the Slovak army showed up at the school and confronted Maria with her "crime." He exploited the issue by offering Maria a choice: if she would join his underground espionage operation against the Germans, he would find another hiding place for the lady and her son, and would see no charges were made against Maria.

Maria had little choice. The bargain called for her to move to Banska Bystrica to live with another couple, and accept a job as a dressmaker with an elderly Russian émigré. These people all were underground sympathizers bent on aiding the overthrow of the Tiso regime.

In Bystrica, Maria launched into a career of dressmaking. Her employer, a talented seamstress, made elegant clothes. The job was an excellent cover as Maria now was in the dangerous business of espionage.

Pollack told her he had been "losing" couriers, but assured Maria that she would be effective and safe because she was young and "innocent looking." Maria was not so sure. But she was dedicated to the idea of getting Slovakia out from under the German yoke. And she was intrigued. She would realize more fully later that she was by nature drawn to difficult and dangerous challenges, even when the consequences might be fatal.

Maria was given the code name "Gita," and sent on her first mission to Turciansky Sv. Martin, 65 miles northwest of Bystrica. Pollack advised her not to be afraid to talk with the Germans – mostly officers – whom she would meet on the trains. She was comfortable doing this as her Viennese-accented German seemed to suggest to Germans that she was somehow sympathetic to them and their cause. The Germans tightly controlled the Slovak train system, and Slovaks frequently came under suspicion while traveling.

August, A Dangerous Mission.

Pollack sent her to Bratislava where she was ordered to pick up a suitcase. She had no idea of the contents. This was not so routine. Getting on the train to return to Bystrica, Maria nearly was forced to submit her luggage for inspection, which would have been fatal.[1] She smiled coquettishly at a German *SS* Officer and accepted his invitation to join him in his compartment. He carried her suitcase. She bid goodby when they arrived in Bystrica, only to see she was going to face another baggage inspection upon leaving the train. Then she saw the *SS* officer again, smiled, and he walked over and picked up her suitcase and carried it out of the station. She accepted his invitation to dinner that evening in the *Narodny Dom Hotel*, but didn't show up.

This had been too close. Now, she realized just how dangerous her work was. Yet, at the same time, she felt somehow immune from getting caught.[2]

Another issue began to disturb her. She began to wonder which was the bigger danger to Slovakia, fascism or communism. Once in Trencin, Maria met an old friend with whom she had taught school. At dinner, Maria was startled when her friend's husband, a CFI Army officer, disclosed that he was an ardent Communist. Maria never ceased to be astonished that intelligent, educated Slovaks professed an allegiance to Communism.[3]

Back in Bystrica, Pollack showed up at the dress shop one day with bad news. Maria stepped outside to talk with him and learned Pollack believed that the security forces of the Slovak Army now suspected both him and Maria. "There are reports coming across my desk asking who you are and why you are in the city," he told Maria.[4]

Maria panicked for a moment, but Pollack said she simply would be under surveillance for the time being. He gave her a new assignment. A driver took her to Captain Pavel Pavlovich who had just come from the USSR. In training for five years, he had just parachuted into Slovakia.

Pavlovich was hiding with a couple outside of Bystrica. Maria delivered Pollack's message to him that he was assigned to be the liaison officer between the CFI and the Czech Brigade. A few days later, Pollack's driver advised Maria in Bystrica that she definitely was being followed and it was unlikely she would be used as a courier. She asked the man what she should do. "Just be grateful you're still alive," he replied.[5]

Pavlovich had his own problems. He narrowly escaped capture when government security police raided his hiding place a few days later. He informed Maria they both must both be careful as the Uprising was about to start. Pavlovich ordered Maria to carry a message to two Partisan commanders in the mountains east of Bystrica, informing them that he was in town.

With Slovak guides, Maria headed for the Lower Tatra Mountains, and found the camp of Captain P. A. Velichko. This was the same Velichko whose men had seized and murdered the 17 German officers in Turciansky Sv. Martin on August 26-27.

That evening, Velichko, a large burley man, preached to Maria about a "Stalinist future" for Slovakia, which left her both disgusted and depressed. Velichko convinced her that Soviet aid to Slovakia was not altruistic, although she said nothing. He was the first Russian officer she had met.[6]

The next day, she was led on a four-hour walk to Captain Igor Yegoroff, another Russian officer, whom she liked immediately. He was a natural leader of men, Maria noticed. Yegoroff seemed relieved that she spoke Russian as his Slovak was poor. He had spent two years in combat, and this was to be his last assignment before going home on leave. He and Velichko were organizing Partisan units in the mountains.

Captain Studensky.

When the CFI secured Bystrica a few days later, Maria returned and was informed by Pavlovich, now a major with a driver and a car, that she was being assigned to the Russian mission in the Velitelsvo as an interpreter. Pavlovich took her to meet her new boss.

Captain Studensky was a cavalry officer whose face was scarred from a wound he suffered in hand to hand combat in the battle for Smolensk in 1942. He made a point of wearing riding britches, and she noticed his boots always were polished to a high shine.

Here Maria was integrated into the Russian intelligence operation, and she didn't like what she saw. Velichko's words about "Father Stalin" were still on her mind. Now she met another Russian she didn't like, Sergei Popov, the political officer. He conducted himself in the old fashioned *NKVD* commissar style, intimidating people and abusing his authority. He continually insisted that Maria translate the Banska Bystrica newspapers so he could compile a records of names and activities. In her eyes, Popov personified the sinister characteristics of the secret police.

Tamara[7] a Lieutenant in the Red Army, was the Russian code clerk. She and Maria became friends. The wife of a Russian officer, she was a stunning copper-haired beauty who worked long hours encoding messages that Maria translated from Slovak to Russian. Studensky edited the messages which were forwarded to Marshall Koniev's headquarters in Kiev. The work load was so great Maria slept on a cot in the office. Tamara was under such tight security she was practically locked in the code room. She was under orders to associate with no Slovaks or non Russian personnel, except for Maria.[8] This favored position Maria held later would be a problem for her.

As each day passed, Maria learned that the Russians had developed a plan to take over as much territory as possible in the west. They were not interested in Slovak independence, and spoke contemptuously of democratic governments. When the Americans arrived, Maria noticed that the Russians avoided them.

Maria Meets The Americans.

Maria was intrigued with the Americans. Although they were hard workers and focused on their work, they also were relaxed and friendly. She recalled years later a conversation with Sergeant Joe Horvath who told Maria how he had proposed to his wife in a drive-in theater. Maria had never heard of drive-in theaters. She was amazed that American cars had heaters.

As the Germans approached the city, Studensky and Popov began preparing to abandon the city. Studensky gave Maria and Tamara money to go into the city to buy boots for the likelihood of hiking through the mountains. He already had told the women that they might not be able to get out of the city by plane.

On October 26, Maria picked up the boots for her and Tamara. They had ordered warm clothes but they were not ready. Maria complained to the Americans and Lt. Tibor Keszthelyi gave her a warm American coat with a fur hood.[9]

---

[1] Maria learned in 1989 that she was carrying a radio.
[2] Maria Gulovich, Telephone interview with the author, September 20, 2000.
[3] Ibid.
[4] Ibid.
[5] Ibid.
[6] Ibid.
[7] Ibid. Maria has forgotten Tamara's last name.
[8] Ibid.
[9] Ibid.

1. Tri Duby Airfield, October 7, 1944. Jim Street's B-17 in the background. Unloaded ordinance for Slovak army in the foreground. (courtesy of SNU museum). **2.** Jim Street. (courtesy of Jim Street). **3.** Tri Duby, October 7, OSS Master Sergeant Jerry Mican, left; British Major John Sehmer, SOE, back to camera, Lt.(USNR) Holt Green on the right. (courtesy of SNU museum). **4.** Tri Duby, American airmen wait on the grass for the arrival of the six B-17s from Italy, October 7. (courtesy of SNU museum).

1. Banska Bystrica, October 19. Front row, left to right, Frank Bulfin, Ladislav Rosina, Partisan officer; Jack Wilson, British SOE agent; Jan Lesak, Partisan officer; Richard Rippon. Standing, left to right, Ben Raczka, John Kaczaja, Howard Coleman, Bob Hede, Keith Hensen, British SOE radio operator; George Fernandes, and Guy LaFatta. All but the two Partisans and Wilson were captured on November 11. Wilson was captured with the OSS team on December 26, 1944. (courtesy of George Fernandes). **2.** Newspaper clipping, unknown origin, Charles Muller, escaped POW, flown back to Italy, October 7 (courtesy of Charles Muller). **3.** Sergeant Howard Luzier, missed October 7 flight, captured on November 11. (courtesy of Howard Luzier. **4.** Theron Arnett, newspaper clipping, unknown origin. Captured by *Abwehr* unit, November 11. (courtesy of Jean Arnett). **5.** Tri Duby, October 7. Left, LTC Gil Pritchard, B-17 commander of sixplane B-1 7 flight; Major Walter Ross, behind Pritchard; Lt. (USNR) Nelson Deranian, Lt. (USNR) Holt Green, looking up at P-51's buzzing the field. Others unknown. (courtesy of SNU museum).

1. OSS agents, (left to right) Charles Heller, Joseph Horvath, and Robert Brown, await the B-17's on October 7. (courtesy of SNU Museum). **2. and 3.** "Swamp Angel" sits camouflaged at Tri Duby where Bill Coloney attempted to restart the engine. In the second photo, 1st Lt. Alex Watkins sits on the wing of the same plane earlier at his Italian airfield. (courtesy of Mrs. Alex Watkins). **4.** Captain Jack Gorman piloted the B-17 which became stuck in the mud on October 7. Partisans spent an hour freeing Gorman's plane which he flew back to Italy without escort. **5.** Lt. Holt Green makes a point with Lt. Nelson Deranian on October 7. Major Walter Ross, center, and Jim Gaul listen. Deranian and Ross flew back to Italy with LTC Pritchard that same day. (courtesy of SNU Museum).

1. Downed B-17 pilot Lt. Jack Shafer was rescued by the OSS but later fell into the hands of the Germans. (courtesy, Jack Shafer). **2.** New Zealander Gordon Follas, center, pictured with Slovak Partisans in Brezova. (courtesy, SNU Museum). **3.** Lt. Francis Perry, OSS DAWES mission, captured at Dolna Lehota, later executed at Mauthausen concentration camp. (courtesy, Frances Frost Hutson). **4.** OSS Sgt. Joe Horvath, left, with OSS U.S. Navy Photographers Mate Nelson Paris And a Soviet Red Army soldier, center, in happier days. Bucharest, Romania, August, 1944. The Americans were executed at Mauthausen. (courtesy, Jim Gabriel).

1. and **2.** 1st Lt. Bill McGregor. Weapons trainer, DAWES mission. Captured on November 11 with airmen. (courtesy of Sandy Woods). **3.** 2nd Lt. Ethan Allen Smith, crash-landed at Tri Duby Airfield, September 17. (courtesy of E.A. Smith). **4.** Joe Morton, Associated Press war correspondent, is shown here interviewing Vlado Zecevic, Minister of Interior in the Yugoslavian cabinet of Tito, May 12, 1944. Morton, widely popular, was an aggressive reporter after the "biggest story of his life" when he went to Slovakia. (courtesy of The Associated Press).

1. Horvath children, Polomka, Slovakia, 1927. Joe is standing at the right. Anna, his cousin, is sitting on the chair with his brother, Frank. Anna secretly delivered food to Joe for the OSS team in Polomka in December, 1944. (courtesy, Rudy and Frank Horvath). **2.** Joe Horvath's high school graduation photo, 1941. (courtesy, Rudy and Frank Horvath). **3.** Photo taken shortly after leaving Donovaly on the Prasiva Mountain. Joe Morton on the left. Holt Green, center, Jerry Mican on the right. (courtesy SNU museum). **4.** British Major Anthony Hunter, the SOE commander in the Kolasin, Yugoslavia, region, and Lt. Holt Green, who reported to Hunter, circa May, 1944. (courtesy, Frances Frost Hutson).

1. Charles Heller, Specialist 2nd Class, USN radio operator, HOUSEBOAT mission. 2. 1st Lt. Tibor Kesthelyi, BOWERY mission, sub-unit of DAWES mission. 3. Nelson Paris, Photographers Mate, USN DAWES mission. 4. Lt. Jim Gaul, USNR, deputy commander, DAWES mission. 5. Captain Edward Baranski, commander, DAY mission. 6. Major John Sehmer, British SOE commander, WINDPROOF mission. 7. Daniel Pavletich, DAY mission. 8. Jan Schwartz, commander, HOUSEBOAT mission. 9. Master Sergeant Jerry Mican, DAWES mission. 10. Lt. Holt Green, USNR, commander, DAWES mission. (all photos, NARA).

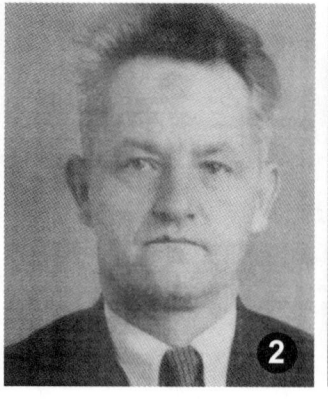

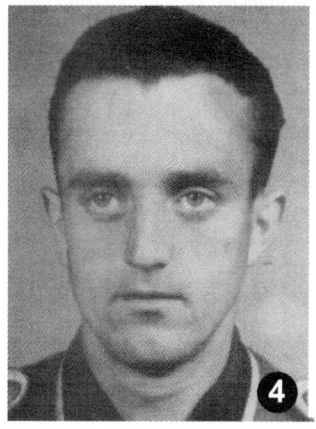

1. Major Erwein *Graf* Thun-Hohenstein, commander, *Abwehr 218.* (courtesy, *Graf* Franz Czernin).
2. Colonel Josef Witiska, commander, *Abwehr Grupp H*, Bratislava. (courtesy, *Bundesarchiv Berlin*). **3.** *Gestapo* director Dr. Manfred Schoeneseiffen. (courtesy, *Bundesrchiv Berlin*).
4. Josef Niedermayer, *SS* officer, Mauthausen concentration camp. (courtesy, *Archiv KZ - Gedenkstaette Mauthausen*).
5. *Hauptsturmführer* Georg Bachmayer on right with unidentified *SS* officer, Mauthausen. (courtesy, *Gedenkstaette* Mauthausen). **6.** *SS* Chief Heinrich Himmler, left, and RSHA Berlin *SS* Chief Ernst Kaltenbrunner, as *SS* Colonel Franz Ziereis points out the buildings at Mauthausen in a 1941 visit of the Nazi leaders. Himmler committed suicide at the end of the war; Kaltenbrunner was tried and hanged at Nurnberg, and Ziereis was mortally wounded by U.S. troops in a shootout, May, 1945. (courtesy, *Gedenkstaette* Mauthausen).

Chapter 19

Rain, Fog and Gunfire

October 27, Donovaly.

The village was teeming with soldiers and refugees. Donovaly was situated in one of only two passes in the Lower *Tatras* where roads connected the Hron Valley, which ran east and west, with the parallel Vah Valley to the north. The *Tatras* were a relatively flat, forested 50-mile long ridge with few roads or settlements. It seemed a natural area from which the Partisans could operate.

The OSS team settled in at a resort hotel which General Golian and General Viest had commandeered as their headquarters. The American airmen were quartered at Motycky, a settlement of only a few houses four miles south.

The Americans awoke before sunrise after a fitful night. The ominous gunfire in the distance was unsettling. As the sun came up, the *Luftwaffe* came out in force, and the Americans were soon witness to an airshow that continued without let up.

The *Luftwaffe*— *Stukas and Focke-Wulfs* — swept through the sky, strafing and bombing the long lines of vehicles and throngs of people still escaping up the Stare Hory Valley. The raids went on hour after hour, resulting in the wounding and killing of hundreds of men, women, and children. The survivors staggered into Donovaly, describing the massive carnage along the entire length of the road.[1]

Down in the valley in and around Bystrica, the *Schill Brigade* cleaned up pockets of resistance. That German patrols would soon reach Donovaly was a foregone conclusion, and the Slovaks were digging in. A Russian officer with an English-speaking interpreter ordered George Fernandes, Bob Hede, and Ernie Coleman to go on a reconnaissance patrol. The American airmen refused, asserting they could take orders only from their commanding officer, Lt. Holt Green. The conversation ended abruptly when a German plane dropped bombs near-by. One of the bomb fragments struck Fernandes in the ankle, causing a minor wound.[2]

Cecilia Wojewoda and Husband Desperate To Flee.

That night Joe Morton and Jim Gaul met with Cecilia Wojewoda and her husband. The Polish couple begged to accompany the Americans into the mountains. Gaul discouraged them, pointing out that they would be safer hiding on their own in some nearby village. Morton gave Cecilia a map of the surrounding mountains, a wool military scarf, and a Roman Catholic Virgin of Lourdes medal. He told her some French nuns had given it to him and assured him that no harm would ever come to him as long as he had it. She refused to take it, but Morton insisted.

A half century later she poignantly wrote to the author. "Later when I knew that he was dead, to my grief was added the terrifying thought that he gave away the key to his life. Would he have survived if he had not given me the medal? We shall never know the answer, but . . . [he] was the kind of man who did not think of himself when he saw someone else in danger."[3]

After the sunset, German patrols began to infiltrate up the mountain and prowl through the woods. Holt Green and Bill McGregor agreed to post their own guards rather than rely on the disorganized Slovaks. McGregor shivered through the night in a shepherd's hut. He observed a German patrol which he didn't challenge and there was no shooting.[4]

Only a few miles north, Dirlewanger's Brigade advanced on Slovak positions south of Liptovska Osada. Dirlewanger moved to encircle the pic-

Rain, Fog, and Gunfire

turesque hamlet to prevent a Slovak breakout.[5] Everywhere, the Germans continued to move aggressively. *SS* General Hoefle had ordered his commanders to capture or destroy without delay all the remaining elements of the scattered CFI forces and Partisans.[6]

No one doubted that in fleeing, the CFI, Partisans, and Americans would have to move higher into the Prasiva range. Travel now would be by foot with the aid of a few pack horses. The Americans were forced to abandon more of their gear. Joe Morton set about burying two trunks, two bags, and a Navy sack which held all his possessions.[7] Nelson Paris left his cameras with a civilian. Others discarded all but their vital belongings.

Maria Gulovich, meanwhile, located the Russian mission. Major Studensky apologized for not keeping his promise to come back and get her. She asked what he and his staff were going to do. His major concern was to get Tamara to the Russian lines. If captured, Tamara would be brutally tortured because of her knowledge of Russian codes.[8]

Maria later ran into the Americans outside the hotel. Jan Schwartz and Joe Horvath spoke to her in Slovak and asked her for news on the military situation. She told them the CFI command and the Russian mission appeared to be disorganized and there was confusion about the Germans. Although the troops were digging in around Donovaly, she believed the senior officers intended to retreat when the attack started.[9]

October 28, Americans Leave For The High Country.

This was a day of reckoning. At 3 AM, Holt Green sent a final, grim message to Bari. "Believe situation getting worse. Possible we may discard radios. . . .Have arranged to split into four groups . . . Three with radios. Organized resistance rapidly deteriorating." [10]

Three hours later, Green assembled the Americans— 43 strong — and split the men into groups. The men stirred around waiting for the sun to come up, although they could see in the dawn a red glare on the horizon to the northwest where Dirlewanger's troops apparently had burned buildings in Liptovska Osada. They listened to the scattered gunfire in the distance.[11] The *Schill Brigade* was closing in.[12]

George Fernandes' group was assigned to Lt. Bill McGregor, and Jack Shafer and his men were with Lt. Ken Lain. Holt Green and Lt. Frank Perry led the two other groups. They loaded up their heavy packs in a light rain and headed east. Before leaving, they destroyed equipment. Nelson Paris, the Navy Photographer's mate, destroyed several thousand feet of exposed 16 mm film. George Fernandes remembers helping destroy the film.[13]

Paris was a dark-haired 29-year-old native of Portland, Oregon. He had accompanied Lt. Nelson Deranian to Romania the previous August to make a photo record of Operation GUNN. Sending Paris along with the DAWES team indicated that the OSS wanted a film record of as many of their missions as possible. Unfortunately none of Paris' film survived the mission.

"We were more or less just following the crowd," Ken Dunlevy later wrote. It was tough going. After two hours near the village of Korytnica, they were forced to lighten their loads. Elements of Dirlewanger's Brigade were less than two miles away to the west and they could hear scattered gunfire.[14]

The muddy trail soon became an endless quagmire. Men began discarding equipment and even food supplies. Lt. Frank Perry ordered Steve Catlos to destroy the heavy radio. Their few pack horses were carrying food.[15] Some of the Slovak officers rode horses. Piontek had found a pack horse for Joe Morton to carry his gear. But, a short distance up the trail, the horse bolted and Morton's possessions were scattered in the mud.[16]

When Lt. Tibor Keszthelyi learned the radio had been destroyed, he was furious at both Perry and Catlos. Tibor — as he was always called — asserted that the radio could have been disassembled and carried in parts by several men. Radio contact was essential in the wilderness.[17]

As the group struggled on, they stumbled into hundreds of fleeing Slovak troops and Jewish refugees. The Americans were amazed to see the vast numbers of refugees in the woods. The weather began to turn worse.

Rain, Fog, and Gunfire 155

Incessant raid continued on into the night. They slept in the open without tents or shelter.[18]

The Slovaks and the Russian mission left Donovaly two hours behind the Americans. Before leaving, they set fire to several hundred vehicles and blew up dozens of artillery pieces. Sporadic automatic weapons fire a few hundred yards away signaled the nearness of the Germans.

The Slovaks headed southeast down through the hills toward Slovenska Lupca on the Brezno road. A mile or two on the trail, they ran into Partisans who said Germans were up ahead. Retracing their steps, the Slovaks were unable to take time to eat. Later, after several hours of sloshing along the muddy trail, their advance guard now reported that a German patrol was just ahead of them. Germans were all over the mountain like ghosts ready to appear at any moment. Refugees, coming and going, added to the confusion. Unnerving gunfire sporadically echoed through the woods in the distance.

Darkness soon fell, and the Slovaks and Russians were able to slip around the Germans. They reached the Czech Brigade camp at 10 PM. The group noticed that General Golian was missing.[19]

Sunday, October 29.

The Americans rose before dawn and ate a meager breakfast. Refugees streamed by, not knowing where they were going, but desperate to avoid the Germans. Back on the trail, the Brigade ran into General Golian and his staff. Golian was rumored to have been captured but somehow had escaped. The group continued on toward the *Prasiva* Mountain Range. Fog kept visibility to only a few feet. The sounds of gunfire and shelling boomed up the mountain from Korytnica where desperate Slovak units were fighting a bloody rear guard action against Dirlewanger's troops.[20]

As they ran into different trail heads and junctions, the combined force of Americans, Slovaks and Russians continually were forced to make wrenching decisions. General Viest and his staff, for example, disagreed strongly with Major Studensky at one point and finally separated to head south in the direction of the Polana mountain. Studensky believed it was a mistake and struck out for Dumbier Mountain. Viest's decision proved to be a fatal blunder.[21]

An hour later, troops from the *Schill Brigade* again caught up to the group and began firing wildly into the fog. Maria joined the others and ran when the gunfire erupted. The Slovaks and refugees scattered into the woods. Maria later recorded the scene:

I crouched behind a tree . . . and I saw the boots of a soldier standing just around the tree where I was hiding. I could tell he was a German by his boots.[Later] as we climbed into the mountains, the rain turned to sleet. Our wet clothes froze. We wanted to reach Dumbier, but some retreating Partisans met us and said Dumbier was infested with Germans. We kept going and found a Partisan camp in which bunkers had been constructed. There was no room there, so we decided to continue toward the valley. We ran into a Partisan on a horse, and he told us where the Americans were. We pressed on . . . [22]

Walking In The Fog and Rain.

The group slipped away again. The Germans had their own problems. The fog and the rain and the mud were allies of no one. The Americans walked for seven hours.[23] The situation was chaotic. They would wander up a trail only to be confronted by a Slovak patrol fleeing Germans from the other direction. Then they would backtrack and wait. Groups of refugees jammed the trails. One of the Brigade patrols finally returned, reporting that it had found Captain Yegoroff's Partisan group.

The Americans, meanwhile, had already reached Yegoroff's Partisan camp near the crest of a 6,000 ft. ridge. Discarded guns, ammunition, grenades, and German gear, littered the trails even at this altitude.[24] At points, the climb had been steep and the men had to rest every 100 yards. Desperate civilians struggled up the mountain and mixed in with the

Rain, Fog, and Gunfire

Partisans and the Americans on the ridge. Occasionally, one of the men would assist a sobbing, struggling Jewish child. Dead horses lay along the trail.[25]

Yegoroff's group occupied several bunkers they had constructed, and the Americans were forced that night to sleep in the open. There was no water or fire wood. Garbage and excrement littered the ground.[26]

Finally the Slovak patrol led Maria's group into the Jegoroff camp just as it was getting dark. There was no room for them either, and they walked off the ridge a short distance to establish a camp near the Americans.[27]

That night, Maria walked over to the American group where she was greeted warmly by Joe Horvath and Tibor. Even though everyone was tired, they began a far ranging discussion around the campfire. The Americans questioned Maria about her feelings toward the Russians and her past work for them. "Was she a Communist?" they asked. The Americans wanted to accept her, but there was some hesitancy.

Maria reminded them that Russia originally was the only nation willing to assist the Slovaks when the Uprising began. Pro-Uprising Slovaks naturally had been loyal to the Russians. Nevertheless, Maria was not surprised that some of the Americans didn't trust her. She was used to being questioned by the Slovaks about her association with the Russians. She soon made clear her strong anti-Soviet views, distinguishing the Soviets from the Russians.[28]

Maria Invited To Join the Americans.

Speaking through Joe Horvath, Bill McGregor changed the course of the conversation and abruptly asked her to stay with the Americans. He told her he believed the Americans couldn't survive without someone who spoke Russian. Maria replied she would need General Viest's approval. Holt Green saw Viest immediately, and returned to welcome Maria into the DAWES mission. Maria was unsure if she had made the right decision. [29]

Maria had become disillusioned with the Russian acts of politicizing every situation. Two causes still motivated her: . Defeat the Germans; and 2.

Support the goals of the failed Uprising. She had concluded that the Russians wanted to take over her country. Despite that, she had performed her work of translating documents and newspapers and other items in a professional manner for the Russian mission.

Maria sat up all night talking to Tibor, Joe Horvath, Holt Green, Jim Gaul, and Bill McGregor. "I [increasingly] felt more secure with Lt. Green and his group than either the Russians or the Partisans," she wrote later. Finally, escaping another night in the rain, Maria would share a tent with the Americans that night.[30]

The rigors of the day's hike had exhausted the Americans. They shared their food and tried to maintain a positive attitude. Josef Piontek remembered the kindness of Jerry Mican who had given him a piece of chocolate at lunch. Joe Morton and Piontek shared some hot chocolate and "some nuts." It was a cold, rainy night. "We were promised a cottage [hut]. Where is it?" Piontek plaintively recorded in his diary.[31]

Meanwhile, the Germans had taken 3,000 prisoners in the Donovaly-Liptovska Osada-Korytnica area. General Hoefle's command acknowledged in their official combat reports that Partisan resistance had been intense.[32] The Germans reported the next day that the Slovaks were "in flight," but that they were still resisting strongly. In Bystrica, Hoefle began organizing shipments of prisoners to Germany to work as forced laborers.[33] The Third *Reich* now had central Slovakia in its grip and slave labor was one of the grim results.

---

1   Kenneth Dunlevy, OSS Report.
2   George Fernandes, Unpublished manuscript.
3   Cecilia Wojewoda, Letter to the author, September 5, 2000, from Warsaw Poland, where she now lives.
4   Dunlevy, OSS Report.
5   *Wehrmacht* Diary, October 28, 1944.
6   Ibid.
7   Josef Piontek Diary.
8   Maria Gulovich, Telephone interview with the author, September 22, 2000.
9   Ibid.

10 NARA, RG 226, Entry 190, Box 116, Folder 407, Message 216.
11 Kenneth Dunlevy, OSS Report.
12 *Wehrmacht* Diary, October 29; Piontek Diary.
13 George Fernandes, Unpublished manuscript.
14 Kenneth Dunlevy, OSS Report; *Wehrmacht* Diary, October 29, 1944.
15 George Fernandes, Unpublished manuscript.
16 Piontek Diary.
17 Maria Gulovich, OSS Report.
18 Dunlevy, OSS Report.
19 Maria Gulovich, Interview with William Miller; Maria Gulovich, OSS Report.
20 *Wehrmacht* Diary summary.
21 Maria Gulovich, OSS Report.
22 Ibid.
23 Ibid.
24 Kenneth Dunlevy, OSS Report.
25 Josef Piontek, Diary.
26 Ibid.
27 Maria Gulovich, OSS Report.
28 Ibid.
29 Ibid.
30 Ibid.
31 Piontek Diary.
32 *Wehrmacht* Diary, summary.
33 Ibid.

Stare Hory Road, October 25

Chapter 20

Over the Precipice

October 26, Muran, 25 Miles East of Brezno.

British Major John Sehmer and three of his men and Margita Kockova, the Slovak-American he had recruited, had left Banska Bystrica on October 13. Sehmer knew the city would fall to the Germans, and made a clean escape early. He notified Lt. Colonel Threlfall in Bari that he was being forced to get rid of his radio. "Huns everywhere," he reported in his last message.[1]

The following day, Sehmer met with Lt. Dymko Voknuk, a deputy commander of a Russian-led Partisan group, and learned the Slovak army no longer existed "as a fighting force." Sehmer decided to stay with the Partisans.[2] Presumably, Threlfall notified the OSS in Bari of the Sehmer messages. Bari already knew Green had fled Bystrica.

October 29, OSS Headquarters, Bari, Italy.

Twenty-four hours had elapsed, and Major Walter Ross and Lt. Deranian had no news from Green. Ross notified 5th Army headquarters in Caserta that Bari was attempting to get a precise location on the DAWES team. He had little to go on. Ross alerted the 15th Air Force to stand by to make a supply drop.[3] Where, of course, he had no idea. He could only guess at Green's desperate situation. Deranian, Lt. Colonel Chapin, Robert Joyce, and Ross conferred daily about the plight of their men with no idea whether they were dead or alive or in the hands of the enemy.[4]

October 30, German-Occupied Banska Bystrica.

The Germans now had collected 10,000 prisoners in the Bystrica-Zvolen-Donovaly area. They were rounding up rail transport to ship them to Germany as forced labor. General Hoefle's *Wehrmacht* headquarters estimated 4,000 Slovak personnel in flight on Dumbier Mountain and another 2-3000 in the Detva-Polana region.[5] The German intelligence net actively interrogated prisoners, meaning there were few secrets the Wehrmacht didn't possess.

On the *Prasiva* Range, the Russians informed Holt Green they were pulling out to head for the Red Army lines. German intelligence already knew this from captured prisoners. The Czech Brigade, however, decided to remain and convinced Green to stay with them. Was this a mistake?[6]

The Americans welcomed the chance to stay in the vacated bunkers and escape the cold. The Brigade had the same idea. Each bunker was designed for 150 men, but nearly 400 squeezed in. That first night, few were able to sleep. They awoke hungry and weary. Later that day, the Partisans caught a German soldier who claimed — after being beaten by the Slovaks — that he was a Dutch national and a deserter. He was assigned to the Americans and ordered to guard their provisions.[7]

October 31, Holt Green Divides The Gold.

The Americans again rose early. Partisan patrols reported that German troops were not far away. Green had brought from Bari several thousand dollars of gold Napoleon coins. He now distributed them among the men. To this point, only officers had been carrying gold, except for a few men who carried bulk amounts. Every man was issued ten coins, each worth $20.00, plus 1000 Koruns of Slovak currency. The men were able to purchase provisions from the Czech Brigade, paying in gold, when necessary.[8]

November 1, Partisans Discard Equipment.

The day started badly. Maria and Lt. Frank Perry discovered their bags

Over the Precipice

had been stolen. Frustration and recriminations against the Partisans ensued. By noon, Green had the group organized, and they moved out, heading east toward Mt. Chabenec. It was cold and windy and the seven mile walk would be another difficult day. "Our clothes were frozen and our shoes were hard as stone," Maria remembered. Again she was disgusted at the sight of Slovak soldiers and Partisans throwing away equipment and deserting. For Maria, quitting was never an option.[9]

They walked for 15 hours, climbing continuously. A steady rain fell most of the day. Then it turned to snow and soon after was made worse by the wind. When the rain and snow finally stopped, a dense fog settled over the mountain. Everyone was exhausted. Maria walked beside Tibor, the handsome Hungarian who had become her protector. Maria's feet became badly frostbitten, and Tibor assisted her up the more difficult inclines.[10]

Darkness fell. At 8 PM, they finally reached the ridge, a narrow promontory with sheer drops on each side of the trail. The foggy weather had given way to a gale as an icy rain fell, whipped into a torrent by the wind.[11] Visibility ranged from only inches to a few feet. Realizing they were lost, they sent out scouts. Some didn't return. The men began looking for a way off the ridge to escape the misery without success. Minutes turned into hours, and their feet began to freeze. Pneumonia now was on everyone's mind.[12] Some of the men believed they were going to freeze to death, and morale was at rock bottom.[13]

Individuals dared not sit down for fear of falling asleep. Lt. Jack Shafer got his crew together and told them they wouldn't quit or give up. He moved around to each of his crew, extolling them not to sit down. He imposed his will: stick together or die. Shafer had seen Slovaks sitting in the snow, huddled together and drifting into sleep. Shafer knew those men would be dead by morning.[14]

After much agonizing, Holt Green and Jim Gaul made a tough decision. The group would go over the side. It was 1 A.M. They unloaded the pack horses and collected their gear and what little food they had left. They gingerly stepped over the side into the abyss and began sliding and slipping down the slope.[15]

The members of the Czech Brigade milled around, gripped by indecision. Finally, they too began to follow the Americans. Those on horses dismounted and began whipping their animals to force them over the edge. Shafer directed the airmen to stay to the left side of the main group.

The Americans started down slowly, chopping foot holes. Some slipped and fell against the large rocks. They could hear the horses above them, falling and screaming. Some crashed by, rolling through to the trees below.[16] One missed Jim Gaul "by inches ." Men were shouting, struggling to get firm footholds. Large boulders came loose and crashed down the slope. One nearly struck Joe Morton.[17]

They moved a half mile down the slope into the tree line. It was 3 AM, still dark. The cold was less severe but still miserable. They stopped to rest, grateful to be out of the wind. Two hours had passed since they had left the ridge. Behind them, small groups wandered down. Some of the Brigade members were injured, a few seriously. Most of the horses had been killed or injured. Holt Green couldn't locate the airmen. He and others called out, but there was no answer.[18]

Separated, Jack Shafer, George Fernandes, and other airmen had descended the steep slope several hundred yards away. It was now starting to get light, and Shafer recalled years later that when they reached the other Americans, they took off their soaked shoes. "We tucked our feet under each other's arms and huddled together under blankets. We slept, completely exhausted."[19]

November 2, Another Miserable Day.

They awoke to another miserable day. Their shoes were frozen and "rang like bells" when they hit them together. Shafer cut a hole in the ice on a pond nearby and they all soaked their feet and hands in the water to thaw them out. They cut up blankets to wrap their feet to walk until they could get their boots back on.[20]

At sunrise, the famished Americans now had to come to terms with their hunger. They hadn't eaten for 18 hours. The Partisans and Brigade members began shooting the crippled horses. The Dutch prisoner with the pack horse had disappeared with their rations, both probably dead up on the slope. Several dead horses lay in the stream where they had been shot. There was talk of butchering them. Maria and some of the others decided they were not so hungry that they were ready to eat horse meat. She and Tibor went out to find some food and were given some beans and "a little flour" from some Partisans. She cut up a beef bone and made soup. Tibor shared some crackers.[21] They still were unable to get warm. Joe Morton used some of his papers to start one of several fires. They collapsed and slept around the fires.[22]

Joseph Piontek later made some tea from young spruce leaves for himself and Joe Morton. Morton was delighted and cheerful as ever. Piontek, an optimist like Morton, noted in his diary that it was All Saints Day. They had been on the move for four days and nights, and now they looked forward to getting some rest. Morton gave Piontek some Koruns to buy food from the Partisans, but the Partisans had nothing to sell.[23]

Morton and Piontek ate the last of their bread and sausage that night. Piontek recorded that watching the bright fires gave him a good feeling for the moment.[24] Later, it began raining in the afternoon and continued all night. The pursuing Germans were on everyone's mind.

Some of the airmen decided to butcher one of the dead horses. Their hunger had reached desperation levels. Shafer laughed years later that "as an old farm boy, I suggested we butcher a horse. We found one and I dressed out a hind quarter and cut steaks that we could cook on sticks over the fires."[25] Maria recorded later that they reluctantly decided to roast the horse meat that night.[26] Bill McGregor recalled that everyone was "really hungry. We chopped up that whole horse and ate every damn bit."[27]

Later That Day.

Around noon, they moved down into the valley and found some huts occupied by Partisans. Maria and some of the men slept under a lean-to. Joe Morton and Piontek went to a larger hut which McGregor, Schwartz, Lain, Horvath, and others had acquired from the Partisans.[28]

Although relieved to find a hut, the prospect of German patrols left them uneasy. "Lt. Drezner and Staff Sergeant Jurgen (probably John Brinser and Eugene Yeargin, both members of Shafer's crew) were very ill," and they were in no condition to make a forced march.[29]

Holt Green decided to keep the group in camp and rest. During the next few days, he and several of the men, plus Maria, sneaked into the villages and farms to buy food. Although the presence of German patrols made the trips dangerous, Lt. Jack Shafer, along with several airmen and Jan Schwartz also made a number of food forays. (See map following page 221.)[30]

November 3, Russians Attempt To Recruit The Americans.

The Russians spoke to Green about bringing the Americans into the Russian military organization to fight the Germans. Jerry Mican and Jan Schwartz interpreted for Green who turned down the request, arguing that the Americans were not trained to fight as infantrymen or guerrillas. Jan Schwartz supported Green's decision.[31]

November 4, Foraging For Food.

After a reasonable night's sleep, Maria, Holt Green, Bill McGregor, Joe Horvath, and some airmen headed toward the valley to find food. They found several abandoned houses. After hiding in the woods for over an hour, watching for Germans, they cautiously entered one of the houses. They found beans, flour, and sugar. Horvath discovered a calf, some chickens, and potatoes in the cellar.

Overjoyed at their find, they were collecting their booty, including some pans and blankets, when McGregor stepped out on the porch and noticed a German patrol approaching 200 yards away. He calmly gave the alarm. Horvath already was up the trail, dragging the stubborn calf. The airmen ran out the back door and broke in a run as Horvath struggled with the calf. He made it back around noon with his prize, much to the elation of the group. Miraculously, the Germans never saw them.[32]

McGregor recalled the incident in the 1960's when he recorded his recollections. The airmen with the group "were really shook, but Maria was without fear. She looked at this incident as a joke."[33]

Maria immediately prepared a soup with carrots, potatoes, cabbage, and chicken. She recalled later that "The boys were nearly crazy from hunger." That night they butchered the calf. All 38 members later stood in line as Maria dished up the meat into their messkits.[34]

George Fernandes was now having trouble walking because of his ankle wound. He had been wounded slightly during the bombing attack back at Donovaly and then aggravated it coming down the ridge. Now it was infected. Two Partisan doctors operated on him, cutting out the infected area and packing it with sulfa. Maria assisted and gave Fernandes some Slivovica during the operation.[35]

The Partisans continued to slaughter their horses daily. Barbecued horsemeat topped the menu. Food remained the chief concern.

Maria Is Alienated by the Russians and Partisans.

Maria increasingly became disenchanted with both the Russians and the Partisans. Talking with Major Studensky on one occasion, she took offense when the Russian officer failed to offer her some lamb he was eating. Just the day before she had shared some food with him. Additionally, he forced Tamara to carry her heavy radio equipment without ever helping her. This disgusted Maria. She objected to the Partisans who spoke suggestively to her. She resented their attitude that they had the right to sleep with any female who happened to be with a group of men. She was happy to be with the Americans.[36]

During this period, the airmen lived several hundred yards apart from the OSS group. They had found a large, run-down shed which they patched up. Jan Schwartz was with them. They began making trips for food down into the valley. It took a day to get down and two days to hike back.

On their first trip, in a group led by Lt. Jack Shafer, they stopped at an isolated cabin where a woman lived alone. She prepared them a sumptuous meal, cooking them a large goose. She also fed them baked bread. Shafer was so moved by the experience that he pulled out his GI issue New Testament and read the 23rd Psalm. He remember it well years later.[37]

A Slovak Partisan had also hiked down into the valley, and had returned with food and medicine. Because so many of the airmen were ill and suffered frostbite, Shafer and others made another trip. They spent the night in a hut with a Russian doctor. Because of waist deep snow, they didn't reach their camp until late the next day.[38]

November 5, Another Difficult Food Run.

After another day of rest, most of the group had regained their strength. Maria and three others attempted to go to Liptovsky Svaty Mikulas, a larger town ten miles to the north. They spent the night with a forester and his wife and were fed another excellent meal. But, the deep snow forced them to turn back the next day. The forester took her into a village where they purchased four liters of cognac, five kilos of salami, five loaves of bread, two pounds of cheese, jams, fish, tomatoes, salt, and flour. Maria and the forester carried the food out of town, but stopped overnight at a private home where they slept on the floor. On the way back to the camp the next day, they ran into dozens of Hungarian Jewish refugees in the valley.

That night, Maria made soup again. The men were so overjoyed that, led by the former college fraternity boy, Bill McGregor, they serenaded her with "Mary, Mary, It's a Grand Old Name."[39]

Back in the camp, Joe Morton, and Piontek discovered they could barely get their boots on. Their painful feet were infected from frostbite.

This was unsettling as they knew they had to keep moving. The Germans, pursuing relentlessly, were closing in again. A beleaguered French Partisan group wandered into the OSS camp. Many of them were ill, and Holt Green gave them a warm meal.[40]

Later That Day.

The Czech Brigade decided to move, relocating up the mountain about an hour away in an abandoned lumber camp. Jerry Mican was sent by Holt Green to stay with them to act as a liaison. The rest of the group remained in their huts. Men continued to go on patrols. One group found an abandoned German radio truck and salvaged some batteries, gasoline, a charger, and some souvenirs. They also found two machine guns.[41]

Holt Green asked Major Studensky to radio Bari. He promised to do so, but no one was sure he did.[42] Many of the men were ill.

The OSS group moved a short distance into a barn. Maria suspected that Ken Dunlevy and one of the airmen had pneumonia. During the night, a group of Partisans moved into the barn with them. When they left in the morning, Tibor discovered his revolver was missing. Maria shared his anger and stole a sack of their flour the Partisans had left in the barn.

"Lt. Green was disgusted with me, but flour, after all, was something very valuable to have," she wrote later.[43] Four Jewish refugees spent the night with them. Tibor then became ill and Maria feared he too might have pneumonia.

November 6, Maria Continues To Amaze The Americans.

Before daybreak, Maria, Holt Green, Joe Horvath, and "Baba," a Slovak girl Jan Schwartz had met in Donovaly and brought along, went to forage for food. Maria, despite her frostbitten feet, was gamely trudging through the snow, looking for villages and isolated farms in which to buy food. The men were amazed not only at her stamina, but at her courage. She could have slipped away and hidden with a Slovak family in any one of the villages or farms, but she chose to stay with the Americans.

"Everybody was in love with Maria. She was really a brave young woman, making all those food runs," Bill McGregor remembered years later. They were astonished at her loyalty to the Americans.[44]

Despite the heroics of this desperate band, the specter of the German army hung over them. Major Erwein *Graf* Thun-Hohenstein, the *Abwehr 218* commander in Banska Bystrica, was coordinating operations designed to eliminate the Partisan activities. Thun-Hohenstein's counterintelligence organization had recruited a large number of Slovak and Russian deserters, including a number of Ukrainian troops, the so-called "Vlasovites." These Ukrainians were named by the Slovaks after the Soviet general, Vladimir Vlasov, who had defected in Russia after his capture by the Germans.

German agents had identified and probably photographed the members of the DAWES mission when they landed at Tri Duby on September 17 and October 7. Thun-Hohenstein, an Austrian nobleman, knew they were trying to make it to the Red Army lines and was determined to head them off. For *Abwehr 218*, the Americans would be a great trophy.

---

1 PRO, HS4/40.
2 Ibid.
3 NARA, RG 226, Entry 190, Box 116, Folder 407, Message 1219.
4 Walter Ross, Interview with William Miller, 1984, courtesy of his daughter, Marilyn Miller.
5 *Wehrmacht* Diary, summary.
6 Kenneth Dunlevy, OSS Report.
7 Maria Gulovich, OSS Report.
8 George Fernandes, Unpublished manuscript.
9 Maria Gulovich, OSS Report.
10 Maria Gulovich, Telephone interview with the author, September 27, 2000.
11 Piontek, Diary; Kenneth Dunlevy, OSS Report.
12 Maria Gulovich, OSS Report; Kenneth Dunlevy, OSS Report.
13 Josef Piontek, Diary.
14 Jack Shafer, Interview with the author, April, 1998.
15 Ibid.
16 Ibid.
17 Kenneth Dunlevy, OSS Report.
18 Josef Piontek, Diary.
19 Jack Shafer, Interview with the author, 1998.

20 Ibid.; Theron Arnett, Letter to Veterans Administration, February 10, 1993, courtesy of his widow, Jean Arnett.
21 Maria Gulovich, OSS Report.
22 Theron Arnett, Letter to Veterans Administration; Jack Shafer, Interview with the author.
23 Ibid.; Josef Piontek, Diary.
24 Ibid.
25 Jack Shafer, Interview with the author; Theron Arnett, Letter to the Veterans Administration.
26 Maria Gulovich, OSS Report.
27 Bill McGregor, Telephone interview with the author, September, 1999.
28 Josef Piontek, Diary.
29 Kenneth Dunlevy, OSS Report.
30 Maria Gulovich, OSS Report; Kenneth Dunlevy, OSS Report.
31 Jan Schwartz, Interview with William Miller, 1984.
32 Bill McGregor, Recorded remarks, circa 1960's, courtesy of his daughter, Sandy Woods; Maria Gulovich, OSS Report.
33 Bill McGregor, Recorded remarks.
34 Maria Gulovich, Interview with William Miller, 1984.
35 George Fernandes, Unpublished manuscript; George Fernandes, Telephone interview with the author, 1999.
36 Maria Gulovich, OSS Report.
37 Jack Shafer, Interview with the author, April, 1998.
38 Ibid.
39 Maria Gulovich, OSS Report; Bill McGregor, Telephone interview with the author, September, 1999.
40 Josef Piontek, Diary.
41 Kenneth Dunlevy, OSS Report.
42 Josef Piontek, Diary.
43 Maria Gulovich, OSS Report.
44 Bill McGregor, Telephone interview with the author, September, 1998.

Escaping on the Prasiva Range

Chapter 21

Rosauer Lände Prison

November 7, On the slopes of the Prasiva.

Jack Shafer, Jan Schwartz and four members of Shafer's crew moved cautiously down the *Prasiva* mountain along with several Slovak soldiers. Hunger was their constant companion, and Shafer had another goose dinner on his mind. He and Schwartz had gold and Slovak Koruns to pay for food and medicine, but foraging into these villages was risky. The *Abwehr* commander, Major *Graf* Thun-Hohenstein, knew the Americans were up on the ridge and that they had been making these supply runs down into the villages in the valley. The Austrian nobleman had begun setting traps.

A mile below the camp, Shafer and the Americans walked cautiously along a winding trail next to a stream. The Slovaks had gone ahead. The area was an old logging site with piles of weathered logs stacked on both sides of the trail between the bank and the edge of the woods.

When Shafer reached the last pile of logs, a German soldier suddenly stepped out and stuck a rifle in Shafer's midsection. The American pushed it aside and pulled out his .38 caliber revolver. He was about to shoot his assailant when he noticed other Germans in the trees and rocks above him pointing their weapons at him. Shafer knew it was over and handed his gun to the soldier.

Sergeant Edwin Zavisa, the last man in the group, recalled the incident years later. The Americans were all armed – Zavisa had a carbine — and he and the others were ready to resist, but Shafer yelled, "Forget it." Resistance would have been futile. The Germans meanwhile began shooting at the Slovaks who had been allowed to pass through the hidden German patrol. The Germans got what they wanted: the Americans alive. Thun-Hohenstein wanted to talk to them.[1]

The Germans descended the slope and disarmed their prisoners, frisking them and taking their watches, rings, and jackets.[2] The Germans also took their boots and gave them their well worn ones.[3]

Jan Schwartz Faced A Crisis.

Jan Schwartz was an OSS agent. Worse, he was carrying an OSS radio code on a small card in his wallet. Believing no one saw him, Schwartz slipped his wallet out of his pants and dropped it on the ground. It landed near Sgt. Theron Arnett, Shafer's radio man. One of the Germans saw it and picked it up, moved to the side and took the money. He put the wallet in another pocket. The German was unaware Schwartz had noticed.[4]

The Germans took their prisoners to their headquarters in an isolated farm house a few miles down the mountain where they stayed and took their meals. The Americans were locked in a barn with several Jews, older men, and some boys. The Germans had been beating all of them. The Americans were roughed up a bit also. Shafer was shocked at the condition of the Jews who were dressed in rags and bruised and beaten.

That evening the Americans were moved into the farm house, and an older German captain invited them to share a meal with him. Shafer was surprised at the sudden hospitality. After a few minutes, a young German soldier burst into the room, armed with a *Schmeisser* machine gun and threatened to shoot them.

"The *Hauptmann* got up and decked him," Jack Shafer remembered. The officer ordered his men to restrain the young soldier after which they resumed their meal. Shafer remembered the "*Hauptmann*" as a decent fellow, except for his treatment of the Jews. The Americans spent the night in the barn. The next day, four Germans took them in an open cart to Ruzomberok.[5]

They were surprised to be confronted by a German officer in Ruzomberok who spoke Oxford-accented English. He told Shafer he was the only German officer in the region who spoke English. This probably was Major Thun-Hohenstein.[6]

As the interrogation of the Americans continued, Sgt. Theron Arnett handed Sgt. Guy Haines a piece of paper. He promptly chewed it up and swallowed it. The Major was furious. He ordered his men to beat Haines, which they did unmercifully. He had swallowed a piece of paper with a radio code that Arnett had been carrying, Sgt. Edwin Zavisa told the author years later.[7]

Jan Schwartz, however, said in 1984 the paper Haines swallowed was simply a statement in Slovak that said they were Americans who would appreciate the help of Slovak citizens. It was designed to be given to Slovaks by Americans who did not speak the language. The prisoners were kept in Ruzomberok overnight and then transported to Bratislava.[8]

Bratislava Prison.

In Bratislava, they were placed in a prison which contained a large number of Slovak soldiers who had participated in the Uprising. *Obersturmbannführer* (Lt. Colonel) Josef Witiska, commander of *Einsatzkommando Grupp H*, vigorously interrogated Shafer, Schwartz, and the others. He wanted to know why Schwartz had no dog tags.[9] On the way to Ruzomberok the day before, Schwartz had worked it out with Shafer and the crew that he would pose as a waist gunner on a B-17 who had lost his dog tags. The colonel happened to ask where Schwartz lived in the States. He replied the Bronx near Fordham Road, and the German responded that he had lived in the Bronx once. Schwartz was shocked. Concerned the officer would notice how poorly he spoke English, Schwartz restricted his replies to yes and no answers.[10]

During an exercise period the following day, Schwartz met a Slovak officer he knew, and asked about escaping. He told Schwartz it "was possible." But, the next day after three days of interrogation, they were put on a train for Vienna. The *Gestapo* had been notified and wanted to talk to these Americans.[11]

After a 50 minute ride, they got off the train in the Vienna outskirts and were marched across the Danube to the *Rosauer Lände* prison, an old stone structure. On the way they passed a column of German soldiers marching east, singing robustly and obviously enthusiastic about going to the Russian front. This was the same *Wehrmacht* enthusiasm Maria had once observed.[12]

In Vienna, the Americans at first were interrogated every day. Shafer and Arnett were accused of being part of the British WINDPROOF mission. Someone obviously had been talking. Schwartz on one occasion was taken to the *Gestapo* in the *Metropol Hotel* in the heart of the city where a *Gestapo* agent in civilian clothes questioned him. They beat a Yugoslav prisoner in front of him, pulling out much of his hair and beating him, leaving him bleeding on the floor. Schwartz was told he would suffer the same fate if he didn't talk. He knew, however, he was a dead man if he told them who he really was.[13]

Theron Arnett Interrogated.

Sgt. Theron Arnett also was closely interrogated about the HOUSEBOAT code. The Germans were not sure who had dropped the paper with the code when the men were captured back on the *Prasiva*. Arnett later said that one of the men had disclosed to the Germans that Arnett was a radio man on the crew of the B-17. The *Gestapo*, he believed, concluded that Arnett actually was an OSS agent. He was beaten almost daily with a rubber hose and with fists and kept in a small cell where he could neither sit up nor lie down at night.[14]

Arnett was kept in the cubicle for three weeks as his interrogators tried to break his resistance. He knew he was starving to death. In addition he had amoebic dysentery and was huddled in his own filth. The *Gestapo* apparently

Rosauer Lände Prison 177

feared he would die before they could break him, and they sent him to the medical room where he was given some food and charcoal to stop the dysentery. Arnett was the only one of the Americans who was beaten, he believed. Finally, he was brought back to the interrogation room and told that if he didn't tell them what they wanted to know, the entire crew would be shot. This was the first news that the crew also was in the same prison. His account of this event was different from the story told by Schwartz.

According to Arnett and Shafer, all the Americans including Schwartz were brought together in the prison basement. Some of the *SS* men who had captured them were there. The Americans were told to admit their identities or face execution.[15]

Arnett maintained later that Schwartz stepped forward and volunteered, "I'm your man." The Germans took him away, and the Americans heard a few days later he had been shot. Thirty years later, Schwartz told writer William Miller he had been identified by the crew as "not one of us." Although Shafer and Arnett had learned by this time that Schwartz survived, they never communicated with him.[16]

Shafer recalled later the confrontation in the prison basement, remembering that Schwartz admitted he was not a member of the crew.[17]

Shafer and the crew were then shipped to Frankfurt, Germany, in an open freight car and had to keep running in place to keep from freezing. In Frankfurt, Arnett was placed in a military hospital because of his emaciated condition.[18]

How had the German interrogator learned about HOUSEBOAT? Three other American airmen had been in the *Rosauer Lände* Prison, having arrived two days before the Schwartz-Shafer group. Their circumstances were different. They had been hiding in a cave at Modra north of Bratislava for eight weeks before they were captured on November 13 (See chapter 4).

Richard Moulton's Unique Vienna Experience.

Richard Moulton, the youngest of this group, has described in his unpublished account an interesting story about his journey to the *Rosauer Lände* prison. When the snows began to fall, Moulton and his buddies hoped someone would lead them back to Italy. Their promised guide never appeared. The Uprising had come and gone, and German troops now were everywhere. The Americans recognized their vulnerability, especially the problem of leaving tracks in the snow around the cave which German patrols would eventually notice. The Michal Mihalek family was feeding the Americans, and Mihalek was nervous, aware that the penalty for hiding airmen was death.[19]

The seven men in Moulton's crew left together, dressed in ragged clothes trying to look like Slovaks. When they left, they promised Mihalek they would urge the U.S. government after the war to reimburse him for all the assistance they had been given. After a few hours, Moulton and the two other enlisted men broke off and walked together while the four officers walked together in another group. Mihalek had given them a note in Slovak to show people if they needed help. They spent the first night in a barn, but the farmer sent them on their way before sun up.[20]

At noon they ran into a German patrol of a dozen men and greeted them in Slovak. The Germans, who spoke no better Slovak than Moulton and his group, ignored them. That night they slept in a home with a couple who had two children. Moulton noticed the people were nervous, not without reason, of course. The next night they slept in an abandoned factory, but then returned to the original family. The Slovak betrayed them and led them to another location and right into the hands of pro-Tiso Slovak troops. Fortunately, the Slovak troops were neither brutal nor unfriendly.[21]

When German soldiers arrived to take possession of the Americans, events took an ugly turn. Brandishing *Schmeisser* machine guns and shouting, the Germans were aggressive and threatening. They yelled "*Bolshevik Schwein*" at the Americans, and the prisoners took care not to provoke their captors. The Americans then were taken by train to Bratislava. That Moulton did not have his dogtags (see Chapter 4) was a problem. The Germans wanted to know what they had been doing since they had been shot down, particularly the previous eight weeks. They were told they could be shot because they were out of uniform. Their interrogators beat them with rubber hoses, but the Americans did not betray the Mihalek family. They were put in a jail with Slovak army prisoners who had been supporters of the Uprising. Obviously, the Germans suspected Moulton of being an OSS agent.[22]

November 15, Moulton And His Buddies Are Captured.

Two German MP's showed up and marched Moulton and his buddies through town to the train station. Moulton recalls being intimidated by the sight of the MP's who wore the metal breast plates signifying they were police. Their train ride lasted just over an hour. The train was crowded and they had to sit on the floor. Moulton noticed other American prisoners who were wearing olive drab uniforms, some with officers' infantry insignia on their collars. Moulton wasn't able to talk to them. When they arrived in Vienna, the Americans were marched first to the *Gestapo* headquarters in the *Metropol Hotel* and later to the *Rosauer Lände* Prison.

The *Metropol*, seized by the Nazis in 1938, was an elegant four-story hotel which the *Gestapo* used as an interrogation center and a jail. Moulton still recalls the hotel's lavish marble stairway. When the prisoners were transferred, they were taken by the *St. Stephan* Cathedral and across the Danube River. Moulton and his buddies were separated and never saw each other again until after the war.[23]

They were put in cells on the third floor of a large building at *Rosauer Lände*. Moulton shared a cell with 15 other men. Two wore striped prison uniforms and were "skin and bones." Moulton soon realized most of the prisoners appeared to be political prisoners. None of them spoke English, but one of the Yugoslavs knew Moulton was an American and subsequently protected him for the 45 days Moulton was locked up, giving him extra food and not allowing other prisoners to steal from him.[24]

Moulton Meets An American OSS Agent.

Moulton's guards told him he was going to be hanged. He was taken downstairs, interrogated and beaten. His interrogator accused him of being a Russian spy who had aided in the Slovak Uprising. Moulton recalls that after he had been in the prison for "several weeks," he happened to meet another American prisoner. Moulton had become seriously ill and was taken to the infirmary to receive treatment, crude and inadequate as it was. There he met an American who was wearing corporal's stripes. We now wonder if it were Theron Arnett of Jan Schwartz.

The American told Moulton he had been with an OSS group in Banska Bystrica, and remembered seeing Moulton on the train from Bratislava. He explained how the Uprising began and why it failed. When the Germans besieged the city, they had been forced to flee into the mountains, he said. The soldier complained that the commanding officer, a Naval officer, was so concerned about the gold in their possession that he believed it led to their capture. The man told Moulton they had hid considerable gold in a cave. The only corporal on the DAWES team was Robert Brown, Holt Green's radio operator. But, Brown was not captured until December 26, and Moulton and his buddies rode the Bratislava-Vienna train on November 15.[25]

The possibility exists, perhaps, that Moulton had seen the Shafer-Schwartz group on the train from Bratislava originally, and certainly may have spoken to Theron Arnett or Schwartz in the medical wing. Yet, according to Jack Shafer and John Brinser, they were in the Bratislava prison by November 15. Moulton may have seen Bill McGregor and Kenneth Lain, both Army First Lieutenants wearing the infantry crossed rifles insignia on their collars, on that train to Vienna.[26]

In prison, Moulton later became seriously ill and was sent again to the infirmary where he was treated. He was told by a guard who spoke some English he would be shot as soon as he recovered. Through the nuns who were nurses in the infirmary, Moulton met a British soldier who was caring for several severely wounded American airmen. They were awaiting repatriation to Switzerland through the International Red Cross. The soldier told the Red Cross representative on his next visit about Moulton who shortly thereafter was released to the *Luftwaffe*. Moulton was able to meet the other Americans and thanked the Englishman who probably saved Moulton's life.[27]

During this period of late November and early December, 1944, the rest of the airmen and the OSS team in the Lower *Tatra* Mountains were dealing with one setback after another. They had three adversaries: the cold, the hunger, and the *Abwehr* major, the Austrian nobleman, Erwein *Graf* Thun-Hohenstein.

---

1   Edwin Zavisa, Telephone interview with the author, April, 1998; Jack Shafer, telephone interview with the author, April 1998.
2   Shafer, Telephone interview.
3   Jan Schwartz, Interview with William Miller, 1984.
4   Ibid.
5   Ibid.
6   Ibid.
7   Edwin Zavisa, Telephone interview with the author, October 24, 2000.
8   Ibid.
9   This probably was Josef Witiska head of *Einsatzkommando Grupp H*, a German-Czech from Moravia and former *Sicherheitsdienst* commander in Prague and *Gestapo* chief in Vienna.
10 Schwartz, Interview with William Miller.
11 Ibid.
12 Jack Shafer, Telephone interview with the author, December 3, 1997.
13 Schwartz, Interview with William Miller.
14 Theron Arnett, letter to Veterans Administration, February 10, 1993.
15 Ibid.
16 Ibid.; Arnett felt guilty for years that he somehow was responsible for forcing Schwartz to confess.
17 Jack Shafer, Telephone interview with the author, December 3, 1997; Schwartz, interview with William Miller. One discrepancy in Schwartz' story was that he claimed the confrontation with Shafer and Arnett took place in March, 1945. Shafer and Guy Haines had been in *Stalag Luft I* in Barth, Germany, for over six weeks by that time. Also, there is some confusion whether this confrontation took place in the *Metropol Hotel* or the *Rosauer Lände* prison.
18 Ibid.
19 Richard Moulton, Unpublished manuscript, March 14, 1998.
20 Ibid.

21 Ibid.
22 Ibid.
23 Ibid. The *Metropol Hotel* later was destroyed by the artillery shelling of the Red Army in the last weeks of the war.
24 Ibid.
25 Ibid.
26 Richard Moulton, Telephone interview with the author, August16, 1997.
27 Ibid.

Chapter 22

Bad Luck on Dumbier

November 11, On the Prasiva.

After Jack Shafer and Jan Schwartz and other members of the food detail were captured, both the Czech Brigade and the Americans tightened their security. They would take no chances of falling into the hands of the Germans.

Colonel Vladimir Prikryl, commander of the Czech Brigade, decided to relocate. At 9 AM, he gave the order to move out, and his Brigade officers began snapping commands. Holt Green was caught off guard because the departure time had been moved up two hours. The Americans hurriedly loaded their packs, realizing they had to leave behind some of their rations. The wind was gusting, and the frost on the ground and the bite in the air signaled that the *Prasiva* was about to punish its trespassers again. There would be no relief for frostbitten feet.[1]

Prikryl's scouts had told him the day before that Thun-Hohenstein's troops were closing in. The brigade could ill afford to stay put. Prikryl believed, and Holt Green concurred, that they had no choice but to retreat up to the ridge below Dumbier mountain.[2]

The Partisans had been given permission to disband and disperse. Many milled around, not knowing where to go. Prikryl also informed the members of the brigade they could leave. Believing they were no match for the Germans, the men were eager to fade away in hopes of fighting another day.[3] This lack of will to resist disgusted the Americans.[4]

Heavy snow began to fall, and the wind picked up, swirling and gusting. The line of suffering men – and the three women –started up the mountain. Many wore the fur hats that George Fernandes had purchased in Banska Bystrica. The column was an uneven, irregular line. A hundred French Partisans, who had escaped from German POW camps, had joined them.

With the French, they now totaled over 600 people. They struggled up the mountain one step at a time, slipping, sliding, and falling, getting up, cursing, and doggedly moving ahead. The fresh snow on top of the old snow had frozen into ice. Conditions worsened as the temperature plummeted, and what had been a snow storm became a blizzard. Eyebrows froze and icicles hung from beards. The full fury of winter lashed out at the pathetic group, dark figures in great coats with blankets and shawls over their shoulders leaning into the wind. Maria Gulovich again had lost some of the feeling in her feet. She repeatedly fell down.[5] Several of the flyers were ill. The exertion of climbing seared their burning lungs.

Only 500 yards uphill, gunfire suddenly swept over the column, causing dozens of Czechs and Partisans to break and run. The Americans were astonished at the disorder.[6] McGregor later described the morale of the Slovaks as "near zero," beaten men cowed by the pursuing Germans and overwhelmed by the weather. Maria was shocked at the conduct of her countrymen.[7]

Small arms fire continued to whistle over their heads. "We were climbing single file. McGregor was leading and I was behind him," George Fernandes later recorded.

He turned and told me to pass the word to hold the line in our column. We continued to climb. Not one of our men broke ranks. A group of partisans near us broke and scattered in all directions. They were leading their horses. I saw two horses fall and roll down the mountain in the snow. One Partisan, tugging at the reins, tried without luck to get his horse on its feet.

At the end of the line below us on the slope were the French Partisans. Disciplined and well armed, they kept up continuous fire.[8]

That was the last they saw of the French. Fernandes concluded later that they sacrificed themselves to save the others.[9]

The flyers, who had lagged behind, finally caught up with Green and the other OSS personnel. Their lungs were bursting and their legs ached as they reached the limits of their endurance. Only the fear of being overtaken by the enemy kept them going. As the group moved still higher above the timber line, the column was fully exposed to the Germans. The Americans could see them — little dark figures, inching up the mountain below.[10]

Fear and Panic.

Maria Gulovich remembers the fear and panic and the burden of the heavy packs. Individuals slipped off the trail, "but no one seemed to notice. Our clothes and shoes were frozen," she later wrote. It was every man for himself.[11] They were forced to keep moving or die.

Exhausted, the group reached the top of the ridge at noon and stopped to eat a desperate meal of raw venison. The French were nowhere in sight, but neither were the Germans. The group resumed the march, but visibility was now less than ten feet and the wind drove the snow horizontally, whipping it this way and that. Around two o'clock, a number of the suffering airmen began to falter as they struggled through knee-deep snow. Dunlevy thought two of the flyers were delirious. The men approached Holt Green about breaking off and going back on their own. Two flyers, Howard Luzier and Wesley Rawbolt, remembered being in a village down the mountain to the northwest when they were with the Russian-led Partisans. They persuaded the other men that would be a safe place to go.[12]

The discipline of the Czechs and the Partisans continued to disintegrate. The airmen were not doing any better, complaining and demanding to be allowed to separate from the main group. As the Partisans and Czechs continued to slip away, the morale of the flyers sank lower and lower. The airmen did not fear, as did the OSS, capture by the Germans. The cold and fatigue had taken their toll.[13]

"We had seen a number of deer, and we felt we could shoot one or two for food," Fernandes recalls. "Green had given each of us 20 gold Napoleons, worth about $200 total, so we felt we had plenty of money to buy food from the villagers."[14]

The flyers were on the verge of revolt. Sergeants Howard Luzier and Wesley Raubolt spoke up, urging the airmen to break off from the OSS. Brought in my Soviet Partisan officers, they had only arrived in Banska Bystrica on October 23. The two men had spent several weeks in safe valleys where they had seen no Germans. They now argued it was suicide to continue in the blizzard conditions. Luzier recalled years later that Holt Green threatened to have them court martialled after the war if they broke off. Luzier said the will to live was stronger than the fear of a courts martial.[15] The other airmen agreed.

Maria listened and shook her head. Tibor translated for her and she watched the body language of the angry men. She knew there were Germans all over the *Prasiva*. The *Einsatzkommando* and *Abwehr* units regularly sent their patrols into every hamlet.[16] Holt Green urged the men to stay and follow the Czech brigade to the Red Army lines.

A heated argument ensued, but Holt Green finally gave in. Bill McGregor sided with Green, although his buddy, Ken Lain, agreed with the flyers. McGregor decided to accompany Lain and the airmen as it was clear they needed the two tough infantry officers. Green reluctantly allowed the two officers to go.[17]

British Agent Goes With the American Airmen.

Keith Hensen,[18] the British agent, also went with the flyers. Jack Wilson (Wanndorfer) hesitated but decided to stay with main group. Tibor Kesthelyi nearly joined the airmen, but apparently influenced by Maria, he stayed. She believed it was a mistake to go back.[19] The blizzard, meanwhile, was howling as everyone stood shivering in the cold. Maria described the scene.

> I will not forget that day for the rest of my life. The wind was blowing so hard that it turned people over. Our eyebrows and hair changed into bunches of icicles. Our clothes and shoes were frozen, hard as a stone. I didn't have any gloves and could feel my hands freezing stiff. I couldn't do anything about it. In the afternoon, we were all dead tired, but we didn't dare sit down even for a moment. We later saw those Partisans who tried it—and froze stiff. We later counted 83 of them.[20]

The flyers descended slowly down the ridge and then headed west toward Zelezno. There was no sign of Germans. After a mile they turned northwest. Just before dark they stumbled upon a deserted log cabin in a clearing. McGregor saw no tracks in the snow, so they concluded there were no Germans in the area.

The airmen decided to spend the night there. As dusk settled, McGregor noticed a light in the woods about 400 yards down the mountain. He and two others went to investigate. Half way there on the trail, they ran into a man whom McGregor at first thought was a Partisan, indistinguishable in a bulky overcoat. He was wrong. Three Germans stepped onto the trail behind them. McGregor was shocked. Hands in the air, they were taken to the hut with the light.[21]

When McGregor left to investigate, a few men began to clean the log cabin and a small stove while others went out to forage for firewood. Fernandes was about 100 yards from the cabin picking up fire wood when a German soldier stepped from behind a tree and swung his rifle like a club, hitting him in the stomach. Stunned, Fernandes looked up and saw a bundled up German soldier. Fernandes recognized the familiar German helmet. Fernandes raised his hands. He noticed about 20 Germans crouched in a ravine a short distance away, advancing slowly toward the cabin. Another 40 Germans who were out of his sight were approaching from other side of the cabin.[22]

Fernandes asked his captor if he were a Slovak. The soldier shook his head. He then asked him if he were "*Deutsch*," and the soldier replied, "*Ja, Ja, Deutsch.*" "I remember the miserable feeling that came over me."[23]

Bob Hede was cleaning out the stove when rifle and machine gun fire hit the cabin. "They nearly blew the roof off. I was standing there with pieces of raw venison in my overcoat pockets, looking forward to cooking the meat. The flyers surrendered quickly as a German burst into the cabin. "He was only a boy," Hede remembered.[24]

The Germans took the prisoners down the mountain about a half mile to a building which was the their headquarters. Ernie Coleman was the last American in line. A guard struck him from behind as they struggled awkwardly across a fast-moving icy stream with their hands in the air. Coleman fell into the water. That night he shivered and shook and developed a fever. They spent the night in the headquarters building which was actually a barn.[25]

About 100 Germans, most of them young men, milled around in the building. The unit included arrogant, haughty Germans and also Austrians. The Austrians were relaxed, even friendly at times.[26]

The commanding officer, a captain, was an Austrian with a quiet manner. One of the Austrians told Fernandes that the Germans wanted to strip them naked and tie them up outside in the snow. The captain questioned the Americans closely, inquiring about the Czech brigade. Talkative, the captain confided later to the flyers that he felt the war would be over in six months.[27]

Germans Threatened to Shoot The Prisoners.

The Germans threatened to "shoot us on the spot," McGregor remembered, but they calmed down.[28] Howard Luzier remembers that the Germans drank heavily that night. "They had taken the gold we were carrying as well as our wrist watches. Keith Hensen spoke fluent German and he was telling us what they were saying. They wanted to shoot us. One German, an officer, objected, saying, 'We have all this gold and their watches. I'll get a detail in the morning and take them down the mountain.'" The German officer knew Major *Graf* Thun-Hohenstein wanted these prisoners alive.

Lt. John Brinser, Jack Shafer's co-pilot, also recalled a German lieutenant telling them they probably would be shot in the morning. Brinser also remembers the Germans' hostile attitude. One of flyers had a small American flag which a German threw on the ground and stepped on. The flyer reached down to pick it up and was struck with a rifle butt.[29]

The following morning the captain ordered his men to return the wedding bands to the married flyers. He directed a corporal and a few men to march the men to Zelezno and then on north to Ruzumberok. Fernandes noted that the corporal was one of the arrogant "SOB's" from the night before. He astonished the flyers by apologizing to them for suspecting that they were "partisan bandits." Had he known they were Americans, he said, he would have treated them differently. On the march, a number of men were troubled with diarrhea, and to the surprise of all, the Germans allowed the men to relieve themselves whenever necessary without being harassed or hurried. Fernandes remembered in amusement later how important little comforts could be. The first time he stepped off the trail he thought he might be shot and closed his eyes as he squatted down.[30]

Ernie Coleman also was suffering. A German soldier noticed him trying to warm his hands and gave him a pair of gloves. Coleman recalls that the German soldiers were decent unless an officer was around.[31]

Bob Hede wasn't able to walk, and the Germans put him on a truck and drove him to a German military hospital at Liptovsky Svaty Mikulas, 16 miles east of Ruzomberok. Fernandes and Hede said goodby and it would be three years before they would see each other again. Hede was well treated in the hospital for two weeks before he was sent to Ruzomberok where he was held 54 days in solitary confinement as a suspected Partisan. A friendly Slovak guard finally arranged for him to be sent to a German POW camp.[32]

November 12, Ruzomberok City Jail.

McGregor and the others were put in the city jail at Ruzomberok and then transferred to another jail where they were interrogated by an "SS colonel." The officer questioned McGregor "in perfect Oxford English," and calmly called him a liar. The German refused to believe the Americans were simply trying to rescue downed flyers. He was polite and never raised his voice, and warned McGregor to "be careful," which surprised the American. He told McGregor he believed they were part of an intelligence mission.[33] After two days in Ruzomberok, the prisoners were transported to Bratislava.

The Brigade, Holt Green, and the OSS personnel, meanwhile, had continued on after the flyers left. Visibility was so bad on the ridge, however, that they became lost and decided to return down the mountain southeast to the Hron Valley. Around 5 PM, they started down a narrow, steep trail. Those who slipped and fell knocked down several people on the trail below.[34] Getting below the timberline, they came to a stand of bushes, so thick they had to crawl on their hands and knees to get through. As they got lower, they crossed a stream several times which bisected the trail. Wading through the icy water, they knew they would soon be dealing with frostbite. Many of the people had difficulty walking. Morale was "very low."[35]

Just before midnight, they reached a point on the west slope of *Mt. Skalka*. Chilled to the bone, they built a fire by a stream. Maria took off her boots only to discover one of her feet was frozen black. A Jewish doctor with the Brigade told her to rub snow on the foot. Several men – Holt Green, Lane Miller, Nelson Paris, Frank Perry, Joe Horvath, and Charles Heller – also all had frozen big toes. Later, Maria couldn't get her boots back on. Joe Morton had the same problem. They wrapped their feet in rags. Some put on wooden sabots.[36]

The howling wind and sub zero temperature left them suffering another miserable night. The next morning, the OSS discovered that some of their food had been stolen by Partisans and Brigade personnel. Holt

Green was furious and cursed the Partisans as a "bunch of bandits." He tried to buy food from Colonel Prikryl who merely laughed at him. Prikryl told Green they had no food, but Green and the others knew the Russian was lying.[37]

A Brigade patrol returned and reported that they were only a few kilometers from the village of Jasenie, west of Podbrezova located on the Brezno road.[38] They resumed the march that morning. Joe Morton could hardly walk. His feet had bleeding, open sores. Morton waited for one of the OSS men, but was so weak he needed help from his interpreter, Josef Piontek. Both Green and Jim Gaul had excellent boots and did not have problems with their feet although Joe Morton suffered greatly. Everyone was using sulfur to treat the sores on their feet. Maria Gulovich's feet were so damaged by the cold that they remained permanently scarred.[39] The four mile walk to the forest above Dolna Lehota took eleven hours. Gaul, who was strong and in good physical condition, wanted to push on faster, but Green was not up to it. Nor were the others.[40]

---

1 Kenneth Dunlevy, OSS Report.
2 Maria Gulovich, OSS Report; Kenneth Dunlevy, OSS Report.
3 George Fernandes, Unpublished manuscript.
4 Kenneth Dunlevy, OSS Report.
5 Maria Gulovich, OSS Report.
6 Kenneth Dunlevy, OSS Report.
7 Bill McGregor, Telephone interview with the author, September 1998.
8 Fernandes, Unpublished manuscript.
9 Ibid.
10 Kenneth Dunlevy, OSS Report.
11 Maria Gulovich, OSS Report; Kenneth Dunlevy, OSS Report.
12 Dunlevy, OSS Report.
13 Ibid.
14 Fernandes, Unpublished manuscript.
15 Howard Luzier, Telephone interview with the author, April 19, 2000; Howard Coleman told the author, June 14, 2001, that he had disregarded the threat by Holt Green.
16 Maria Gulovich, OSS Report.
17 Robert Hede, Telephone interview with the author, 1997; Fernandes, Telephone interview with the author, 1997; Dunlevy, OSS Report.
18 Hensen's real name may have been Frank Hensque.
19 Maria Gulovich, Interview with William Miller, 1984.

20 Maria Gulovich, OSS Report.
21 Bill McGregor, Telephone interview with the author, April, 1998.
22 George Fernandes, Unpublished manuscript.
23 Ibid.
24 Bob Hede, Telephone interview with the author, April, 1998.
25 Ernie Coleman, Telephone interview with the author, April, 1998.
26 George Fernandes, Unpublished manuscript; Hede, Telephone interview.
27 George Fernandes, Unpublished manuscript.
28 Bill McGregor, Telephone interview.
29 John Brinser, Telephone interview with the author, 1997.
30 George Fernandes, Unpublished manuscript.
31 Ernie Coleman, Telephone interview.
32 Bob Hede, Telephone interview.
33 Bill McGregor, Telephone interview. This probably was Major Graf Thun-Hohenstein, but may have been Colonel Josef Witiska, head of Einsatzkommando *Grupp H* in Bratislava.
34 Maria Gulovich, OSS Report.
35 Kenneth Dunlevy, OSS Report.
36 Maria Gulovich, OSS Report.
37 Kenneth Dunlevy, OSS Report.
38 Maria Gulovich, OSS Report.
39 Josef Piontek, Diary; Maria Gulovich, telephone interview with the author, November, 2000.
40 Josef Piontek, Diary.

Chapter 23

Disasters and More Suffering

As the Anglo-American group scrambled through the *Tatra* Mountains during the collapse of the Slovak Uprising, their superiors in Bari sought to put pressure on their higher commands to provide more aid for Slovakia. The issue became mired in the politics of image and the intrigues of international diplomacy.

October 26, London.

Lt. Colonel Perkins, SOE London, notified General Leslie Hollis of the British general staff that the Foreign Office appeared to be "wavering" about sending aid to the Slovaks. The issue was whether it could be done without the aid being promised with "His Majesty's Government being responsible for the success or failure of the Uprising." Perkins clearly had aligned himself with Lt. Colonel Threlfall's position in Bari that some kind of aid should be extended to the desperate Slovaks. Perkins was concerned that ". . . we should not place ourselves in the invidious position of being the only major ally which has not rendered assistance."[1]

October 27, A "Russian Affair."

There would be no British aid. General Hollis informed Frank Roberts of the Foreign Office that the Chiefs of Staff had met that morning and decided not to intervene in Slovakia. They had concluded that the chances of success of the Slovak army were "very poor." It was a Russian affair, Hollis pointed out, and he reported they were taking "took pains" to avoid irritating their ally by trying to support "distant risings." The British generals agreed that it was futile to attempt to rescue an uprising that appeared doomed.[2]

Major John Sehmer and his WINDPROOF mission, caught in the middle of the Uprising, therefore, were expendable, forced to fend for themselves. Politics became more important in this instance than noble gestures to a desperate people. Sehmer's superiors in Bari were sympathetic to his plight, but the lack of incentive from London, coupled with the bad weather in Italy, precluded any significant efforts of support.

November 1, In the *Tatra* Mountains.

Sehmer did not realize he was being abandoned. He radioed Bari that he needed arms for 200 Partisans. He reported the Germans controlled all the villages and roads. He signed off by asking for cigarettes, tobacco and "rum . . . repeat rum."[3]

November 3, Move To Polomka.

Sehmer and his small group had moved west and found a refuge on the mountain slopes above Polomka. Sehmer had no idea where the Americans were. They had struggled through the deep snow up the mountain to a small, isolated hut.[4] Sehmer radioed Threlfall that they had lost their supplies and had joined 200 Partisans. He radioed they were short of clothing, arms, ammunition, and had little food.[5] Lt. Zenopian in a later message said they carried their radio into the villages of Helpa and Polomka to get power to send messages.[6]

Sehmer radioed Bari on November 6 they were spending most nights in the open. He described the snow conditions and pleaded for warm clothing. " . . . please hurry sorties."[7]

More Suffering

November 12, Maria Advised To Leave The Americans.

Twenty miles to the west, the Americans were still with Colonel Vladimir Prykryl's Czech Brigade. That morning, Major Studensky visited the American camp to see Maria, and informed her the Russians were leaving for the Red Army front. He advised her to find a peasant family, get some civilian clothing, go into hiding, and wait for the Russians.[8]

The Americans also decided to move, but not to follow Prykryl. Most of the men had trouble walking. Holt Green, Jim Gaul, and Steve Catlos were the strongest. Green and Catlos didn't suffer from frostbite that slowed the others. Gaul seemed superhuman and often carried Joe Morton's gear. Snow fell intermittently and the temperature hovered around zero. They reached Dolna Lehota, but hesitated before moving in too close. Green and Gaul stayed in the woods to wait until daylight to see if it was safe to enter the village. Joe Horvath and Tibor usually participated in these decisions.

Josef Piontek considered leaving and striking out on his own. One of the Slovak officers advised him to slip away and find a village in which to hide as Maria had been advised. He was reluctant to leave, but Joe Morton told him to go. The young soldier had friends in a nearby village, and he concluded he could do the Americans no more good. Joe Morton bid him goodbye.

Piontek and another Slovak soldier later hid in a farmer's barn under a haystack. He wrote the Associated Press after the war that German patrols were rounding up Slovaks in every village, and it was nearly impossible to move about. Before Piontek left the Americans, they had exchanged addresses and promised to keep in touch after the war.[9]

Green gave Maria and Tibor permission to go immediately with three Slovak soldiers to the village to buy food. Maria thought she could locate the home of a friend, Terka Pajedova, a former teaching colleague. Cautiously walking down the streets in the dark, they were ready to flee at the slightest noise. No Germans were in sight. Maria located Pajedova's home at the edge of the village, and she welcomed them warmly. Maria and Tibor spent the night there after a warm meal. The Slovak soldiers purchased food from other families.[10]

Back in the main camp, morale was at rock bottom. Green and Gaul tried to cheer up the group. At 3 AM, the Slovaks finally returned with three sacks of food, and the Americans were able to heat some beans which they ate half-cooked.[11] The next day the group went to Pajedova's house and they were fed. Maria and Tibor made several contacts in the village, inquiring about hiding places, but the people were afraid of housing the Americans.[12]

Major Sehmer's radio still was not working properly. He notified on November 15 Bari that the hand generator for the radio was broken and they had to go to a "distant village" to charge their batteries.[13] Sehmer and the Americans still did not know each other's whereabouts.

November 16.

The Americans moved four miles up the mountain to some antimony mines. The huts around the mines were occupied by Partisans and the Czech Brigade. Colonel Vladimir Prikryl ordered a one-room hut vacated for the Americans. The suffering Americans collapsed into the hut, grateful again to be out of the elements. Two Partisan nurses treated those with frost bite. One related how her parents had been murdered by the Germans. Maria remembered the kindness of the two women.[14]

Prikryl assigned two soldiers to the Americans to cook and keep them supplied with rations. Maria recalled later that life became relatively "pleasant" for a few days. "Pleasant" meant that all things were relative. Most regained their health although some still had infected fingers, feet, and legs. They needed medicine, but Maria was reluctant to seek out a hospital for fear of running into Germans. Joe Morton had some sulfa powder which he shared. Two days later they moved to another larger cabin. Here they listened to the BBC on their radio, cheered by the news of the Allies advancing on all fronts. They learned also that Franklin Roosevelt had been re-elected to a fourth term. They tried to contact Bari, but their make-shift batteries

More Suffering 197

were too strong and they burned out the radio. That was a blow which depressed Holt Green and Jim Gaul.

November 23, Thanksgiving of Hope.

They celebrated Thanksgiving with a good meal which featured a baked cake and a fruit salad. Their cabin had a stove, and Maria roasted a pig she had purchased in Dolna Lehota.[15]

Jim Gaul gave a moving prayer where he thanked God for His protection. The desperate people prayed together for relief and salvation. Gaul spoke of the need to remember the Americans who had been captured or had departed. They often wondered what had happened to Bill McGregor, Ken Lain, Jan Schwartz, and the airmen.[16]

The prayer was written down by Lt. Stefan Zenopian and kept by him until he subsequently reached Allied lines. It read as follows:

> Oh God, we who are gathered here in thy name and by thy name and by thy blessing on this day of Thanksgiving do offer with deep gratitude our most heartfelt thanks for our deliverance from the blizzards and high winds of the wintry mountains and from the cruel snows fallen upon us and from the perils of the black night in dark valleys.
> Gratefully we thank thee for preserving our group together and for maintaining our physical health and strength and for buttressing our wavering courage and for providing good even in our darkest days and we ask thy blessing on us and our allies, particularly the Slovak nation and thy mercy on our comrades who are missing by enemy action and wintry storm. Amen.[17]

Morton's frostbitten feet were in bad shape. He was forced to wear wooden sabots. Years later, Maria recalled him with the snow often caked two or three inches thick on them. He was repeatedly taking them off to clean the soles. Maria remembered him looking "ridiculous," and they often joked about his "platform shoes." Morton always was good natured and always laughed at himself with the others.[18]

Twice a week, peasants from Dolna Lehota brought them food, eggs, butter, a goose, and a calf. Most of the party began to get their health back, although Joe Morton had a severe case of dysentery. One of the Jewish doctors advised Maria to go to the hospital in Brezno to get treatment for her foot. The open sore was so bad she could see the bone in her foot.[19]

That night, Major Sehmer surprised them when he showed up at the mine headquarters, having learned their location from Partisans. A Partisan had seen a "tall blond American" with a jacket with USNR on the back and had followed him along a trail into Dolna Lehota. He reported back to Sehmer who knew it had to be Jim Gaul. Sehmer had notified Bari and got a reply. Morale soared. Help was on the way.[20]

Sehmer complained bitterly on November 24, telling Bari to "buck up and send sortie . . ."[21]

They continued to recover their strength, although some still could hardly walk. Men, usually led by Joe Horvath and some Slovaks, went down to Dolna Lehota at night to buy food. The Germans controlled the village by day and often at night. The food runs were risky. Maria could barely walk. She was unable to accompany them.

November 28, Disaster at Dolna Lehota.

Sehmer suggested to Holt Green that his group travel to Sehmer's new hiding place, a ski lodge called Velky Bok, up the mountain from Polomka 20 miles east of Dolna Lehota. Sehmer convinced Green that it would be safer there. Green, Joe Horvath, and Robert Brown left with Sehmer to investigate. Jim Gaul was left in charge.

The next day Lt. Frank Perry and a Slovak officer went to Dolna Lehota to buy some food. They didn't return. The next morning Tibor and Jerry Mican went down to Prikryl's headquarters to see what he could learn.

Less than an hour later, the Americans heard gunfire. Slovaks came running up the mountain, shouting that Germans were attacking the headquarters. Maria, Joe Morton, and the others frantically packed their belong-

More Suffering 199

ings, gathered up food and prepared to flee. To her horror, Maria could not get her shoes on. Her feet were swollen. She found some rubber boots and sliced them to get them on her feet. She had difficulty walking. Nelson Paris and Joe Morton waited to assist her up the steep trail.[22]

Joe Morton hobbled along in his wooden shoes, hardly able to climb. They moved slowly. Gunfire echoed through the trees. The bursts of automatic weapons fire had a chilling effect. Maria struggled to keep up but walking was painful. Morton and Catlos helped her. Jerry Mican and Frank Perry were missing. Steve Catlos went back to look for them. Mican came into view, wandering up the trail as if he were lost. Perry was nowhere in sight. Mass confusion prevailed.

Jim Gaul and Tibor were at the headquarters when the attack began. Gaul took off running, but Tibor was in the latrine and was left behind, an ignominious position in a crisis of life and death. Jerry Mican also was left behind, and no one knew what happened to Lt. Frank Perry.[23]

Prikryl had failed to post guards and the Germans had infiltrated extremely close to the camp before they attacked. The Germans went on a rampage, burning the headquarters building and also homes and huts between the mining camp and Dolna Lehota. They killed 38 Slovaks and wounded dozens of others. The wounded who failed to escape were thrown into the burning houses by the Germans. They later shot the two nurses who had treated the Americans suffering from frostbite two weeks earlier.[24]

Slovak Major Jan Stanek, one of the battalion commanders who was attacked by the Germans, and his men fled in disorder.[25]

The Americans soon found themselves in chest high snow as they fled up the mountain. They couldn't go on. After waiting a few hours, they retraced their steps and cautiously returned to the camp. Steve Catlos half-carried Maria who could not walk unassisted. The Germans had left. The Americans rested overnight, and then left in the early morning hours for Myto.[26]

November 30, Myto.

Myto, ten miles distant, was another grueling hike. They arrived at 9 PM. It was dark and cold and they were forced to spend the night in the open. Maria recalled that Nelson Paris was so miserable and in such pain that he began to cry. A half century later she remembered wiping the tears away from his face as he suffered. That night they learned that the Germans had ambushed Major Stanek's men who had regrouped after the disaster at Dolna Lehota. The Germans captured a large number of Slovaks, but Stanek escaped with 35 of his men.[27] Because it was unsafe to enter Myto, Gaul decided they would stay in some stables outside of the village.[28]

Maria could barely walk, and Joe Morton was hobbling in his wooden shoes. Lane Miller and Nelson Paris, weak and seriously ill, moved with the others to a primitive sheep herder's hut. No one was comfortable, and Jim Gaul, seeking a better refuge, discovered a Slovak farmer who agreed to take three of them to his house. Gaul returned to get Maria, Miller, and Paris. It took them two hours to make what normally would have been a 15 minute walk. But again, Gaul showed he was a tower of strength.

When they reached the farm house, Maria again had to cut the boots off her feet. Then, the Slovak, afraid of being caught by the Germans, lost his nerve. He ordered them to leave, and at 2:45 AM in the biting cold, they headed back to the stables. They arrived at 6 AM, exhausted. Maria could no longer walk and had crawled the last few hundred yards on her hands and knees. How much more could they endure?[29]

Feeling guilty, the farmer returned the next day and led them to a hunting shack in the woods where three Jewish boys were hiding. The group remained here for two weeks.[30]

December 2, Struggle Through The Cold.

Jim Gaul and Steve Catlos went to Polomka to see Holt Green to get permission to move there. There, Major Sehmer and his team were able to send messages to Bari but had to sneak into Polomka to get electrical power to operate their radio.

In Myto, Maria and Tibor and the others bought food from boys from the village. The Slovak youths brought food to a designated spot in the woods where the Americans left money. The distressing news from the village that Frank Perry had been captured by the Germans in Dolna Lehota left them shaken. On top of this, the grisly accounts of the Germans throwing the wounded into the burning buildings reinforced once again their hatred of a barbaric enemy.[31]

Now they had a few days to rest. And for some, to reflect. Their conquest over pain and suffering had resulted in strong bonds of unity in the most difficult of circumstances. The love that emerged from this adversity seemed not only to endure but to guarantee a sense that they would prevail. Yet, they had lost Frank Perry. Their travail seemed like some grim, gothic tragedy on one hand and a heroic epic on the other. Some days, they awoke to a gray, overcast morning, depressed and discouraged as they speculated about Perry's fate. Other days, they were greeted by the morning rays of sunshine which broke through the mist bringing welcome relief from the cold. Some days the men to took off their shirts and sunbathed. Although dealing with lice, they now were able to clean up.

The gleaming white snow lay on the mountain, reminding them of past, happier times. Idle conversation and reminiscing about playing in the snow as children highlighted their days. Now, the utmost pleasure was being able to wash in heated water, although hunger gripped them daily and interminably.

Their dignity was gone. The awful consequences of dysentery saw to that. Their appearances were appalling. Filthy and louse ridden, their faces wind-burned and their health threatened by utter exhaustion, they had, in spite of all this, been drawn together. The men shaved when they could and trimmed each other's hair. They never totally relaxed, knowing that catastrophe could befall them at any moment. *Einsatzkommando* hunting parties,

Abwehr 218 and Major *Graf* Thun-Hohenstein, were just beyond the next stand of timber, just beyond the next village.

With what food they had, Joe Morton prepared the breakfasts with care and good humor while Tibor and Maria cooked the other meals. In this appallingly cruel weather, they had managed to persevere, struggling through one wintry crisis after another, surviving the hikes, each worse and more tortuous than the last. Partisan patrols regularly reported the movements of the enemy which raised the level of anxiety. Despite this, the mood in the camp was generally calm. As they luxuriated in the warmth of their evening campfires, their love for each other now equaled their primal urge to stay alive. They had acquired a new dignity.[32]

December 10, Jim Gaul Returns From Polomka.

Jim Gaul walked into camp with Aba Berdichev (cover name, Lt. Robert Willis), one of Major Sehmer's men. Gaul, the iron man who could overcome anything, had been gone eight days and was a welcome sight. He and Berdichev had been up at Velky Bok with the British and a group of Partisans.

Gaul carried a letter written by Margita Kockova. An American citizen of Slovak birth, she also was with the British mission at Velky Bok. Kockova's letter was to a village priest in Myto who she thought would be able to supply pack horses.[33]

Jim Gaul directed Tibor and Mican to walk to Myto and deliver the letter the next evening. They left after dark. Maria had a foreboding about this trip and begged them not to go. She had forged an emotional bond with Tibor, and she was especially fond of Jerry Mican. She feared for their lives and told them so. The men only laughed at her. She looked at them wistfully as they departed. How quickly their fragile security could dissolve into peril. A simple mistake could mean disaster. Gaul ordered them not to stay the night.[34]

More Suffering

1. PRO, HS4/42.
2. Ibid.
3. PRO, HS4/40.
4. Ibid.
5. Ibid.
6. PRO, HS4/42.
7. PRO, HS4/40.
8. Maria Gulovich, OSS Report.
9. Josef Piontek, Letter to the Associated Press, July, 1945.
10. Maria Gulovich, OSS Report.
11. Kenneth Dunlevy, OSS Report.
12. Ibid.
13. PRO, HS4/40.
14. Kenneth Dunlevy, OSS Report; Maria Gulovich, OSS Report.
15. Maria Gulovich, Interview with William Miller, 1984.
16. Maria Gulovich, OSS Report.
17. James Sehmer sent a copy of the prayer to the author, part of a letter Stephan Zenopian wrote to the Sehmer family after World War II, August 21, 1997.
18. Maria Gulovich, Telephone conversation with the author, October 27, 2000.
19. Ibid.
20. Kenneth Dunlevy, OSS Report.
21. James Sehmer, Letter to the author; Steve Catlos, conversation with Harriett and Harvey Gaul (parents of Jim Gaul) as reported by them in a letter to Holt Green's family, October 16, 1945, courtesy of Frances Frost Hutson.
22. Maria Gulovich, OSS Report.
23. Kenneth Dunlevy, OSS Report; Maria Gulovich, OSS Report.
24. Ibid.
25. Stanek's written statement, Courtesy of Maria Gulovich Liu, November, 2000.
26. Kenneth Dunlevy, OSS Report.; Maria Gulovich, interview with William Miller.
27. Stanek's account.
28. Maria Gulovich, OSS Report; Maria Gulovich, Telephone interview with author, October 27, 2000.
29. Maria Gulovich, OSS Report.
30. Kenneth Dunlevy, OSS Report.
31. Maria Gulovich, OSS Report.
32. Ibid.
33. Ibid.
34. Ibid.

Chapter 24

Betrayal

October 10, Zvolenska Slatina.

While Holt Green, Jim Gaul and the others were trying to stay alive on the *Tatras* in October and November, Captain Edward Baranski, Daniel Pavletich, Emil Tomes and Tony Novak were twenty miles south gathering intelligence in the area east of Zvolen. Lt. Lane Miller, a member of Baranski's team, had gone to Banska Bystrica and was with Holt Green.

Baranski had left Banska Bystrica October 10 to set up operations in this small town, seven miles east of Zvolen and 21 miles southeast of Banska Bystrica. Lane Miller, a pilot, went to Tri Duby the next day and checked out Alexander Watkins' P-51 Mustang. "She is in excellent mechanical condition with few minor exceptions," Baranski radioed Otto Jakes in Bari. Baranski also urged Bari to pressure the 15th Air Force to commence strafing missions [in support of the Slovaks].[1] Baranski was less concerned about being evacuated than providing intelligence enabling the 15th Air Force to attack the Germans.

Miller recognized the vulnerability of Tri Duby, and hustled around to find alternate airfields. Baranski notified Jakes of Miller's efforts.[2] On October 17, to make communication with these airfields possible, Baranski asked Bari to send ten "Walkie Talkie's" (WWII hand-held radios) and a case of flashlights.[3] Two days later, Baranski informed Bari that the Germans had bombed Tri Duby, and that ground forces were moving north out of

Krupina, 16 miles south of Zvolen.[4]

Baranski and his men were keeping track of the German advance. Two days later, he informed Bari that the enemy was now five miles north of Krupina. Also, he gave dimensions of a dirt airfield near Brezno.[5]

Novak was the chief intelligence collector for Baranski. Steve Catlos in an interview with Jim Gaul's parents in October, 1945, described Novak as a "Gypsy." Catlos said Novak played the violin beautifully and regularly entertained the men at Bari before they left on the mission. He was a popular person, but one known to exaggerate his accomplishments.[6]

Holt Green informed Bari on October 24 that Zvolen Slatina and Tri Duby would fall to the Germans in two days.[7] Green requested Bari on the same date to advise him where Baranski was located.[8] Sometime between October 15 and October 25, Lane Miller had rejoined Holt Green in Banska Bystrica.

Tony Novak had been scouting around and through the German lines, recording troop movements and then returned to Zvolenska Slatina. The Zvara family told him on October 23 Baranski and Pavletich had left just before the Germans had seized the city. Novak and the other two, plus Emil Tomes, had been in town for two weeks without incident. The arrival of the Germans now changed everything.

Had Baranski and Pavletich returned to Banska Bystrica? Always resourceful, Novak purchased a bicycle and headed for the rebel capital. On the way, he learned the city was about to fall to the Germans. He turned around and set out for the Polana Mountains, 14 miles to the east where some Partisan units were located.

The Germans controlled the main roads. Novak was forced to travel on hiking trails and back roads. He couldn't find Baranski and Pavletich. No one there knew where the Americans were. Novak headed back to Zvolenska Slatina. He was stopped by a German patrol and arrested. Novak, an ethnic Slovak and young, should not have appeared to be a problem to the enemy. But the Germans were taking few chances. A few hours later, Novak was left alone with a single guard. Seeing his chance, Novak jumped the guard and shoved him down a steep embankment. He took off running and made his escape. He returned that night to the Zvara family. They still could tell him nothing about Baranski and Pavletich.[9]

November 7, Zvolenska Slatina.

Unknown to the others, Baranski, Pavletich, and Emil Tomes actually had been with one of the Partisan units in Polana. The Germans moved north from Zvolenska Slatina into the Polana Mountains and scattered the Slovaks. The three-man American team fled, but lost all their gear including their wireless radio and most of their clothes. Tomes was missing, and Baranski feared he had been captured.[10]

Two days later, a detachment of Germans drove into town with "car-loads" of American equipment, including a radio set. Novak actually approached the German sergeant in charge and recognized some of his own clothes. The Germans were selling the clothes to a group of Slovaks crowding around, and Novak was able to buy his own uniform back. Novak learned from the German that they nearly had captured an "American captain."[11] Novak realized the Germans had intelligence sources among the Slovak populace.

November 15, Piest.

After the fiasco in the Polano Mountains, Baranski and Pavletich moved to the village of Piest pri Detva, 15 miles east of Zvolenski Slatina. There is no record when they arrived there. They were able to move in with the Jan Vrto family. A few days later, Baranski sent Vrto to Zvolenska Slatina to the Zvara house with a message. Novak was wary of a trap, and sent Mrs. Zvara back with Vrto to verify that Baranski was really there. She brought back good news, and Novak headed for Piest.

The Zvara and Vrto families were anti-German, and they had put their lives at risk by aiding the Americans. But, they were paid well in gold, the same tender Holt Green was using 35 miles to the north on the other side of the Polana Mountains.

Baranski must have been relieved to see Novak. He described how Tomes had fled in another direction when the Germans attacked and he had no idea where he was. He guessed that Tomes had been captured. Although Baranski had lost his radio, he had been able to destroy the code. Without clothes and equipment, Baranski was helpless. But Novak was a crafty agent and moved easily through the towns of the region without suspicion. He was Baranski's eyes and ears, alert and able to avoid the enemy.

Novak stayed two days in Piest. He, Baranski, and Pavletich discussed heading for the Russian lines, but Baranski concluded it was too far to travel. Also, the snow was waist deep in the mountain passes. Baranski informed Novak he also was considering joining a Partisan unit. During this time, Novak shuttled back and forth to Zvolenska Slatina where he spent most of his time. He had excellent contacts in the town.

At the Zvara house, the indefatigable Novak prepared 5000 flyers and leaflets and distributed them in Zvolen. He was working with a priest, who supplied a mimeograph machine, and a local pharmacist, a communist, who supplied the ink.

December 8, Novak Warned To Flee.

Novak rejoined Baranski and Pavletich and reported on his activities. Despite German patrols everywhere, the situation seemed under control. He left the next day at 2 PM to return to Zvolenska Slatina, but Vera Zvara greeted him in a panic, telling him to flee immediately. Her parents had been arrested, and she was terrified. Novak went to his friend, the priest, who told him the bad news. Under torture, Mrs. Zvara told them where to find Baranski. She also gave them a description of Novak.[12]

Although shaken, Novak remained calm and resolute. He made his way north a few miles to the village of Zolna on back roads. He had a friend return later to pick up Vera. On December 11, she joined Novak and reported that Baranski and Pavletich had been arrested. She told Novak the Germans were looking for him. If Vera's mother had been forced to betray Baranski, Novak knew certainly they indeed would be looking for him. He dyed his hair red, said goodbye to Vera, and left to join the Partisans.

Novak found a Partisan group in Kotmanovo, ten miles east of Piest, and subsequently fought in several engagements. He later claimed he joined an orchestra in Hungary and was able to booby-trap a musical instrument in a tavern on Christmas eve which detonated and killed a number of German troops. Ultimately, he made it to Belgrade and reported to the OSS. He claimed he personally had killed 25 Germans. He had collected their dog tags which he gave to Otto Jakes. [13]

---

1 NARA, RG 226, Entry 136, Box 26, Folder 263.
2 Ibid., Messages 06, 07.
3 Ibid., Message 09.
4 Ibid., Message 12.
5 Ibid., Message 70.
6 Steve Catlos, Interview with Harriett and Harvey Gaul, reported in a letter, October 10, 1946, Harriett Gaul to Hazel Frost (Holt Green's sister).
7 NARA, RG 226, Entry 136, Box 34, Folder 376, Message 199.
8 Ibid., Message 211.
9 Anton Novak, OSS Report, Written by Otto Jakes, Bari, February 14, 1945. NARA, RG 226, Entry 190, Box 22, Folder 1.
10 Ibid.
11 Ibid.
12 Ibid.
13 Ibid., Catlos, interview with Harriett and Harvey Gaul.

Chapter 25

"Things Don't Look Right"

December 12, Myto.

Maria spent a sleepless night waiting for Tibor and Jerry Mican to return. Jim Gaul had specifically ordered them not to stay overnight in Myto. He knew it was always tempting to stay in a warm house and a comfortable bed. But the German patrols frequently were out making surprise searches and break-ins. At first, Gaul was not worried, but by the end of the day, he decided to take Maria and find out what had happened to the two men.

Maria and Gaul didn't go straight to the priest's parish house. Gaul stayed in another house nearby. Maria went to see the priest. No one answered the door. Finally, Dr. Stefan Katlousky, the priest, answered Maria's knock. He was suspicious and guarded in what he said, and Maria sensed he was lying. Then, his wife entered the room in tears.[1]

She confirmed that Tibor and Mican had been captured. She told them she had fed the two men and invited them to spend the night. In the early morning, she sent her 16-year-old maid, Anna Engler, to show them a safe way back to their hut.[2]

Engler led the two Americans through several back yards in the dark. They then stepped out on the main street, but less than 100 yards up the street, they ran into a slow-moving vehicle coming their direction. It was filled with Germans. They walked by the patrol, but after a few yards, the Germans stopped and called back to them.

It was all over, too late to run. Engler did not understand German, but the two Americans answered them. Engler slipped away. The two Americans surrendered without resistance. Several of the German soldiers returned to the priest's house a few minutes later. Aware she was in danger, the Engler girl had taken off her street clothes and climbed back into bed. The Germans had been confused in the dark about who had been on the street.[3]

The prisoners were taken to Brezno and that night to Banska Bystrica. Determined to capture the rest of the Americans, a small German force led by a pro-German Slovak prepared to head for the American camp. It had been snowing all night and the drifts were waist deep. After going only a short distance, the Germans turned back. Gaul and Maria had no choice but to struggle on. They reached the base camp at midnight, unaware they had narrowly avoided capture. Maria was seething because she was convinced that the priest had betrayed the two Americans. Gaul knew they had to break camp and move. The Germans would be coming. After a brief rest, they headed for Polomka.

One More Struggle Through Savage Conditions.

It was another trial through the ice and the snow, 20-miles and two-and-a-half days of torture. Some, like Joe Morton, wore sabots. They hobbled along, suffering. Their frostbite worsened. Sores opened up again on nearly everyone's feet. Maria's legs became swollen, and the excruciating pain in her feet left her gasping. Morton could hardly walk. Jack Wilson, although older, surprisingly seemed to endure the elements without much pain. Ken Dunlevy, Lane Miller, and Nelson Paris suffered terribly. Although in misery, Morton never allowed the ordeal to dampen his spirits. Jim Gaul continually inspired them to struggle on.

The group crept through the woods next to the road, forced to travel in a wide arc around the villages in order to avoid the Germans. Near the village of Gasparovo, they were surprised to see a German patrol coming toward them. They dropped down in the snow. Maria could not believe they avoided being seen. After dark, despite their painful feet, they enjoyed the luxury of walking on the main road. They still were wary of the occasional nighttime German patrols.[4]

Their guide was a young boy Jim Gaul had hired who kept them informed about which villages were occupied by Germans. Later that night they slept in the snow outside of the town of Benus. They dared not risk starting a fire. The next day they reached the mountain slope above Polomka around 3 PM. They still faced another four-hour walk up the mountain to the hut where Holt Green and the others were staying. It was a difficult climb, requiring them to ford icy streams, struggle up steep banks and then slide down others. The ravines were filled with snow drifts.[5]

The streams were treacherous obstacles. A fall into the icy water could lead to pneumonia. Steve Catlos assisted Maria. Joe Morton helped Nelson Paris. Lane Miller and Jack Wilson struggled up slowly. Ken Dunlevy was weak, but doggedly kept up. Jim Gaul's strength seemed boundless. Steve Catlos, Joe Horvath, and Aba Berdichev maintained the pace. As they worked their way up the mountain in silence, their thoughts were still on Tibor and Jerry Mican.[6]

December 14, Relief On The *Homolka* Mountain.

As it turned dark, the group was on the verge of collapse. Jim Gaul, the eternal cheerleader, had kept them moving, encouraging, cajoling and physically assisting individuals over rocks and through the waist deep snow. They finally reached the hut at 6,000 feet elevation.

Their warm reception was joyous and thrilling as Holt Green and the others greeted them with laughter and jokes. Even in the grimmest of circumstances, everyone seemed to maintain a sense of humor. They immediately were treated to a hot meal, and their spirits soared, sobered, however, when they reported the grim news about Tibor and Mican.

The hut had been covered with branches and was now well blanketed with snow. Difficult to see, it was secluded off the main trail. The British lived a mile and a half up the mountain in the Velky Bok ski lodge. Roughly 100 Partisans were there also. Most of the Slovaks at Velky Bok were wounded, but they were rowdy and noisy and frequently fired their weapons into the air with little reason. Some remember the lodge as a ski resort. Others said it was a sanitarium.

Margita Kockova, the American-born Slovak with the British group, was staying in the hut with the Americans. She and Maria diligently washed all the men's clothes which gave them relief from the rampant lice. " . . . our clothes were almost walking with lice," Maria remembers. But Maria and Kockova didn't get along. Kockova was in her 30's, and Maria felt she was overbearing.

Kockova, remembered as having average looks, may have been jealous of Maria who was younger and attractive. Maria received a lot of attention from the men. Also, Maria had a mind of her own. The biggest issue, however, was the letter Kockova had written to the priest in Myto which Tibor and Mican had delivered and which led to their capture. Maria held Kockova responsible.[7]

The group was able to secure food from people in the Polomka village. Joe Horvath established contact with his uncle and other relatives. This proved to be a huge benefit as his cousin, Anna Horvath, would leave milk and other food at pre-arranged sites in the woods. Horvath would hike down and pick up the supplies.[8]

Major Jan Stanek, who at times stayed in the hut with the Americans as well as at Velky Bok where his men were recuperating, was able to get food from the villages. His Slovak unit consisted of the survivors of the disasters at Dolna Lehota and Myto on December 2. Stanek had escaped with only 35 men. They had fled east to Velky Bok where the British group and Holt Green were staying. Other Partisans, remnants of other units, were billeted there also.[9]

The group now began eating reasonably well, and life became moderately pleasant. They believed at first their isolated hut was safe. They did

"Things Don't Look Right" 215

their best to nurse their frostbitten feet. Joe Morton and Maria had become close friends, although they spoke in simple English which Maria was beginning to learn. Morton treated her feet each day with some sulfur powder. Maria never forgot his kindness and attention. The men, meanwhile, fighting off boredom, played chess and a game called "Battleship."[10]

December 16, Final Message To Bari.

Major Sehmer's messages to SOE Bari were the first news the OSS had received about the DAWES group. Major Walter Ross and Lt. Nelson Deranian were still trying to figure out how to bring aid to their beleaguered men. They checked with the 15 Air Force Operations office daily, hoping to get a re-supply mission into the air.[11]

Sehmer put through his final message on this date to SOE Bari. He described their group as exhausted, hungry, and suffering from frozen feet.[12] Before his radio failed, Sehmer had sent their location to Bari with instructions on how signal fires would be set at night on top of the mountain ridge. He told them he needed a new radio, plus, "extra heavy" clothing, general supplies and ammunition. Everyone looked forward to the re-supply airdrop.

Before the Americans arrived, Lt. Zenopian and Bill Davies would go down to Polomka to charge the radio batteries. It always was a dangerous operation with German patrols intermittently prowling the region. But they were able to send their last message.[13]

Both SOE and OSS Bari now learned the plight of their people.[14] The message was "garbled," but Bari learned that the main group was near "Dolnialehota . . . no news Baranski, Novak, and Pavletich (sic), McGregor . . . all equipment lost . . . majority in bad condition because of exposure. Frozen feet . . . exhaustion." Ross and Deranian probably thought they had learned the worst, but the worst was yet to come.[15]

Walter Ross years told William Miller in 1984 that, "A day didn't go by from the time we lost close contact with those people that we didn't sit down . . . and have lengthy discussions with high ranking people in the 15th

Air Force and the responsible people in the OSS. We were very, very upset about it."[16] The weather either was bad in Italy or adverse over Slovakia. The 15th continued to cancel all flights.[17]

On December 18, SOE Bari radioed Sehmer that three planes were ready to fly the first night of good weather. Lt. Colonel Threlfall asked him if they could receive daylight flights of fighters dropping canisters. He also asked if they could receive bombers by day with a strong fighter escort. He emphasized the importance of ground recognition signals and spelled out the procedure.[18]

On the *Homolka* Mountain each night, a few people went to the peak to set signal fires. Although the weather had been clear for three days, the group waited in vain for aircraft to appear.

Plans To Celebrate Christmas.

As Christmas approached, they planned a celebration. Jim Gaul was the organizer of these festivities. Gaul, Ken Dunlevy, Joe Morton, Joe Horvath, and two Slovaks made arrangements to go down to Polomka to get a cart full of food. The practice of the Slovaks in Polomka was to hide food under a wagon load of hay or manure. Horvath had learned that there were no Germans in the town, and he and the others agreed not to carry their weapons.[19]

The rendezvous was in an open field. The group had to come out of the woods, cross a cleared field, ford a small stream, and walk to the road to the wagon. It was a risky operation. When they had just paid the Slovaks in gold and were lifting their sacks of food, which included a small pig, a German patrol appeared. Horvath and the others dropped the food and sprinted for the woods. The Germans began firing. Morton had the most difficulty running due to his sore feet and the wooden shoes.

Morton carried a Beretta pistol which he fired at the Germans. It was a small caliber gun and was comically feeble against the Germans. Dunlevy, Gaul, and Horvath broke out laughing when they stopped to rest after several hundred yards.[20]

By the time they retreated deep into the woods, Morton could not keep up. His wooden shoes were caked with snow which left him clumsy and barely able to walk. He sat down and told them to leave him and run to the hut. Gaul ordered him to his feet. Gaul told the rest of the men to keep going and insisted he would take care of Morton.

Dunlevy and Horvath reluctantly left. A few minutes later, they heard a great fusillade of gunfire and assumed that Gaul and Morton had been killed. They kept going and it soon became dark. An hour later, Gaul and Morton came up the trail, reporting that the Germans simply had fired wildly into the woods. When the Germans left, the two came out of hiding and had calmly hiked up the trail.[21]

When Gaul and Dunlevy failed to reach the hut before dark, Maria and the others feared another tragedy had happened, but tragedy had been averted. Gaul gleefully told the story of Morton and his Beretta. The humor and laughter about a deadly scene where one group of men was trying to kill another had become routine. The next day, two of the Slovaks went down and recovered some of the food left by the Germans.[22]

December 22, Germans Occupy Polomka.

As Christmas approached, their situation changed. Three thousand retreating German and Hungarian troops arrived in the region and were garrisoned in Polomka and Helpa, a smaller village nearby. The Anglo-Americans now lost their chief source of food. Fortunately, Margita Kockova knew people in Maluzina, a village a few miles to the west on a mountain road leading south to the Hron Valley. Holt Green, John Sehmer, Robert Brown, and Lt. Zenopian set out to go there and get additional food for their Christmas dinner. Meanwhile, Joe Horvath had cut down a small Christmas tree, and Maria decorated it with red and blue paper stars. They cut up a candle and attached the segments to the tree. The scene in the tiny hut was warm and cheery.[23]

Green, Sehmer, and the others returned with food halfway through dinner that night. They also had a fresh supply of Slivovica. Sehmer prepared "Sunaginsky chai," which was a drink he learned about in Yugoslavia. They sang and danced. Lt. Zenopian sang "Pistol-Packing Mama," partially in Slovak and Hungarian, and everybody laughed and had a good time.[24]

December 25, A Somber Christmas Celebration.

Another celebration and meal were organized on Christmas Day. Jim Gaul hiked up to Velky Bok and brought back the Americans and British, plus another stock of liquor. Aba Berdichev, Robert Brown, Steve Catlos, Lt. Zenopian, and two Slovaks came down from the "big house," as they called it. They had been staying at Velky Bok in order to set the signal fires for the expected relief plane. Holt Green normally stayed at Velky Bok while Jim Gaul stayed in the hut.

Maria and Kockova actually baked a cake for the party. After dinner, Gaul led the group in prayers. He borrowed Dunlevy's pocket Bible for the service.[25] "We prayed to God to help us all, to help us stay alive. But our prayers were not answered . . . " In his prayer, similar to the one he gave at Thanksgiving, he mentioned Bill McGregor, Ken Lain, Tibor, Jerry Mican, and the airmen by name. The group had a round of solemn toasts. Most of the group ate standing up while others sat on the bunks.[26]

Maria recalled sitting next to Joe Morton. " . . . [He] had a faraway look in his eyes. His baby daughter had been born while he was overseas, and I imagined he was thinking of her. Nobody said anything. Their thoughts were all elsewhere." Jim Gaul wrote a poem which mentioned each individual in the group. They sang Christmas carols, followed by a meal of soup, sausages, and bread.[27]

The Christmas spirit touched them all. The next morning brought a beautiful, clear day, and the snow glistened in the sunlight. They strolled about in the serene setting. Despite the deprivations they had endured and their terrible frostbite sores, they savored a magical moment in this remote spot in the mountains. They were comrades of one mind with neither anxiety nor fear. They shared stories about their families at home and the different things they had done as children during Christmas. Major Sehmer told charming stories about England. Dunlevy remembered him later as an extremely sociable British officer. "He never seemed serious and was always charming." Nevertheless, in his relationship with Holt Green, Sehmer seemed to "call the shots," Dunlevy remembered.[28] In retrospect, Sehmer's relaxed and confident attitude may have affected Green's judgment about security.

Indeed, the Americans had become careless. Joe Horvath had made a friend of a *Volksdeutsche* shoemaker in the village. Horvath's Polomka relatives later concluded later that this man may have betrayed the Americans.[29] The close scrape with the Germans at the wagon incident surely had given the Germans proof that the Anglo-Americans were on the mountain.

Polomka Civilians Warn The Americans.

Anna Horvath, Joe's cousin, and other family members and friends in Polomka, also concluded that the Americans had been too casual about their security at the cabin. Anna told Joe on one occasion, "Get out of here." A half-century later, she recalled that Joe replied, "No, a plane is coming. We're going to get out later."[30] Obviously Holt Green and John Sehmer believed they had to wait for the re-supply drop which they had set up during their last radio messages to Bari. If they moved, they had no hope of getting another radio.

Maria recalls Joe Horvath discussing the issue of security. He wondered about the reliability of the Slovak guards. Holt Green was giving Dymko money, and it was Maria's understanding that the payment in part was for providing protection for the Americans.[31]

During the Christmas day meal, another conflict occurred between Kockova and Maria. Kockova had criticized Maria for the way she was dividing and serving the food. A terrible spat occurred, and Maria said she had had enough. She told Holt Green she was going to move up to Velky Bok, and he agreed it would be for the best.[32]

Later that afternoon, Maria left for the lodge with Zenopian, Catlos, Davies, Dunlevy, and one of the Slovaks. Green, Sehmer, Berdichev, and Brown said they would come up the next day. There was to be another party that night. A lot of drinking was going on, Dunlevy recalled. He decided to leave.[33]

Joe Morton walked up the trail for about a half-mile with Dunlevy, Catlos, and Maria. The hut was about a 75-minute hike from the lodge. Morton and Maria said goodby to each other and she kissed him on the brow. Morton merely shook his head slowly as he said goodby to Maria.[34] It was another, poignant, ominous parting. Maria had a bad feeling about the situation.

Dunlevy remained with Morton a few minutes to talk. Morton told him, "Things didn't look right." They agreed that the group should move, that security was bad. They shook hands and parted, never to see one another again.[35]

---

1 Maria Gulovich, Interview with William Miller, 1984.
2 Anna Engler Kochanova's 1999 interview with Martin Bubeliny's parents, March 1999, in Polomka, courtesy of Martin Bubeliny.
3 Ibid.; Maria Gulovich, OSS Report.
4 Maria Gulovich, OSS Report.
5 Ibid.
6 Ibid.
7 Ibid.
8 Frank Horvath, Telephone interview with the author, September, 1999, in which Horvath recounted a conversation with his cousin, Anna, in Polomka in September, 1999.
9 Jan Stanek report, Courtesy of Maria Gulovich, November, 2000.
10 Maria Gulovich, Interview with William Miller, 1983.
11 Walter Ross, Interview with William Miller, 1983.
12 PRO, HS4/40.
13 Stephan Zenopian, Interview with Walter Ross, March 3, 1945, NARA, Entry 190, Box 116, Folder 407.
14 NARA, RG 226, Entry 124, Box 28, Folder 221. Message from Walter Ross and Nelson Deranian to Lt. Colonel Howard Chapin, Caserta, with a corrected version of Sehmer's "garbled" message of December 16, 1944
15 Ibid.

16 Walter Ross, interview (taped) with William Miller, 1984.
17 Ibid.
18 PRO, HS4/40.
19 Kenneth Dunlevy, Interview with Harriett Gaul, reported in a letter, October 5, 1945, to Hazel Frost.
20 Ibid.
21 Ibid.
22 Maria Gulovich, Interview with William Miller.
23 Ibid.
24 Ibid.
25 Kenneth Dunlevy, Interview with William Miller.
26 Ibid.; Maria Gulovich's OSS Report.
27 Maria Gulovich, OSS Report.
28 Kenneth Dunlevy, interview with Miller.
29 Ibid.; Frank Horvath, Joe's brother and a resident of Ohio, visited his cousins in Polomka in September, 1998, and reviewed these matters at length with the family.
30 Ibid.
31 Maria Gulovich, telephone interview with the author, January 2, 2001.
32 Maria Gulovich, OSS Report.
33 Kenneth Dunlevy, interview with William Miller.
34 Kenneth Dunlevy, OSS Report.; Maria Gulovich, Interview with the author, January 2, 2001.
35 Kenneth Dunlevy, Interview with Harriett and Harvey Gaul.

ESCAPE ROUTE OF THE DAWN

Liptovska Mikulas

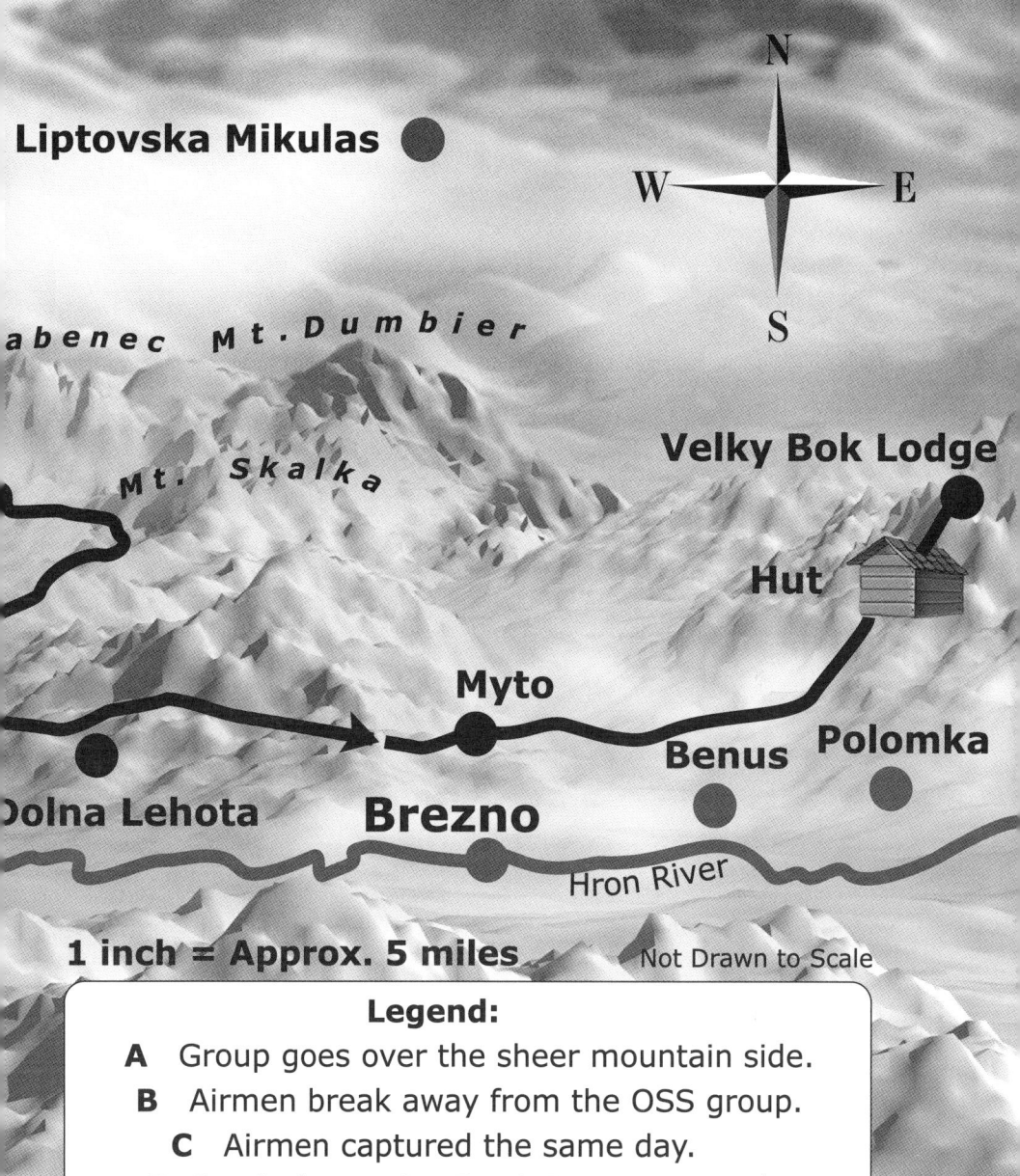

abenec Mt. Dumbier

Mt. Skalka

Velky Bok Lodge

Hut

Myto

Benus **Polomka**

Dolna Lehota **Brezno**

Hron River

1 inch = Approx. 5 miles   Not Drawn to Scale

Legend:
- **A** Group goes over the sheer mountain side.
- **B** Airmen break away from the OSS group.
- **C** Airmen captured the same day.
- **Dolna Lehota** Lt. Frank Perry captured.
- **Myto** Lt. Tibor Keszthelyi and M/Sgt. Jerry Mican captured.
- **Hut** Lt. Holt Green, Major John Sehmer, and others captured.
- **Velky Bok Lodge** Maria Gulovich and others escape.

ISSION IN THE LOWER TATRAS.

Chapter 26

"Some Devil is Coming"

Christmas Day, 1944.

Major Erwein *Graf* Thun-Hohenstein and his *Abwehr 218* unit knew the Americans and the British were somewhere up on the *Homolka* Mountain, and they were closing in on their prey.

In the eyes of one of his colleagues, The *Graf* was "an exceptional, fascinating personality," and a dedicated German officer. He had served in Italy with *Abwehr 212*, a counterintelligence unit in the Rome area during most of 1943 and until August, 1944, when the historic city was about to fall to the U.S. Fifth Army. Thun-Hohenstein then spent time in Florence, Italy, before being selected for a special mission to Slovakia.[1]

Thun-Hohenstein apparently was picked for the Slovakia mission by Otto Skorzeny, the legendary *SS* colonel who commanded *Abwehr II* in the *Reichssicherheitsdienst* (RSHA) in Berlin. Skorzeny, a native of Austria, was the Waffen *SS* officer who had recently led the daring rescue of Benito Mussolini from the mountain top *Gran Grasso Hotel* in Italy. Only 36, Skorzeny also had taken over the control of the *Reich* Chancellery in the confusion during the hectic hours following the July bomb plot on Hitler's life.[2]

Skorzeny, born in Vienna to an aristocratic family, and, like Thun-Hohenstein, he was the graduate of an elite military academy. Thun-Hohenstein was a graduate of the *Kavallelrie-Kadettenschule* in *Mährisch-Weisskirchen* in Morvavia, then part of the Austro-Hungarian empire. He was fluent in Czech and Slovak and also spoke English, Russian and Polish.

Sometime in early September during the initial weeks of the Slovak National Uprising, Thun-Hohenstein, according to one account, parachuted into Slovakia. Disguised as either a British or Canadian intelligence agent, he allegedly made contact with Slovak partisans and stayed with them briefly. As the German *SS* units moved to crush the Uprising, Thun-Hohenstein left the Partisans and assumed command of *Abwehr 218*, working closely with Colonel Josef Witiska's *Einsatzkommando gruppe H* in Bratislava.[3]

As The Germans reeled in thousands of prisoners, Thun-Hohenstein was able to learn a great deal about the DAWES and WINDPROOF missions. He recruited Slovak defectors for his *Abwehr* unit as he moved into the Lower *Tatra* Mountains behind the fleeing Americans. Certainly Thun-Hohenstein had been able to interrogate Tibor Keszthelyi and Jerry Mican. What he may have learned from them is unknown, but the Graf knew they were part of the DAWES mission.

The *Graf* Thun-Hohenstein's *Edelweiss* Unit.

Thun-Hohenstein's *Abwehr 218* was known as the "*Edelweiss*" unit, a highly motivated force, roughly one-third German, one-third Ukrainian, and one-third *Volksdeutsche*. The *Graf* ultimately awarded the Iron Cross to thirty of his men who conducted over 50 anti-partisan operations. They were resourceful, aggressive, and motivated in part by being allowed to keep whatever loot they captured.[4]

When Thun-Hohenstein arrived in Brezno on December 21, one of the *Edelweiss* officers, a captain who was a Ukrainian deserter, told the *Graf* he had been scouting up and down the Hron Valley and had spotted smoke up on the Homolka. The Ukrainian believed it was coming from a hut occupied by the Anglo-Americans.[5]

The *Graf* had been frustrated earlier when the Anglo-Americans slipped away at Dolna Lehota and Myto. From newly captured prisoners, Thun-Hohenstein learned the number of Americans and British, their arms, their general location and their physical condition. Besides Keszthelyi and Mican, he certainly must have questioned the captured airmen accompanying Bill McGregor, as well as the Jack Shafer group. Later, he got his hands on Frank Perry.

We have no idea exactly what Thun-Hohenstein learned from the hundreds of captured members of the Czech Brigade and the Partisans. Certainly they had passed on information about both the Americans and British. Additionally, the Germans had numerous sympathizers and informers among the Slovak population. Slovakia was different from Yugoslavia. In Slovakia, Holt Green and his men were operating in largely hostile territory.

With the news of the hut on the Homolka, the *Graf* saw his chance and was ready to pounce. He was determined to see that the Anglo-Americans didn't escape this time. Thun-Hohenstein also had an ace up his sleeve. A Partisan named Bandi Gönder had been involved in a dispute with an officer at Velky Bok and returned to the valley.

Some rumored the dispute was over a girl. Others said it was about a promotion. Whatever his grievance, Gönder sold his services to the *Abwehr*. He agreed to lead the *Edelweiss* force to the hut. After the war, Maria learned he had been paid 50,000 Koruns by Thun-Hohenstein to betray his comrades.[6] Also, a Slovak captain called Niznansky, who had been captured in October, had gone over to the Germans and was given a command in *Abwehr 218* by Thun-Hohenstein.[7]

Although isolated deep in the woods, the Americans had left tell-tale tracks in the snow. Horvath and others increasingly became concerned about their security. Joe Morton's comments to Dunlevy on Christmas day indicated that he too had been influenced by Joe Horvath.

December 26, Polomka.

Slovak-speaking Germans pounded on the doors of several families in the small village around 2 AM. Inside, they ordered the men to get dressed. The Germans were in a "cruel mood," one of the Slovaks recalled in 1998.

The Germans took the men to a warehouse which the Germans had converted into their headquarters. Others were detained in a school.[8]

Before dawn, the German *Edelweiss* unit, dressed in Slovak uniforms, began the advance up the *Homolka*. The Polomka civilians were forced to carry the heavy weapons and ammunition. Bandi Gönder reputedly walked at the head of the column with Major Thun-Hohenstein. The *Graf* interestingly was wearing traditional Austrian civilian hunting clothes, knickers, and a green jacket, according to one account. The Ukrainian members of the column prodded the Slovak men of Polomka with rifles and *Schmeisser* machine guns as they marched up the mountain.[9]

A guard from Velky Bok who had been stationed near Polomka saw the column and ran up the mountain to alert the Slovaks at the lodge. He allegedly ran by the entrance trail to the hut where the OSS was hiding without stopping. The guard reached Velky Bok around 8 AM.[10]

Thun-Hohenstein led his men in a circuitous route in order to attack the hut from above. The trails leading to both the hut and Velky Bok had been heavily booby-trapped, and only someone familiar with the mines and traps would be able to get through without incident. Gönder knew the way.

Thun-Hohenstein Cuts Off Escape Route.

Thun-Hohenstein reasoned the Anglo-Americans would flee toward Velky Bok, and he wanted to cut off that escape route by coming in above them. Capturing them proved to be much easier than the *Graf* had imagined.

When they reached the hut around 8:30, Lt. Lane Miller was washing in the stream a few yards from the building. Several *Edelweiss* members, pretending to be Partisans, walked down to the hut and shouted, "We are your friends." According to one account, they pointed their weapons through the open windows. They also pointed their weapons at Miller, and he raised his arms. The attackers allegedly fired only a few rounds into the hut.[11]

The accounts of Major Jan Stanek and Pavel Kamenesky, who were in the hut, later presented a different version of the events of that day. Stanek

"Some Devil Is Coming" 229

was the Slovak Army commander and Kamenesky was his "batman" (valet). They reported that there was a burst of machine gun fire and slugs came through the roof of the hut. The people inside huddled in the corners of the room. Stanek and Kamenesky were wounded. Holt Green and Jim Gaul also suffered gunshot wounds in the arms.[12]

Kamenesky was standing at the stove, making a fire with Joe Horvath when the attack began. Kamenesky believed if he were captured, he was a "dead man." Hence, he grabbed a *Schmeisser* and ran out the door. When the weapon became entangled with the camouflaged trees leaning against the building, he dropped it and took off running as bullets ripped the snow around him. It was unclear whether he was wounded in the hut or later as he ran away.[13]

Were The Americans Preparing to Move?

In his interrogation by the Soviets after his capture in 1945, Thun-Hohenstein recalled that some of the persons in the hut were washing when they were taken. Some were shaving, and the *Graf* believed "They were getting ready to go somewhere."[14]

After the surrender of the Anglo-Americans, the *Graf* asked them in English and German if any spoke German. Major Stanek, Joe Morton, and Margita Kockova replied in the affirmative. The major asked them what they were doing on the *Homolka*, and Stanek replied that they were "studying agricultural problems." Thun-Hohenstein, astonished (and probably amused) by the bizarre reply, asked for specifics about what they were studying. Stanek replied he "didn't know." The prisoners must have looked on in amazement as this nobleman in Austrian hunting clothes addressed them.[15]

Thun-Hohenstein allowed them to get dressed. After about twenty minutes, he ordered a squad of men to escort them down to Polomka. Several civilians were ordered to carry Holt Green and Stanek because of their wounds. They collected the documents in the hut and stuffed them into five rucksacks. They found a briefcase filled with documents, a camera, a typewriter, four maps of Europe and Czechoslovakia printed on silk, two large American and British flags, a machine gun, four pistols, and a short wave radio.[16] No mention was made of the gold, but that probably went into the pockets of Thun-Hohenstein's men. They set fire to the hut and left.

Thun-Hohenstein then proceeded up the mountain toward Velky Bok. The civilians again were forced again to carry the heavy weapons and the ammunition.

Flight From Velky Bok.

Maria was working in the kitchen at the lodge when Lt. Dymko Volnuk rushed in and said, "Tell your people to get ready." She didn't know what he was talking about. "Why," she asked. "Who knows? Perhaps some devil is coming," he replied.

A sentry, who was a Russian Partisan, had heard and seen the Germans shooting at the hut below and had run back to the lodge. About 45 minutes later, they saw the German column advancing toward them. Dymko ordered three bursts of machine gun fire. "If they are friends, they won't shoot back," he said. In a few minutes, Dymko got his answer when several rounds of artillery fire boomed up from the valley below. The German column also began firing mortars at the lodge.

Maria, Dunlevy, Catlos, Zenopian, and Davies, preparing to flee, already had been packing their possessions into ruck sacks. The Partisans prepared to make a stand, but the German force of over 200 men was too large. The Anglo-Americans knew it was a no-win situation. They left when they saw the Partisans beginning to fade away. Later, they heard one of the Partisans say he saw Gönder among the attackers.[17]

The *Edelweiss* unit, meanwhile, led the Anglo-American prisoners down the mountain. In Polomka, the citizens were ordered to come to the main square of the village to witness the prisoners being loaded onto trucks to be taken to Brezno. One Slovak, Josef Skalos, recalled from accounts from his family and friends that the prisoners looked depressed.[18] Skalos had

"Some Devil Is Coming" 231

attended elementary school with Joe Horvath before the Horvath family immigrated to the States.[19]

For Joe Horvath, it was a grim, ironic experience. He had been warned by his cousin, and had taken the warning seriously. Perhaps Holt Green was planning to move, as Thun-Hohenstein later believed. If only the re-supply flight had arrived the day before Christmas. Apparently, they were reluctant to move until the re-supply drop came.

We know Joe Morton had been concerned. The author was told in 1998 by the former wife of one of the OSS survivors that there may have been too much drinking in the hut. Morton was worried, but probably still believed he would survive. Jack Wilson, an SIS agent and a Jew, knew if he were captured, he was doomed. Sadly, their false sense of security had led to their downfall. One is reminded how at Donovaly, Bill McGregor convinced Holt Green not to rely on Partisan sentries. McGregor reacted instinctively as an infantryman. Green and Jim Gaul put their security in the hands of Partisans with disastrous results.

---

1 Franz *Graf* (Count) Czernin, Letter to the author, January 20, 2001. Czernin is Thun-Hohenstein's son-in-law and resides in Vienna. Czernin quoted Joachim Engelmann, a noted military author in postwar Austria and a close friend of Thun-Hohenstein, in a letter to Czernin in 1982. Engelmann and Thun-Hohenstein served together in Slovakia in the fall of 1944.
2 During the Battle of the Bulge, Otto Skorzeny organized an armored brigade, *Jagdverbande 150*, using troops disguised as Americans and employing captured Sherman tanks. They set out to infiltrate American lines and raise havoc during the American retreat. The mission failed, but Skorzeny established himself among the Allies as the "most dangerous man in Europe."
3 Ibid.
4 Soviet interrogation of Thun-Hohenstein, 1945, courtesy of Julian Hendy, Yorkshire Television, United Kingdom. Original is in Slovak at the SNU Museum, Banska Bystrica, Slovakia; One German writer has reported that *Abwehr 218*, like the *SS* combat units in Slovakia, took few prisoners, but was "exceptionally successful in defeating newly formed Partisan units." Nevertheless, *Abwehr 218* also was accused of severe cruelties against the Slovak villagers who were suspected of being partisan supporters. His *Edelweiss* unit destroyed several Slovak villages which had been home bases of Partisan groups. Thun-Hohenstein's men allegedly killed 300 Slovaks and captured another 600 who were sent to concentration camps. Rudolf Melzer, *Erlebte Geschichte* (Vienna: *Karpatendeutsche Landsmannschaft in Österrich*, 1996) p. 504.
5 Soviet Interrogation of Thun-Hohenstein; In 1962 and 1963, the Czechoslovak government in two trials prosecuted a number of Slovaks who had been members of the *Edelweiss* unit. One, a Captain Nizansky living in Germany was condemned to death in absentia. Rudolf Melzer, *Erlebte Geschichte* (Vienna: *Karpatendeutsche Landsmannschaft in Österrich*, 1996) p. 504.
6 There is some confusion about Gönder. The name "Bandi" is Hungarian for Andrej. In a Slovak

language report in the OSS files, there is an interview with Eduard Gönder who claimed the Germans took his three sons, including Bandi, with a group of Polomka civilians. They allegedly traveled on skis to the hut. Eduard Gönder reported that the Slovak who betrayed the Americans and led the Germans to the shack actually was Josef Zajac, a Jew from Benus. Maria Gulovich vaguely recalls a story that a merchant had not been paid for food taken by the Partisans and he, name unknown, may have been the man who betrayed the Americans. Of course, Gönder was eager to save his sons and may have contrived his story, blaming a Jew as a likely scapegoat.

7 Soviet interrogation of Thun-Hohenstein.
8 Slovak witness interviewed by Julian Hendy, Yorkshire Television. Transcript given to the author by Hendy, Yorkshire Television, TV Centre, Leeds, United Kingdom, November 12, 2000.
9 Josef Skalos, Interview with William Miller, 1983, courtesy of Marilyn Miller.
10 Steve Catlos, interview with William Miller, 1983, courtesy of Marilyn Miller
11 Interview with Slovak citizen by Julian Hendy.
12 Kenneth Dunlevy, OSS Report, quoting Kamenesky; Stanek's report, courtesy of Maria Gulovich.
13 Stanek's report.
14 Soviet interrogation of Thun-Hohenstein.
15 Ibid.
16 Ibid.; The radio was without batteries and not operable.
17 Ibid.
18 Josef Skalos interview.
19 William Miller's notes, 1983, courtesy of Marilyn Miller.

Chapter 27

Fleeing Once Again

10:30 AM, December 26, Velky Bok.

Gunfire echoed through the trees as machine gun and rifle fire raked the mountain side. Thun-Hohenstein's well-armed *Edelweiss* unit was determined to capture the Velky Bok. As the fire-fight continued for over two hours, Maria, Ken Dunlevy, Steve Catlos, Lt. Zenopian, Sgt. Bill Davies and two Slovaks saw that the Partisans were preparing to take flight.

When mortar fire from the village began to fall near the lodge, Maria and the others took off through the snow with their heavy rucksacks. Slovaks also took off on the run, leaving the wounded in the lodge. Lt. Dymko Voknuk and the remnants of the Czech brigade were with them. They all fled in a generally south-easterly direction.

The clear, blue-sky day and bright sun gave no hint of the panic that was unfolding on the *Homolka*. As they ran and walked, laboring through the snow, Maria shook her head in amazement at the events of the day. She asked herself, how had it all happened? She could not believe that Holt Green and the others had been captured. After an hour, they ran into Lt. Dymko Volnuk's Partisan group. The group moved into a small valley east of Polomka, about four miles from Velky Bok.[1]

Facing little resistance, Thun-Hohenstein had advanced easily to the lodge. The *Graf* ordered his men to set fire to the structure, leaving the wounded Slovaks to perish in the flames. Guerrilla warfare was warfare with rules or morals. The prevailing standard was ruthless brutality — no quarter given and none asked.

Around noon, Maria and her compatriots looked back toward Velky Bok and saw the column of smoke from the burning ski lodge. Later, as the sun was setting, they reached a forester's cabin. They and about 25 Partisans forced their way into his house. His hostile attitude betrayed pro-German sympathies, although his vehement protests fell upon deaf ears. Furious, Lt. Dymko threatened to steal all his possessions. The forester was fortunate to escape with his life.

Here they met "Sasha," who was a Russian officer in Dymko's command. Boyish looking although he was 27 or 28, he spoke several languages and claimed to have served on the Russian front 17 times. With Sasha the group totaled 12 persons.[2]

A few hours later, some Partisans brought Pavel Kamensky to the cabin. He was suffering from his gunshot wound received during his escape from the Polomka hut, and could barely walk. Kamensky related the full story about what had happened in the hut and how Holt Green and the others were led away by the *Edelweiss* troop. Maria and the men were shocked.

27 December.

The Partisans and the Anglo-Americans planned to build bunkers near the cabin, and stay in the area. The Partisans, however, objected to the labor, and little work was accomplished. Another Partisan group in the area was led by a Russian named Shukayev, a Cossack cavalry raider who had been raising havoc with the Germans in the mountains. His base camp was a short distance away. He had a radio, and the Americans saw their chance of contacting Bari.

Zenopian was eager to join Shukayev's group, but Maria and the others objected. Maria flat out refused to go, and the Anglo-Americans took the same position. They stayed in their own camp. The following day, Maria

Fleeing Once Again

learned that an Allied airdrop had occurred on the night of the 26th, and Shukayev's men found all the supplies. They now refused to share them.[3]

December 31, East of Velky Bok.

While the Anglo-American group was contemplating their next move, a German force surprised and overran Shukayev's camp, forcing him and his men to flee. The Anglo-Americans now realized they too would have to move on. Pavel was unable to walk. Dunlevy and Catlos left eleven gold Napoleon coins with the forester and asked him to care for the wounded Slovak.[4]

That night, after having moved a short distance, they camped out under the trees and listened to the German soldiers in the distance fire their weapons into the air to celebrate the New Year. For the *Wehrmacht*, it was not going to be a good year, but the soldiers seized the spirit of the moment and celebrated.[5]

January 1, 1945, Surrounded by German Troops.

The Anglo-Americans realized their predicament. Surrounded by thousands of retreating German troops, they decided to strike out for the Russian lines, although Lt. Zenopian again objected. A long discussion followed. Sergeant Davies finally defied his superior officer, and informed him that he was going with the Americans. Although outraged, Zenopian decided to come along. They left at 1 AM. The weather was bad, but it gave them an advantage. They were able to walk in the open areas without being seen.[6]

Stefan Zenopian was an interesting individual. He first joined Major Sehmer in June, 1944 in Italy. He had been assigned to the Political Intelligence Department of the British Foreign Office, and was sent to SOE Force 399 when he linked up with Sehmer. They lived together with eight other men in Brindisi until they parachuted into Slovakia on September 18.[7]

Zenopian had been a language instructor before the war and spoke fluent Hungarian. Lt. Allan Daniels, a Canadian of Hungarian origin and a member of WINDPROOF, had jumped into Slovakia with the Sehmer team. They originally were to penetrate Hungary, but when that proved difficult, SOE Bari ordered the team to go to Banska Bystrica.[8]

January 2, "Germans Everywhere."

Leaving before dawn, they moved to the east, and Maria later recalled that "Germans were everywhere," forcing them to wade through icy streams. Their frostbite injuries still hadn't healed, and the hike was another ordeal. The weather was bad and visibility limited.[9] The group now totaled 11 persons plus one Austrian deserter, a Slovak boy, one member of the Czech brigade, and several other Partisans.

They watched German troops practice a river-crossing maneuver over the frozen Hron. They also saw long columns of weary German soldiers marching west. These *Wehrmacht* troops were lucky to have survived the Russian front, but their woes were not over yet. Forced to stay out of sight, the group spent another cold night in the woods.[10]

As they neared Telgart it was still dark, and they nearly ran into a German vehicle. They spent another night out in the open. They had hoped to cross the Hron Valley that night, but gave it up. Despite their current obstacles, Dunlevy believed at this point it was "clear sailing" to the Russian lines.[11]

January 3, Hron River Valley.

They awoke to another cold, clear day. They now had to cross the valley at a point between Telgart and Sumiac. There were German troop columns marching west down the road, one after the other. The Anglo-Americans were amazed at the number of Germans on the move. They came steadily during daylight hours. Also, patrols were combing the wooded slopes, looking for Partisans. The group decided to wait until

Fleeing Once Again

dark to cross the valley.

At daybreak, they crossed the road and then walked on the ice across the Hron. Maria and the others crawled on their bellies in the snow to cross the valley to avoid being seen. They went in pairs. As they were sneaking across the ice, Dunlevy fell though. He was quickly rescued, but it was difficult to dry out in the winter temperatures. A speeding German vehicle came by forcing them to enter the water. They all spent an uncomfortable two hours drying out later to get warm. "God was on our side," Maria wrote later.[12]

The Germans patrolled the road at night. They spent the night in another hunting shack near the top of a mountain. The forester was uneasy about their being there, and feared that the Germans would discover them and he would be shot. His fears were well-grounded. Some German soldiers were staying in a house nearby. Maria could hear heavy machine gun fire in the valley below to the east.[13]

On January 4, they arose early and struck out for Rejdova, nine miles from Telgart and about 25 miles east of Polomka. They arrived around 4 PM in a mountainous region. Because of the deep snow, they were lost much of the time. Their route to Rejdova took them through the Hlboke Valley.

In Rejdova, the people surprised them by feeding them immediately after they arrived. They brought each a glass of wine and refused any kind of payment. Germans were going and coming, irregularly and steadily.[14]

January 5, Rumors of Typhus.

The next day they met with the local notary who typically, in a small village, acted with the powers of a mayor. He was anti-German. Maria was eager to cross the front lines, but he advised them not to. There was considerable machine gun fire in a valley nearby which meant there was fighting going on.[15]

Because there was a rumor of typhus in Rejdova, there were few

Germans around. Nevertheless, Maria was continually overwhelmed by the generosity of the people in Rejdova. One of the woman heated water for her so she could wash up.

They learned that the front was only 20 miles away. Steve Catlos, who spoke Hungarian, decided to remain in the village with the Jan Kusera family. Kusera was surprised that one of the Americans spoke Hungarian, although Lt. Zenopian also spoke Hungarian. Catlos explained to Dunlevy that someone had to survive the ordeal so that the DAWES story could be told after the war. Maria, Dunlevy, and Bill Davies didn't buy that story and were mildly disgusted. They were convinced it was safer to keep moving.[16]

One of the Partisans decided to walk to the Russian front, but the others, including Sasha, who was Lt. Voknuk's aide, opted to remain in the village.[17] The notary, noticing that Maria was educated and multilingual offered her a job. She refused. She had Tibor's diary and decided to leave it with the notary with instructions to give it to the American authorities after the war.[18]

Maria gave up the diary reluctantly. It was her only remaining link with Tibor. She thought about him and the others constantly, but persevered in her efforts to lead the group to the Russian lines.

---

1 Maria Gulovich, Interview with William Miller, 1984.
2 Kenneth Dunlevy, Interview with William Miller, 1983.
3 Maria Gulovich, OSS Report.
4 Maria Gulovich, Interview with William Miller.
5 Ibid.
6 Kenneth Dunlevy, OSS Report.
7 Stefan Zenopian, Letter to Sehmer family, courtesy of James Sehmer.
8 Ibid.
9 Maria Gulovich, Interview with William Miller.
10 Ibid.
11 Kenneth Dunlevy, OSS Report.
12 Maria Gulovich, Interview with William Miller.
13 Kenneth Dunlevy, OSS Report; Maria Gulovich, Telephone interview with the author, January 2, 2000.

14 Maria Gulovich, Ibid.
15 Maria Gulovich, Interview with William Miller; Dunlevy, OSS Report.
16 Maria Gulovich, Letter to the author, October 15, 2000;
   Dunlevy did not directly criticize Catlos after the war for remaining in Rejdova.
17 Dunlevy, OSS Report.
18 Maria Gulovich, Interview with William Miller.

Chapter 28

Ludvik and Igor Nabelek

December 12, Banska Bystrica.

The *Gestapo* jail was filled with political prisoners – mostly Slovaks — when Frank Perry, Tibor Keszthelyi, Jerry Mican and the others were brought in. Among the Slovaks were two young men, Ludvik and Igor Nabelek, members of a special Slovak army unit, who had been there since November 6.

The Nabelek brothers were part of a command that joined the headquarters unit of Generals Viest and Golian in Donovaly in the Lower *Tatra* Mountains in those hectic hours during the October evacuation of Banska Bystrica. From Donovaly, they fled east through the Lower *Tatra* with the same throng of people which included the DAWES and Russian missions. Viest and Golian later opted to break off and head south across the Hron valley to seek refuge in the *Polana* Mountains.[1]

North of the village of St. Ondrej on the Hron River, the Nabelek brothers and part of their unit had been ordered by Viest to go undercover while he and Golian went into the hills to hide in a forester's hut near Bukovec. Everywhere Slovak troops were in flight, hoping to return to their home villages, find friends and relatives, and seek cover. When they reached Bukovec, the Germans unfortunately found the Nabeleks, and later in the day, during a sweep of the village, captured Viest and Golian.

The Nabeleks were identified as the sons of Dr. Ludvik Nabelek, one of the authors of the Uprising Declaration of August 29, and the nephews of three prominent, senior Slovak Army officers, Milan, Mirko, and Milos Vesel. The Nabeleks later were turned over to the *Gestapo*.

Ludvik and Igor had worked in an underground group before the Uprising began. Their father and their uncles were active in this group and were dedicated to the overthrow of the German occupation. The young Nabelek's joined the Army a few days before the revolt erupted, assigned to a special unit attached later to the general staff.[2]

The *Wehrmacht* Captured Hundreds of Prisoners.

As the *Wehrmacht* proceeded to crush the Uprising, the Germans collected prisoners by the hundreds, including many Allied agents. The AMSTERDAM team, an SOE operation, had entered Slovakia at the same time as the first DAWES team. AMSTERDAM was an A Force 199 British mission, commanded by Lt. Colonel Anthony Symonds in Cairo. The mission included several Palestinian Jews — Zwi Ben-Yaakov (cover name, Michael Janay), Rafael Reiss (Cover name, Stephen Rice), and Haviva Reik (cover name, Ada Robinson). Reik had flown in with Holt Green on September 17. Several others had parachuted into Slovakia that same night while some flew in with the OSS on October 7.

What we know about the AMSTERDAM operation comes from Chaim Chermesh (Cover name, Harry Morris), a member of the team who resides today in Israel. The team had traveled to Brezno just before Banska Bystrica fell. Chermesh, originally from Hungary, met with Holt Green and also knew Tibor and Steve Catlos, with whom he conversed in Hungarian.[3]

Ben-Yaakov was the AMSTERDAM commander. The team was tasked to find downed airmen, but they basically set about organizing local Jews in the area to fight the Germans. The lightly armed force moved into the region of Bukovec after Bystrica fell. Eight members of the team were killed in action almost immediately. A day later, Ben-Yaakov was captured with Stephen Reiss and Chaviva Reik. Chermesh, while were aiding another wounded comrade, was able to hide in the woods. Chermesh later made it to eastern Slovakia where he fought with a Partisan group until the Red Army arrived.[4]

Reiss and Reik both had suffered gun shot wounds, and Ludvik Nabelek, a medical school student, treated them in the jail. The Nabeleks, their father a physician, discovered that many of their fellow prisoners were educated and worldly. Crowded into small, dank cells and fed smelly, tasteless food, they were coping with the dread of uncertain fates. Their cells reeked from excrement from a shared corner pot in each of the crowded cells, and the lack of privacy and the interminable hunger ebbed away at their dignity.

Jaques Cransac, one of six prisoners from Captain Georges Lanurien's French Partisan group, had a booklet of poems which he shared with Igor Nabelek and others. They whiled away the hours discussing life, the war, their families, the Uprising, their homelands, and their fates, an endless battle with despair and melancholy. Fortunately, the Slovak guards generally were friendly and allowed the Nabeleks freedom to visit men in different cells when the German overseers weren't around. Citizens in the town were allowed to bring food to the prisoners.

The American prisoners were erudite and sophisticated. Jerry Mican was a university graduate, and Tibor Keszthelyi was multi-lingual and well traveled. Both were friendly, gracious men with much to share and discuss with the Nabeleks.

Ludvik Nabelek spoke daily with Ben-Yaakov who lived in Britain. His wife was expecting a child, and he spoke often of her.[5] Igor Nabelek years later recalled the somber moments in the hours before dawn when the Germans called out names for those to be taken away and shot. "Nobody knew when his name was to be read."[6]

Mid November, Banska Bystrica Jail.

Around the middle of November, Reiss and Reik were taken away with a transport of Jews and others to Kremnicka, just south of Bystrica, where they were executed. Reik, a 30-year-old native of Bystrica, had immigrated to Palestine in 1939. When the British organized the AMSTERDAM mission, she volunteered. Ben-Yaakov, whom the Germans did not realize was a Jew, felt guilty because Reik and Reiss were his close friends. The French prisoners were taken away in the first week of January, 1945, and attempting to resist five of them were shot trying to escape.[7]

Frank Perry, who had been captured at Dolna Lehota, arrived at the jail near the end of November. Perry told Ludvik Nabelek he was a crewmember of a B-24 which had been shot down near Ruzomberok while on a reconnaissance mission. This was the usual cover story that OSS prisoners used.

Circa December 12-13, Banska Bystrica Jail.

The Nabeleks recalled the arrival of Tibor Keszthelyi and Jerry Mican. Ludvik remembered Mican only by his first name. Tibor told Nabelek the circumstances of their capture on the foggy, dark morning of December 12, although they were not to get in touch with either Perry or Ben-Yaakov in jail, Nabelek arranged for them to get together without the jailers knowing about it.

Igor Nabelek today remembers Keszthelyi and Mican vividly. They talked long into the night about their life experiences before and during the Uprising. Igor recalls that the Americans were always relaxed and pleasant, but frustrated that the Gemans kept them locked up. They were convinced because they were still in their Army uniforms that they should, and eventually would be, treated simply as prisoners of war.[8]

The Nabeleks celebrated the holidays with the prisoners. "It was not a happy Christmas, but we tried to make it as pleasant as possible," Nabelek recorded. Friends and relatives brought the Nabeleks gifts, and some Slovaks even brought gifts for the other prisoners.[9]

December 26, Joe Morton Arrives.

Joe Morton was brought to the jail the same day the main group had been captured. He told the Nabeleks the details of their capture. The other members of the DAWES team were kept at a school house where they were interrogated by the *Gestapo*. They were brought to the jail over the next two days singularly or in small groups. The Nabeleks recalled both Holt Green and Jim Gaul suffering from gunshot arm wounds. Igor recalls that Green and the others were suspicious of the Germans because they treated them so kindly, offering them alcohol and other courtesies.[10]

Ben-Yaakov was surprised to discover Major Sehmer was among the prisoners. He was nervous about Sehmer being there, fearing the *Gestapo* would learn they were on the same mission and their stories "didn't jibe."[11]

December 29, American Prisoners Sent to Bratislava.

At noon without notice, the Anglo-Americans were shipped out and sent to Bratislava.[12] At his *Einsatzkommando Grupp H* headquarters, Colonel Josef Witiska, interrogated them there at length. Witiska forwarded a series of interrogation reports to the *Reichssicherheitsdienst* headquarters in Berlin, prompting Heinrich Himmler's men to move the prisoners to Mauthausen concentration camp at Linz Austria, 100 miles to the west.[13]

In Banska Bystrica, the Nabeleks had believed their American friends had been transferred to a prisoner of war camp and did not learn of their actual fate until later. During the few days they were together, the Nabeleks formed strong bonds with the Anglo-American group, bearing "the consequences of defeat," as Ludvik put it.[14]

Because of an act of sabotage in Banska Bystrica, Germans took ten prisoners and announced they would be shot in the main city square. The two Nabeleks were among the hostages, but the lives of all ten were saved through the intervention of the Catholic Bishop of Banska Bystrica and another prominent citizen. Their plea for mercy was accepted by the Tiso government who arranged with the German authorities to spare them.

After the German surrender, Ludvik Nabelek wrote a report for the OSS.[15] The OSS and the Associated Press sought information from all sources. The prisoners had not been shipped to a POW camp, but to the dreaded Mauthausen concentration camp near Linz, Austria.

---

1 Igor Nabelek, E mail to the author, September 6, 1999.
2 Ibid.
3 Chaim Chermesh, Letter to the author, November 25, 1997.
4 Ibid.
5 Ludvik Nabelek, OSS affidavit, NARA, RG 226, Entry 196, Box 34, Folder 75.
6 Igor Nabelek, E mail to the author, February 22, 2001.
7 Ibid.; Jacques Cransac's body was later identified at Kremnicka after the war when this book of poems was found with his remains. Igor Nabelek visited Cransac's parents in Paris after the war.
8 Ibid.
9 Ibid.
10 Ibid.
11 Ludvik Nabelek, OSS affidavit.
12 This did not include Edward Baranski or Daniel Pavletich who actually arrived at the Banska Bystrica jail on this date, apparently from Zvolen. They were shipped out of Banska Bystrica on January 4.
13 *Nazi Conspiracy and Aggression*. Volume VIII. USGPO, Washington, 1946, PP. 606-619. Affidavit of Dieter Wisliceny, January 3, 1946, Direct examination before the International Military Tribunal, Nürnberg, Germany.
14 NARA, Ludvik Nabelek, OSS report.

Chapter 29

Mauthausen

The extraordinary thing about the events at Mauthausen is that so much is known about what happened there. Because Berlin sent down special investigators to interrogate the Anglo-American prisoners, which was unusual, certain surviving members of the Mauthausen staff were able to remember them. One *SS* officer, for example, recalled the day the prisoners arrived in a truck from Bratislava, although Allied prisoners always created special interest.

The camp commandant's subsequent death-bed confession – he had been shot by American troops trying to escape – also provided some information. Additionally, two prisoners in the Mauthausen crematorium, who burned bodies daily, survived and supplied affidavits to OSS investigators. The prisoners identified photos of some of the DAWES personnel.

Also, two *SS* interpreters provided information. One had private contact with several of the American prisoners. Also, three *SS* staff officers and one sergeant who played minor roles in the interrogations and executions provided detailed confessions about their own complicity. They also implicated others. One of the *Gestapo* agents, Walter Habecker, arrested in 1947, admitted being involved in the interrogations.

Describing the Mauthausen events requires reconstructing ugly scenes of sociopath *SS* officers and *Gestapo* agents abusing helpless men. The reader might suspect that the descriptions are exaggerated, the product of a creative writer. But, the eye-witness accounts provided by Germans, countrymen of the most brutal *Nazis*, validate the facts. The *SS* killers were archetypal *Nazis* who killed, not only for the *Reich* and the *Führer*, but for pleasure.

A Few miles east of Linz, Austria, January 6, 1945.

Throughout the Nazi system, Mauthausen was known as "*Mordhausen*," ("*Murderhausen*"). Allied investigators later were convinced that the Austrian residents between Vienna and Steyr had full knowledge about the murders and genocide that occurred there. Civilians in large numbers routinely had assisted the *SS* in rounding up prisoners during mass escapes. Mauthausen actually meant "toll village," a point on the Danube where the barons of an earlier age collected tribute from the river traffic.

Mauthausen may have been the worst German concentration camp, a living hell where the killings exceeded in savagery those at Auschwitz and elsewhere. The latter camp had horrendous numbers of dead, but Mauthausen may have had a higher incidence of brutal behavior by the *SS* staff who were not content to kill, but to kill brutally.

Ernst Kaltenbrunner, head of the *Reichsicherheitsdienst* in Berlin, visited Mauthausen three times and Heinrich Himmler, head of the *SS*, twice. On one visit, Kaltenbrunner witnessed the execution of several prisoners, and then strolled through the gas chamber laughing, one *SS* officer recalled.[1]

Standartenführer (Colonel) Franz Ziereis and his deputy, *Hauptsturmführer* (Lt. Colonel) Georg Bachmayer, commanded *Konzentrationlager Mauthausen (KLM)*. These two *Totenkopf SS* officers' domain was a sprawling prison, a dull grey complex constructed with stone materials from the quarries on site.

According to *Obersturmführer* (Lieutenant) Hans Altfuldisch, Ziereis was influenced by the Nazi *Gauleiter* August Eigruber, the senior Nazi official in the western part of Austria. Eigruber, who visited the camp 26 times, was arrested after the war, tried, and executed by the U.S. Army in 1947.[2]

While the casual observer might have thought *KLM* was a simple factory or construction site, the emaciated prisoners working around the complex betrayed the its awful nature. Lt. Jack Taylor, USNR, a captured OSS agent who arrived there on April 1, 1945, described the prisoners as "half-dead creatures in filthy, ragged stripes and wooden shoes."[3] He soon became one of them, although he miraculously survived the last seven weeks of the war.

Mauthausen was designated as a "work camp" where inmates were literally worked to death. Although not a mass extermination camp like Auschwitz or Treblinka, *KLM* was a "category three" camp, the most severe of the Nazi concentration *KZ* Lagers. Hundreds of armed *SS* guards patrolled the camp which was surrounded by electrified fences. Prisoners sent to Mauthausen were designated *Rückkehr unerwünscht*—Return not desired. Over 150,000 prisoners had been executed there by the end of the war.[4]

Although Commandant Franz Ziereis always was immaculately dressed, carefully groomed, and reputedly a "good family man," he took pleasure in mistreating prisoners. He regularly called meetings of his staff to review new methods of torture and brutality.[5]

A 43-year-old native of Bavaria, Ziereis enjoyed shooting prisoners in the prison yard for amusement. Once he allowed his 12-year-old son to do the same. At Mauthausen, killing was sport. His wife once visited the camp to witness the gassing of prisoners in the crematorium.[6] Small windows on the door allowed persons to watch the writhing of victims in their death throes.

In April, 1945, at an all-night drinking party involving Eigruber, *Obersturmführers* (Lieutenants) Karl Schulz and Martin Roth, and others, Ziereis in a drunken rage personally shot ten prisoners at 4 AM. An officer who had suggested that they postpone the executions until morning was threatened by Ziereis at gunpoint. Two of the victims were British SOE agents. Eigruber confessed later that the story was true.[7]

Jack Taylor wrote an account of some of the sadistic practices of the

Totenkopf ("Death's Head" –note the symbol on the hats of the *SS* personnel in the photos.) *SS* staff at Mauthausen. After his liberation, Taylor opted to remain at Mauthausen to collect evidence for the subsequent war crimes trial of the *KLM* staff.[8]

One incident among many reveals the brutality of the *SS*. In late April, 1945, a 15th Air Force B-24 was shot down only a few miles from the camp. Georg Bachmayer rode out on his horse to direct the capture of the unfortunate Americans. He ordered two of the men tied to a vehicle, forcing them to run behind. Bachmayer rode his horse behind them, lashing them with his whip. A short time later, Taylor witnessed Bachmayer and another *SS* man inside the camp savagely beating the men and four others.

Brutish-looking, as photos attest, Georg Bachmayer was a hard-drinking, carousing individual. He reportedly organized wild sex orgies with female prisoners for himself and other *SS* officers.[9] Mauthausen had a brothel for prisoners, and a separate one for the *SS* enlistedmen. The officers had their "kept" girl friends, pretty young women, pathetic, and degraded female prisoners trying to survive.[10]

Bachmayer also liked to sic his German shepherd dogs on prisoners. Men suffered horribly when the dogs attacked them, often leaving them to bleed to death. Bachmayer's favorite dog, "Lord," was particularly vicious. A common practice involved hanging prisoners 18 inches off the ground and allowing the dogs to rip at their feet and legs. The *SS* guards frequently stood around laughing.[11]

When the American Army War Crimes prosecutor, Colonel William Denson, tried the *SS* staff after the war, he summarized the long list of crimes against the Mauthausen defendants. He stated there was no concentration camp in Germany where conditions were more terrible than at Mauthausen. During winter months, for example, guards often would spray water on naked, unfortunate souls and leave them covered with a sheet of ice as their lives ebbed away.[12]

Lt. Holt Green, Major John Sehmer, and the other Anglo-American prisoners arriving from Bratislava could have had little idea of what they were about to endure, unaware their handlers were among the most vicious German *Reichsicherheitsdienst SS* personnel in Germany.

Mauthausen was run by men who had been criminals and thugs before the war. By contrast, the DAWES and WINDPROOF Americans, Englishmen, and Palestinian Jews, products of the academic and business worlds, were representatives of another world. The Anglo-Americans, the two Jews, and Daniel Pavletich, the Croatian; were introduced to a world of unimagined hell. Nor was Margit Kockova from the WINDPROOF team spared.

Based on the preliminary interrogations of the DAWES-WIND-PROOF personnel in Bratislava by *SS* Colonel Josef Witiska, Ernst Kaltenbrunner selected a veteran team of interrogators in Berlin to travel to Mauthausen to question the prisoners.

Sturmbannführer (Major) Dr. Manfred Schoenenseiffen, a graduate of the University of Bonn, also with a reputation for cruelty, was selected to head the team. Despite his sadistic nature, Schoenenseiffen had, according to one account, a calm, professional appearance. Although only 33 years old, he had worked for the *Gestapo* since 1938. He was the director of *AMT IV B-1-b* in charge of counterintelligence affairs in Holland, Great Britain, and the United States.[13]

Kriminal-Kommissar Walter Habecker was personally selected by *Gestapo* chief Heinrich Müller to be part of the interrogation team. [14] Habecker, 16 years a Berlin detective before he joined the *Gestapo* in 1935. He had an interesting background. Habecker was detailed in 1938 to work on Spanish Civil War matters, and in 1941 actually was sent by the *Gestapo* to Spain to bring back 82 Germans who fought with the Loyalists and were taken prisoner by the Franco regime. After their return to Germany, the prisoners were interned in a camp at Brauweiler near Cologne.[15]

Noted in the *Gestapo* as a torture specialist, Habecker had been a key interrogator of the *Rote Kapelle* (Red Orchestra). This espionage group was apprehended by the *Gestapo* in 1942 and 1943 consisted of some Germans guided by anti-fascist idealism and others by Marxist-Leninist ideology. They had penetrated the German army high command and did immeasurable damage to the German war effort on the Russian front. Most of the accused were "broken" through severe questioning with Habecker playing a major role in the case.

Outraged by the audacity of the "Red Orchestra," Hitler decreed that when the *Gestapo* was finished with them, the prisoners would be executed by being hung on meat hooks by short ropes causing death by strangulation. Others, including several women, were guillotined.[16] Over 100 *Rote Kapelle* prisoners eventually were executed.[17]

Habecker later was one of the lead interrogators of *Wehrmacht* officers and others involved in the bomb-plot conspiracy to kill Adolf Hitler on July 20, 1944. In all likelihood, Habecker questioned Admiral Canaris, head of the *Abwehr*, Pastor Dietrich Bonhöffer, and also Field Marshall Erwin von Witzleben.[18]

Habecker liked to stalk around the prisoners with his hands in his pockets and a cigar in his mouth while he questioned and harangued his victims. His closely-cropped, gray hair and his Hitler-style narrow mustache gave him a brutal appearance, no less so than Georg Bachmayer's.[19]

Heinrich Arndt also was part of the team. He was an *Untersturmführer* (Second Lieutenant) and *Kriminaloberstsekretär*, 43 years old, six feet tall, and a member of Schoeneseiffen's *AMT IV* department.

The Berlin *SS* and *Gestapo* agents took the overnight train from the Anhalter Station to Linz on January 5. To avoid Allied air attacks, most German trains traveled at night. Werner Müller, 33 years old and born in Halle, Germany, was selected to accompany the *SS* men. He wore glasses and had a youthful appearance, and twice had worked in Great Britain before the war. His ability to speak French and Italian, plus excellent English, enabled him previously to work as a receptionist in German hotels.

Another interpreter, Dr. Hans Wilhelm Thost, 55 years old, *AMT VI*, the *RSHA* department handling foreign intelligence, spoke English well and was brought along as a second interpreter. Thost and Müller later would give extensive testimony to the OSS and War Crimes Commission investigators.

Müller, had been assigned to *AMT IV* in Berlin where he worked for Schoeneseiffen. He previously had served in the *Wehrmacht*, but had been discharged because of poor health. He later worked as a civilian for the army and saw service in Paris in the censorship office. In the summer of 1944, he was sent to Berlin to work in the *Abwehr-Leitstelle*, and later was sent back in October to work for the *RHSA* when Heinrich Himmler took over the censorship office.[20]

Enroute to Mauthausen, Müller had learned the interrogations of the Anglo-Americans had been ordered from the *Führer*'s office and were of the highest importance. He had never met the other *SS* men before, and never saw them afterwards.[21]

The Berlin group arrived in the morning of January 6, and the interrogations started the next day. Schoenenseiffen and Habecker, assisted by Dr. Thost, began with the British prisoners.

Jack Wilson was the first. Habecker promptly "hanged" him, suspending him with ropes tied around his wrists. Thost recalled Wilson screaming in pain, stopping only to gasp for breaths.

The "hanging was an apparatus with ropes with two slip knots." Habecker added to Wilson's misery by striking him repeatedly with a whip. Wilson was left suspended for several minutes, finally confessing he was a Jew from Vienna who had immigrated to Scotland and had changed his name from Wanndorfer. He described how his mission was to drop by parachute near Vienna, but he had missed his drop zone and landed in Slovakia 40 miles east.[22] *Obersturmführer* Hans Altfuldisch, who witnessed the interrogation, described to OSS investigators the same details as those reported by Thost. Werner Müller also verified the details.[23]

We don't know if Jack Wilson implicated Keith Hensen, who at that moment was working in the mess hall at *Dulag Luft* north of Frankfurt.

Thost recalled that Wilson spoke German with a Viennese accent. When Thost claimed he told Habecker he disapproved of the torture, Habecker dismissed Thost, saying "the Jew spoke German very well."[24]

Major Sehmer was brought in next. At first the interrogation was conducted calmly. Then, *Kommandant* Ziereis entered the room and asked for an account of the hanging of Wilson. "He showed visible pleasure at this story, and ordered a veritable gallows" installed immediately in the next room where Habecker had "worked on" Wilson.[25]

Ziereis took off Sehmer's glasses and struck him in the face. During the interrogations, the commandant continually shouted, "Hang him, hang him." Ziereis was livid with hate. The SS officers bound Sehmer's hands behind his back and hanged him for 20 minutes. "The spectacle" [of the torture of the prisoners] delighted Ziereis, Thost reported.[26]

Sehmer was evasive in answering questions about the Bari SOE and OSS operations which angered Habecker. When Sehmer was let down, the German pulled out what he called "the Tibetan prayer mill," which he had brought from Berlin. It consisted of three to four sticks of wood the size and shape of pencils which he placed between Sehmer's fingers.

When Habecker squeezed the major's fingers, the pain was unbearable, causing Sehmer to cry out. Ziereis watched with glee and again struck Sehmer. The SS blandly referred to this use of torture as using "force" during questioning, while the *Gestapo* categorized it as "intensive interrogation," one of those masterful Nazi understatements. "Until now," Thost said later, "I had considered stories about the *Gestapo* to be enemy propaganda lies,"[27]

While this was going on, Heinrich Arndt and *Sturmbannführer* Manfred Schoeneseiffen interrogated Holt Green in the next room. Werner Müller assisted. Arndt beat Green with a leather-covered stick which amused Schoenenseifen. When he saw the bruises on Green's forehead, Schoenenseiffen called them, "The aureole (halo) of Jesus." Schoeneseiffen liked to make fun of the prisoners when they were being tortured. At first, Green told questioners he was the only OSS officer in the group and the other Americans were downed airmen. This attempt to shield his men resulted in his beatings.[28]

Habecker entered the room and took over the questioning. He threatened Green with his own leather-covered whip and then began hitting him. Müller pressed Green to tell the truth to avoid the punishment. Müller told Green that Wilson (It could have been Sehmer.) already had told his interrogators about the OSS operation. Green refused, and Habecker continued to beat him across the shoulders and on the neck.

Kommandant Ziereis came in and asked if this was the prisoner who signed a statement under protest in Bratislava, as reported by *SS* Colonel Josef Witiska. "Now we can show him what we can do to him," Ziereis shouted. "We'll hang him too." He ordered Green to take off his jacket and remove the insignia of the U.S. Navy and his lieutenant's bars from the jacket.

"We'll degrade him," Ziereis said. He handed the jacket back to Green and told him to put it on, but Green couldn't because of the cast on his left arm.

Müller stepped forward to help the American officer, but Ziereis stopped him. "What do you want to do?" he snarled.

Müller replied he simply wanted to help the American because his arm was in a cast.

"Are you married?" Ziereis asked. The interpreter said he was not.

"Of course not" Ziereis replied, "otherwise you would know how to treat these people who are killing our women and children." He was referring to the Allied bombing of German cities.

Wilson was brought in to confront Green who immediately admitted he had been lying.[29]

That night at dinner, Hans Thost informed Ziereis, whom he knew had never been to the front, that although he, Thost, had been in combat, he was unable to strike a defenseless prisoner. Ziereis replied, "An enemy was an enemy."

Habecker, who was listening, told Thost, "A cure at Mauthausen would do you [Thost] good." Thost claimed he replied that "God alone, and not [Habecker], would decide." Before they left Mauthausen, Thost and Müller privately discussed the torture and the brutality used in the interrogations. Müller confessed to Thost that watching the torture made him physically ill.[30]

According to Thost, most of the members of the DAWES and WINDPROOF teams were beaten, struck, and hanged by the wrists. Some were also tortured with the "Tibetan prayer mill." Thost reported that the *Gestapo* agents administered torture "in cold blood," and not in anger. All of this was witnessed by *Obersturmführer* Hans Altfuldisch and *Obersharführer* Josef Niedermayer, as they admitted later. Ziereis had ordered Niedermayer, Andreas Trumm, and Altfuldisch to be present during the interrogations.[31]

The last night, January 11, Ziereis threw a party for the interrogation team. Schoenenseifen told how he had taken all stripes and evidence of rank and decorations away from the prisoners and had informed them they would not be treated as prisoners of war, but as agents and partisans and "so would be shot."[32]

When Thost returned to Berlin, he reported to his superior, Dr. Paeffgen at *RSHA* headquarters. Thost complained about the brutality of Ziereis and the others, and that it seemed to him the DAWES personnel should have been sent to a prisoner of war camp.

Paeffgen cautioned him. "We can't do anything about it," he said, "and risk being interned ourselves in a camp. Try to forget the matter. For God's sake, don't speak of it to anyone, otherwise, neither Schellenberg (the director of *AMT VI*) nor [I] will be able to save you."[33]

After the war, American intelligence personnel deliberated over whom and what to believe. Americans joked cynically about Germans who claimed they were only obeying their superiors, and that they had no choice.

Surely, there were good and decent Germans who had been caught up in the war, and the innocent could not safely buck the police-state system.

Individuals with special talents, like Thost and Müller, frequently were drawn into intelligence work, a dirty business conducted by all armies. Even the OSS and other Allied military personnel frequently found themselves in a "take-no-prisoners" situation. The Russians brutalized captured *Wehrmacht* prisoners and German civilians, but American OSS and British SOE personnel never engaged in brutality remotely on the scale of the *Gestapo*, the *SS*, and SD.

---

1 NARA, RG 338, Joseph Niedermayer affidavit, Cases Tried 1945-49-000-50-5-26, Box 349.
2 NARA, RG 338, Hans Altfuldisch affidavit, Cases Tried 1945-49, 000-50-5-26, Boxes 344 and 349.
3 NARA, Jack Taylor Report, War Crimes Trials records, (USAREUR) War Crimes Branch, War Crimes Case Trial 1945-49, 000-50-5-26 through 000-50-5-26, Box 413.
4 NARA, Hans Altfuldisch affidavit.
5 Ibid.
6 One account later reported that Ziereis' son had committed suicide.
7 NARA, Josef Niedermayer affidavit.
8 Ibid.
9 Ibid.
10 Ibid.
11 Ibid.
12 Bard, Mitchell E., Forgotten Victims. (Boulder: Westview Press, 1994), p. 116.
13 NARA, Werner Müller affidavit, RG 153, Entry 8-9, Box 116; Schoeneseiffen was awarded his PhD in 1938. His doctoral dissertation was entitled, "Criminal Justice in Cologne in the 18th Century."
14 NARA, Report by Lawrence Houston, OSS General Counsel, RG 153, Entry 143, Box 116. Müller, one of the most notorious of the high ranking *Nazis*, never was found after the war.
15 *Bundesarchiv*, Germany, Z42 IV 1466, "*Der Offentliche Anklaeger bei dem Spruchgericht, 4a Sp.Js. 548/47*," Courtesy of Anton Seul, *Koblenz Bundesarchiv*.
16 Victims guillotined were executed while lying on their backs to add to their terror.
17 Johannes Tuchel, *Die Gestapo-Sonderkommission "Rote Kapelle*," from *Die Rote Kapelle im Widerstand gegen den Nationalsozialismus/hrsg.* By Hans Coppi, Jürgen Danyel, Johannes Tuchel. (Berlin: Hentrich Publishers, 1994), pp. 148-149.
18 Schlabrendorff, Fabian von, *The Secret War Against Hitler* (Pitman Publishing Corporation), 1965), pp. 303-316. Schlabrendorff survived the war to testify at Walter Habecker's war crimes trial in 1948.
19 NARA, Werner Müller affidavit.
20 There were six departments of the *RSHA*. *Amt I* was administration; *Amt II* was equipment and finance; *Amt III* was the Sicherheitsdienst and SIPO (Security Service and Security Police) and *AMT V* was the Kriminalpolizei (Criminal Police). Ernst Kaltenbrunner was in charge of the whole operation.
21 NARA, SAINT to Chief OSS, Caserta, NARA, RG 141 A, Box 12, Folder 89.
22 NARA, RG 153, Dr. Hans Thost affidavit, Entry 8-9, Box 116.
23 NARA, Hans Altfuldisch affidavit.
24 Ibid.
25 Ibid.

26 Ibid.
27 Ibid.
28 NARA, Werner Müller affidavit.
29 Ibid. German interrogators frequently used the excuse of the Allied bombings of German cities to justify abuse and torture of Allied prisoners.
30 NARA, Thost affidavit.
31 NARA, Hans Altfuldisch affidavit.
32 NARA, Thost affidavit.
33 Ibid.

1. *SS Obersturmführer* (Captain) Hans Altfuldisch, Mauthausen staff, tried and executed by the U.S. Army, 1947. He witnessed and later described to OSS interrogators the torture and execution of the DAWES personnel. (courtesy, *Bundesarchiv Berlin*). 2. *SS Obersturmführer* Martin Roth, commander of the Mauthausen crematorium. Roth evaded authorities after the war, but was tried and sentenced to seven years imprisonment in a German court in 1970. (*Bundesarchiv Berlin*). 3. and 4. Brothers Igor and Ludvik Nabelek were Slovak soldiers captured in November, 1944. They subsequently met the DAWES, AMSTERDAM, and WINDPROOF prisoners in the Banska Bystrica jail. (courtesy of Igor Nabelek and Mira Nabelekova). 5. Letter from Jerry Mican's widow written the day after he probably was executed. She had no idea her husband was a POW. OSS officials routinely gave little information to family members. (NARA document).

> 330 Lionel Rd
> Riverside, Ill
> Jan. 24, 1945
>
> Dear Mr. Jakes,
>
> Thanks for your letter of Dec. 26th, but somehow in spite of your assurances I am getting more worried and nervous than ever. — I do not know what Jerry's work is, but after reading an article about 18 men being apprehended in Cal. — I am imagining and worrying.
>
> Is there any possibility of getting a direct message from Jerry to me?
>
> Please, let me hear some more if you can.
>
> Sincerely yours
> Mary R. Mican

1. *Obersturmführer* Georg Bachmayer was the brutal deputy camp commander of Mauthausen concentration camp who shot individually most of the DAWES team members. Bachmayer shot his family and himself after the German surrender. (courtesy, *Bundesarchiv Berlin*)

2. Maria Gulovich, in Heidelberg, Germany, 1945. After the war, Maria was put on the OSS payroll and given uniform status. She worked in Salzburg, Heidelberg, and Wiesbaden before being brought to the United States. (courtesy of Maria Gulovich Liu).

3. Associated Press correspondent Joe Morton received OSS permission to accompany the DAWES mission in 1944 from Bari, Italy. While the OSS later denied it gave him that permission, the author found a copy of a radio transmission in the National Archives in 1999 which notified the OSS commander in Slovakia that Morton would arrive there on the next flight. Morton told his colleagues he was after the "biggest story of his life." Later, he fled into the mountains with the DAWES team, and was captured by the Germans and subsequently executed at Mauthausen. (courtesy, Associated Press).

1. Maria Gulovich and Cadet Roy Brunhart and three other men await the award presentations on the Plain of West Point, May 25, 1946. Maria and Brunhart both received Bronze Stars, although Maria originally was to receive the Distinguished Service Cross. Later, the award was downgraded to a Silver Star and still later to the Bronze Star. She was the first woman ever decorated at West Point. (courtesy of Colonel Roy Brunhart, USAF, retired, U.S. Army Signal Corps photo). **2.** Cecilia Wojewoda and her husband fled Budapest, Hungary, in 1944 when the Germans seized control of the country. A journalist, Wojewoda met and become close friends with Joe Morton, Holt Green, and Jim Gaul in Banska Bystrica.

Cecilia Wojewoda

1. The Plain at West Point, May 25, 1946. After the presentation of awards, the Corps of West Point cadets passed in review. Left to right, Major General William Donovan (in civilian clothes), former head of the OSS; Lt. General Maxwell Taylor, Superintendent of West Point, three unidentified men, Cadet Roy Brunhart, and Maria Gulovich. (courtesy of Roy Brunhart, Army Signal Corps photo). **2.** Lt. Holt Green before World War 11. Green was a wealthy textile manufacturer in Charleston, South Carolina, technically unfit physically for military service when the war started. (courtesy of Frances Hutson). **3.** A graduate of the University of Illinois and a former high school star athlete, Captain Edward Baranski was a highly intelligent and audacious OSS officer. (NARA photo).

1. Steve Catlos, Ken Lain, Bill McGregor and Jan Schwartz, DAWES survivors, were guests of The Czechoslovakian government in August, 1964. Here President Zbirka decorates Catlos. Premier Nikita Khrushchev was the principal speaker at a huge rally in Banska Bystrica on the same day, but the crowd gave Bill McGregor the greatest ovation when he spoke. Khrushchev left in a huff. (courtesy of the SNU museum). **2.** Maria Gulovich, now living in California, 1952. (courtesy of the Cleveland Press and the Cleveland Public Library).

Maria Gulovich
1952

1. Maria Gulovich Liu and United States Secretary of State Madeleine Albright chat during the 50th anniversary celebration of the Slovak National Uprising in Polomka, Slovakia, on August 29, 1994. Veterans of the Uprising were invited to the celebration which also was attended by Albright and Secretary of the Army Togo Smith. **2.** Maria talks with General Studenko, left, who came from Moscow for the celebration. Maria had worked for Studenko (a cover name) in Banska Bystrica in 1944 until the Germans overran the city, forcing the Soviets, the OSS, the downed American airmen, and thousands of Slovaks to flee into the Tatra Mountains. When they were on the run from the Germans, Studenko advised Maria to put on peasant clothes and go into a small village to hide and await the end of the war. Maria chose instead to remain with the American OSS team. (courtesy, Maria Gulovich Liu).

August 1994
Polomka, Slovakia

Chapter 30

Into Russian Hands

January 6, 1945, Rejdova, Slovakia.

Maria and the group left at 3 AM for the Russian front. Just before sunrise, they narrowly avoided a group of German soldiers who were setting up a defensive position. Steve Catlos had decided to stay with the Hungarian family, convincing Dunlevy that one of them had to get back to Italy, and the odds were better, he argued, if they split up.

The group left with a guide who was nervous, knowing he was a dead man if they were captured by the Germans. They moved cautiously, carefully considering every fork on the dirt trails, and watching for footprints in the snow. They scouted ahead as much as possible, walking in silence, their minds still on their comrades who were now prisoners of the Germans.[1]

They arrived at Petramanovce village around noon. German troops were on all the roads, and *Wehrmacht* vehicles often appeared without warning. The young guide lost his nerve totally, and returned to his village. Before he left, he told them to wait outside the village. He gave Maria the name of a farmer who would find them a place to hide.

Maria entered the village after dark, but the reception was cool. German soldiers had been in the village. They regularly came to the villagers to get for food and fodder for their horses. Everyone in the village was terrified, Maria learned, because the Germans were desperate and unpredictable. The farmer agreed to allow them to stay in his barn, but for one night only.

The next day he suggested they move to an abandoned mine nearby. As they prepared to leave, three truck loads of German troops arrived in the village. Several Germans were on motorcycles. The men wore dirty, dusty uniforms and grim expressions. The farmer, although in a state of panic, struggled to maintain his composure.

By the time the soldiers reached their house, Maria and the others were in the barn, hiding under a haystack. The Germans made a cursory search and left. Everyone relaxed, but these surprise visits carried the potential for deadly confrontations.[2]

Maria, who later was helping prepare a meal in the farmhouse, discovered she couldn't walk. She had injured her knee earlier in a fall. When it came time to move to the mine, Mari still was unable to walk. Stefan Zenopian was upset and cursed at her, shouting that she was jeopardizing the group. Davies blew up at the lieutenant and threatened him physically. Zenopian cooled down when he realized the extent of her injury. But it was another incident which added to Zenopian's loss of respect by the others.[3]

Zenopian was a problem case. At the request of Major Walter Ross (now a Lt. Colonel), Dunlevy later evaluated the British lieutenant for the OSS. Dunlevy explained how grateful the group had been at the Polomka hut for Zenopian's efforts in getting food from nearby villages. But Dunlevy also said Zenopian was physically weak, and often couldn't carry his share of the load. He continually held up the group while walking, commenting, "I wasn't made for walking."[4]

Dunlevy found Zenopian "a difficult person," impossible to reason with. Dunlevy recorded how angry he and the others were about the way Zenopian treated Maria. Dunlevy also found him excessively rank conscious.[5]

Furthermore, Zenopian's later assertions that he led the group through German lines was sharply contradicted by Dunlevy. The American said the credit for this belonged solely to Maria, "our little sweetheart . . . for whom I am and will be grateful forever. To her, it is no doubt that I owe my safety

Into Russian Hands

and perhaps my life."[6]

Bill Davies finally carried Maria on his back to the cave. It turned out to be an old, abandoned mine that had not been worked for 70 years, 50 yards deep but only about four feet wide and four feet high. They arrived at 1 AM. The mine was pitch dark and cold. Water dripped onto the floor continuously. They would spend six days and nights there.

January 6-11, In The *Petramanovce* Mine.

In the first few days, their guide scouted out the front lines and concluded because of the sparsely wooded terrain, it would be too dangerous to attempt to cross the lines. He brought food from the village, bacon, bread, and marmalade. They paid for it in gold. One brought a bottle of rum for the men. Because of the echoes, they only whispered because the sound carried out of the mine. Although they were freezing, they couldn't build a fire because of the lack of air. They lighted a candle only when they ate.[7]

Time passed slowly. They drew weary of talking about food, the smoke, the stench, their ordeal, the cramped space, and what they had been through. Fitful sleep left them edgy. They speculated about the men now in the hands of the Germans – Bill McGregor, the airmen, Frank Perry, Tibor Keszthelyi, Holt Green, Jim Gaul, Major Sehmer, and the others.[8]

The International Red Cross had by this time notified the families those airmen – George Fernandes, Bob Hede, Jack Shafer, and the others – captured in the first part of November that their men were now in German POW camps. The Germans still suspected Bill McGregor and Ken Lain of being OSS agents, and the Americans were being interrogated in a special *SS* facility north of Frankfurt, Germany.

Meanwhile, Maria continued to go out foraging for food. On one occasion, she was picked up by a German truck load of troops, pulling a large artillery gun. Her fluent German allowed her to talk causally with the Germans who stopped to let her off the truck when they reached the village.[9]

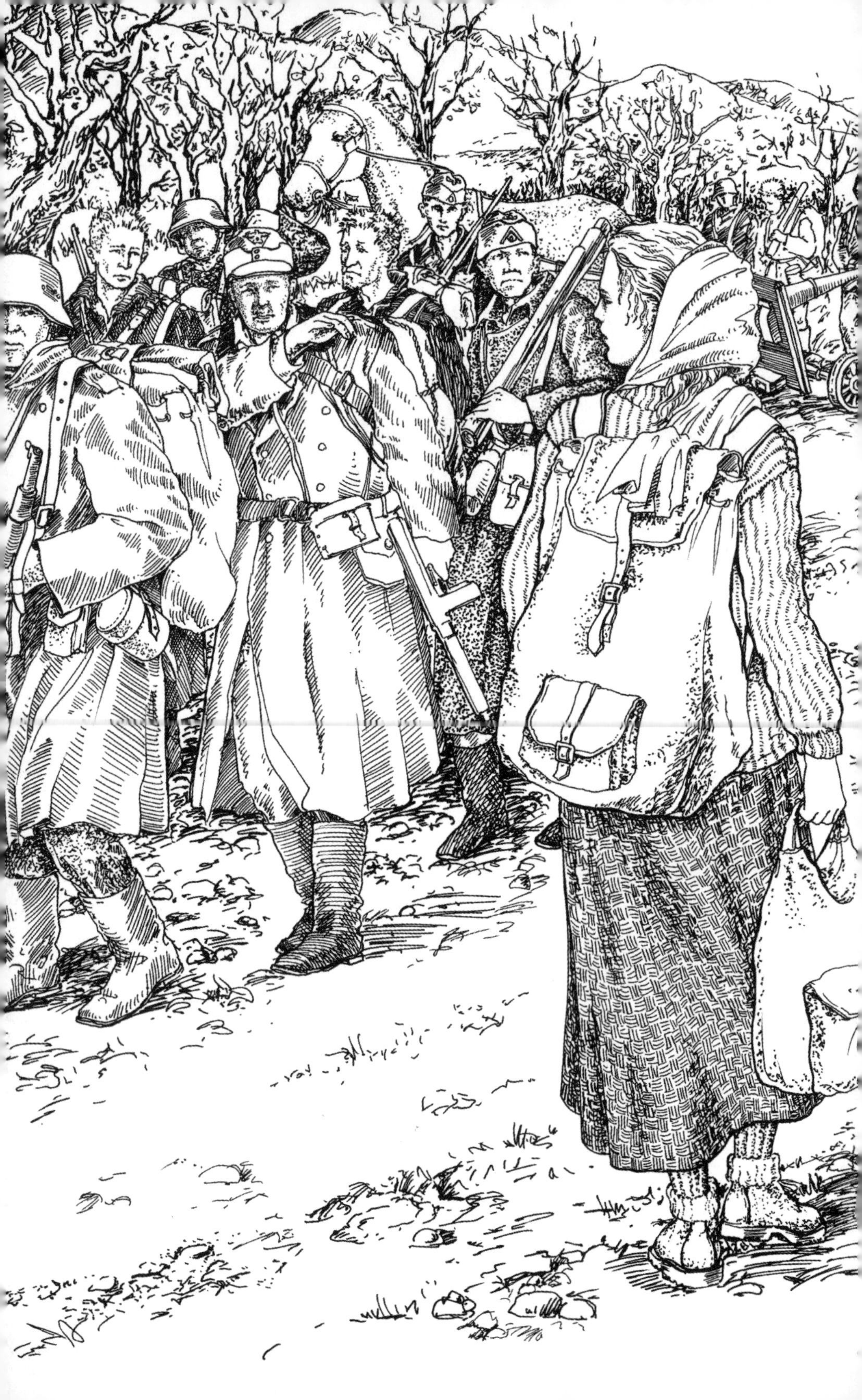

"Look, there's a Partisan"

January 12, Maria Encounters the Germans.

When Maria was able to walk again, she secured some peasant's clothes from one of their helpers in the village, an older man, who happened to be a member of the local Communist Party. Maria walked six miles to the village of Roznavske Bystre with the Communist to find a better place to stay. It was only four miles from the front. They encountered several German patrols who generally ignored the older man and the peasant girl.

On the return to Petramanovce, they passed a German column marching west. One cried, "Look there's a Partisan." The whole column stopped and looked around.

Maria retorted, "Yeah, just like you. If you think so, you're my comrade." The men noted her Viennese-accented German, laughed, and went on their way.

In Bystre, Maria learned of a larger mine where many people were hiding. The next day they moved, and were now closer to the front lines. They could hear the shelling.

The scene in the mine was surreal, a huge cavernous cave like a large tenement house with different levels and seemingly endless tunnels. About 50 persons were hiding there, Partisans, deserters, old men and children, Communists, and other politically endangered people. Fires were going all through the large cave, some being used for cooking, some for heat, and others simply as a focus for a social circle. The air was acrid, and the stench of human waste lingered everywhere. Her new guide, another Communist, knew the mine like his own home. Inside, they had to use a ladder to get to the third level. The men above would lower the ladder after the person below tapped out a special code on a metal pipe. Everyone used carbide lamps.

Maria and the others soon became infected with lice, and their bites had become infected. Their constant discomfort seemed to go on forever. Sleeping was difficult. Among the inhabitants were four Hungarian deserters, sleeping on boards to stay off the wet dirt and the straw. Maria conversed with them. They were desperate to stay alive, although everyone had a sense of fear about the Russians who would arrive soon, particularly the Hungarians.

The Communist's wife made soup for them in large pots which he brought to them. It would last for a few days. Maria, meanwhile, left the cave with the Communist to round up additional food. She continued to pay for the food with gold.[10]

January 17, Confronted by German Soldiers.

Maria crossed the border into Hungary where she was able to purchase from a storekeeper a large bag of bread and bacon. Several German soldiers arrived in the store and asked her, apparently out of curiosity, why she was buying so much food. The lady explained that Maria was her cousin and could not make regular trips to the store since she lived some distance away. Maria left the store and, looking in their army vehicle, saw a can of gasoline which she stole. Maria was a daring risk-taker, always fearful, always living with her nightmares, but always audacious and quick-witted.[11]

The pressure from the Russian advance was mounting. Thousands of German soldiers retreated in horse-drawn carts. They were forlorn and dispirited, but occasionally kind and sympathetic. One German in a truck stopped and gave Maria a ride into town when she was on one of her food runs.[12]

On one trip, Maria walked to the Communists' house and found it occupied by several German soldiers. One made a pass at her. She held him off, only after getting some cigars from him which she took back to Dunlevy. On another trip across the border, some Hungarians denounced her as a spy and refused to sell her food. Maria promptly told them she would denounce them as Communists if they did not sell her the food. She prevailed as always.[13]

January 23, "You're Free, You're Free!"

One of the villagers appeared at the mine and reported that the

Germans were pulling out, although they had not seen any Romanians or Russians. At 11 AM at the opening at the mine, they heard yelling. A man was shouting, "You're free. You're free. The Romanians are here and so are Russian patrols."[14]

Maria and the others – Dunlevy, Catlos, Davies, and Zenopian — were "drunk with joy." They went outside and celebrated. Tears came to their eyes, although Maria recalled later they were sobered by the fact "we knew nothing about the fate of our comrades who had been captured. We never stopped thinking of them." Nevertheless, they felt a great sense of relief. Naively, they believed the Russians would aid them in getting in touch with the American and British missions.[15]

The problem now was to find authorities who would transport them to either the American or British missions. Maria and the men walked four miles to a village where the local Red Army headquarters were located. There she had learned that the main Russian commanders in the area were located some additional distance near the Hungarian border. Failing to get help, Maria walked four miles east to the Romanian army headquarters at Roznavske Bystre to see General Dragomer. He invited the group to dinner, but informed them he had no authority to help them. He was under the control of the Russians.

January 25, Rimavska Sobota.

Later, a Russian captain later took them to Rimavska Sobota in his car. There they discovered they weren't as free as they had believed. "The party now clearly became prisoners in the hands of the Russians."[16] They arrived at 11 PM and were interrogated immediately by Soviet intelligence officers. The grilling lasted until 4 AM. They were questioned every night thereafter, and were the object of intense curiosity, visited several times at all hours of the night by people who simply came in and stared at them.[17]

January 29, Reunited with Steve Catlos.

Steve Catlos showed up suddenly. He had been liberated by the Romanians who later turned him over to the Russians who brought him to Rimavska Sobota. "They talked long into the night." He had much to relate. Catlos had stayed with the Jan Tomasik family until January 26. He had lived first in their house, later in the barn, and finally in a hay bunker in the hills west of Rejdova. The retreating Germans had been a serious threat.

Catlos became ill and was in bed one day when German *SS* troops suddenly entered the house. They inquired who he was, and Mrs. Tomasik told them he had typhus. They left the room immediately without further questions. But this incident with the Germans frightened the family. Jan Tomasik had built a small place for Catlos to hide in the barn above a pen where the family housed sheep during the winter months. Catlos moved in with the sheep.

A German army unit set up a field kitchen in the family's front yard, and Catlos was able to observe them from his hiding place. When the family fed the sheep and their lambs, they secretly brought food for their American guest. The Germans continued to exhaust the hay supply in the barn, and when Catlos' hiding place was in danger of being exposed, he moved into the hay bunker in the hills.

After the Germans retreated west, the family brought Catlos back to the house, pulling him on a sled. As they traveled on the narrow road through the Hlboke Valley, they were stopped by a Romanian army troop with several Russian soldiers. A Russian officer with the Romanians grabbed Catlos and ordered him to come with them to fight the Germans. Jan Kusera immediately went to a Romanian commander and explained who Catlos was. He was given a note which Kusera ran back to the valley and used to "rescue" Catlos. The family had Catlos' rifle and camera for many years.[18]

In Rimavska Sobota, Dunlevy reported later they were surprised at how much Lend Lease equipment they saw the Russians using, trucks, clothes, and a myriad of other items. Dunlevy actually was given a pair of patent leather U.S. Naval Officer's shoes.[19]

February 1-9, Lucenec, Hungary.

The Soviets informed them that because the front had moved west, they would relocate 50 miles to Lucenec. There, they were given rooms in a hotel, a ramshackle building with inoperable plumbing and broken glass in the windows. Some French partisans were there, plus a variety of other people. A Polish partisan girl, who was pregnant, was in the building as well as a variety of other nationalities.

Maria and the others asked to be hospitalized because the bites from the lice had become infected. Maria became so ill, the doctors feared she had malaria or TB.[20]

Everyone went into a Russian hospital. Zenopian complained about being put in a room with people of lessor rank which disgusted Dunlevy and Davies. On February 2, a Russian colonel took Zenopian to the Red Army headquarters at Heves, Hungary, south of Lucenec and east of Budapest. The Soviet officer said he would "straighten out matters."

Captain Georges de Lannurian, the commander of the French partisans in Slovakia, who had showed up at Rimavska Sobota, also was taken to Heves with Zenopian. There were persons of all nationalities there awaiting disposition. Most were scheduled to go to Odessa for repatriation under the terms of the Yalta agreement. Zenopian learned that the British were to go to Bucharest where a British Mission was located.[21]

The hospital was reminiscent of descriptions of American Civil War surgical hospitals. A constant traffic of ambulances with an endless parade of seriously wounded Russian soldiers was treated by the medical staff. Many of the wounded suffered burns, others required amputations, and some had pneumonia. Others had badly infected wounds. Doctors performed operations without anesthesia. Suffering men seemed to be screaming constantly. Dozens lay on stretchers in the hallways, moaning and crying out. Maria was horrified.[22]

They were allowed to take long baths in large tanks before Zenopian left and get their clothing steam cleaned. Their clothes shrank so severely that they had to get new Russian uniforms. Maria sewed on their patches so they could retain their national identity. Dunlevy and Catlos said they could be shot as spies if they were wearing Russian uniforms. Davies complained how silly he would look to his old British comrades. The group was amused when Zenopian's favorite pair of fur-lined gloves came through the wash so badly shrunk only a small child could have worn them. He was furious and denounced the primitive Russians as he suffered the ridicule of his comrades.[23]

February 10, Yaszkiser, Hungary.

After being released from the hospital, the Russians moved Maria and the men 100 miles to the *NKVD* (the Soviet secret police) interrogation center at Yaszkiser, east of Budapest. The entire trip took several hours and was made in a poor weather through snow and wind. Thousands of Soviets were moving west to encircle the Hungarian capital. Red Army trucks jammed roads along with horse-drawn carts, artillery pieces, and marching men. They were witnessing one of the great armies in the history of the world as the procession streamed by, hour after hour.

Once in Yaszkiser, the Russians interrogated Maria at least once every 24 hours, usually around midnight. Dunlevy and Catlos had told her exactly what to admit to and what not to say. Intelligent and crafty as ever, Maria endured the interrogations without making a single mistake, which, of course, could have been fatal. Her interrogators continually asked her if her American and British friends were spies. They wanted to know why she didn't stay in Slovakia. They had never heard of the Slovak Uprising.[24]

Meanwhile, unknown to Maria and the others, their comrades had been undergoing brutal interrogations and worse at Mauthausen concentration camp in Austria.

1. Maria Gulovich, Interview with William Miller, 1984.
2. Maria Gulovich, Telephone interview with the Author, February 15, 2001.
3. Ibid.
4. Kenneth Dunlevy, OSS Report; Maria Gulovich always suspected he had flat feet.
5. NARA, RG 226, Entry 190, Box 116, Folder 407. Stephan Zenopian, Interview by Walter Ross, March 3, 1945. In his report Zenopian used expressions such as, "I made the decision," "I had the situation well in hand," etc., when in fact they were group decisions or ones suggested by Maria Gulovich; See also, PRO Hs4/41, Walter Ross report to Lt. Colonel Chapin, Bari.
6. Ibid. These comments were prompted by a request from Ross, who originally had proposed some sort of military decoration for Zenopian, but said he wanted first to hear from Dunlevy and Catlos. He got an earful.
7. Ibid.
8. Maria Gulovich, Telephone interview with the author, February 15, 2001.
9. Ibid.
10. Ibid.
11. Ibid.
12. Ibid.
13. Ibid.
14. Ibid.
15. Ibid.
16. PRO, HS4/41. Sergeant Bill Davies report.
17. PRO, HS 4/6. Stefan Zenopian report. The Soviets said they had to wait for instructions from Moscow before they released the Anglo-American group.
18. Jan Kristiak, Letter to the author, September 16, 2000. Kristiak is Tomasik's grandson. Catlos apparently did not report all this information to his superiors when he got back to Italy, if Jan Kristiak's letter is accurate.
19. Kenneth Dunlevy, OSS Report.
20. Maria Gulovich, Interview with William Miller, 1984.
21. Ibid.
22. Maria Gulovich, Telephone interview with the author, February 15, 2001.
23. Ibid.
24. Ibid.

Chapter 31

Evil Men

Mauthausen, Sometime after January 11, 1945.

Captain Edward Baranski and Daniel Pavletich arrived after the *RHSA* interrogation team had returned to Berlin.[1] After reviewing the reports, including several from Colonel Josef Witiska from Bratislava, Ernst Kaltenbrunner sent Manfred Schoeneseiffen, Werner Müller, Walter Habecker, and Kriminaloberstsekretär Heinrich Arndt back to Mauthausen on January 23.[2]

Talking with Müller on the train, Arndt speculated that the prisoners might already have been executed or moved to another prison camp. This in fact had not occurred. Berlin's intention was to wring out of the DAWES team what intelligence they could before disposing of them.[3]

January 23.

On the first day of this second Mauthausen session, Müller and Arndt began with an interrogation of Jim Gaul. Surprisingly, the Navy lieutenant himself first directed questions to Müller (Arndt spoke no English.), informing Müller that while they were happy to see him, the prisoners were wondering about their fate.

Arndt directed Müller to tell Gaul they would know in a few days which camp they would be sent to and that they might be involved in a prisoner exchange. Gaul appeared relieved. Müller did not mention the grim alternative. During this conversation, Gaul informed Müller that Holt Green was still suffering from the beatings he had endured the previous week.

Green's neck and face were swollen, and his requests for medical aid were ignored. Müller requested one of the guards to summon a medical aide who applied ointment on Green's neck. Green also was treated with a heat lamp, and expressed his gratitude to Müller.[4]

Interrogators Continue The Torture.

Later, Green was questioned again. *Kommandant* Franz Ziereis participated in this interrogation and was especially abusive. He threatened to "hang him." Ziereis, indifferent to Green's injuries, directed that a rope be put around the American's neck. During the questioning he jerked Green toward him, demanding to know if he was going to tell any more lies. Green answered that he would not.

Obersturmführer Hans Altfuldisch, at Ziereis' suggestion, attached the rope to a hook on the wall. Altfuldisch pulled on the rope which lifted Green upward until he was forced up on his toes causing him severe pain. *Obersturmführer* Karl Schulz and *Obersharführer* Josef Niedermayer also were present.[5]

Müller, meanwhile, repeated to other members of the DAWES team what he had told Gaul. Desperate for any hint of good news, the prisoners' spirits were lifted. Müller and the men shared a relaxed conversation. They told him about the games they played in passing away the time. Müller also talked at length with Holt Green after his interrogation session. He learned that Green had objected to the sending of so many additional OSS personnel on the October 7 mission. Also, they discussed Kenneth Robert's historical novel, "Oliver Wiswell," which Müller was reading. He said he would, if allowed, loan Green the novel, a story about the American Revolution from the loyalist point of view.[6]

Müller and Arndt also interrogated Joe Morton, who also was concerned about his fate. Morton asked permission to send a telegram to the Associated Press in New York. He insisted he was a civilian and simply a reporter with nothing to do with the DAWES mission. Morton suggested that the "press was rather powerful" and this perhaps might affect the negotiations concerning the prisoners. He cited an example of a story he had written about Yugoslavia.

Arndt informed Morton through Müller he would pass on the suggestion. Sadly, Morton was both desperate and perhaps naïve. The SS had no intention of helping Morton. Certainly they had no intention of letting a member of the press go free to tell the world what was happening in a Nazi concentration camp.

Kriminal-Kommissar Walter Habecker questioned Jack Wilson a second time, beating him repeatedly. Altfuldisch, who was assisting Habecker, watched the beating.[7] Müller, shocked at the cruelty, asked Habecker to stop beating Wilson and give him time to answer the questions. Habecker erupted in anger and shouted at Müller not to interrupt him or he would beat him instead. Later, Habecker also severely beat Aba Berdichev, the Israeli prisoner.[8]

Baranski and Pavletich, meanwhile, had been interrogated at Bratislava. Upon their arrival at Mauthausen, they were identified by Lt. Lane Miller as members of the DAY team, the sub unit of the DAWES group. *Standartenfürhrer* Ziereis was present at that confrontation.[9]

Ziereis "Hangs" Edward Baranski.

Ziereis, always the brute, greeted Baranski harshly. "This one we must hang," he said. Baranski had insisted at Bratislava he was a downed airman, the usual OSS cover story when in the hands of the enemy. This angered Ziereis. "Very clever," the German said. "He deserves special treatment."

Müller had become used to the word "*Afihanga*," (Probably "*Aufhange*") the name given the process of hanging prisoners by their wrists held behind their back. It was extremely painful. Müller was told to tell

Baranski he must answer all questions truthfully, otherwise "bad things" would happen. Baranski agreed that he would.

Baranski saw the chain hanging from the beam in the ceiling and turned to Müller and said, "Oh, I know what they're going to do now." The interrogator again asked Baranski if he would answer all questions, and Baranski replied that he would. This was translated to Ziereis who laughed and repeated, "No, first he must hang."[10]

Baranski was forced to stand on the table so his wrists could be secured to the chain. Upset by this, Müller attempted to leave the room, but Ziereis ordered him to remain. He told Müller to ask Baranski again if he would answer questions truthfully. He did and Baranski agreed to do so. The SS guards in the room pulled the table out from under Baranski's legs and left him hanging. Müller, knowing Baranski was in intense pain, was astonished by his composure. Baranski physically was strong. He neither cried out nor complained. Ziereis ordered Müller to ask Baranski again if he would tell the truth. Müller answered "yes" for Baranski because he knew the answer.

This angered Ziereis who demanded that the question be put to Baranski again. The commandant, seeing that Baranski was showing no pain, erupted into a rage and shouted, "I think the fellow still enjoys himself."[11]

Habecker, standing nearby, touched Baranski's leg which spun him around slightly as he hung in the air. Ziereis then ordered one of the SS men in the back of the room to pull down on Baranski's legs. After a few moments, Baranski broke and begged to be let down. He said he would answer every question. This was not enough for Ziereis, and he ordered Baranski to be left hanging for several minutes. *Obersturmführer* Josef Niedermayer, the chief jailer at Mauthausen, later testified he witnessed this torture. His assistant, Willibald Prokasch, and Andreas Trumm, another SS sergeant, also were in the room.

At this point, Baranski, a devout Roman Catholic, began to pray. Bachmayer, Schoeneseiffen, Schulz, Altfuldisch, Niedermayer and Trumm stood watching. Ziereis asked Müller what Baranski was saying. When

Müller told them, they all broke into laughter. Müller was overcome. His eyes filled with tears, but he was helpless to do anything.

Ziereis finally ordered the men to lower Baranski to the floor. The American stood with his arms at his side and his hands drained of blood. He was led into the next room where he sat with his head bowed. He was broken psychologically.[12]

Baranski was given a bottle of mineral water, but he couldn't hold it in his hands and struggled to balance it between his knees. Müller could only stand and watch. Müller later claimed it was the worst 30 minutes of his life.

After the war, Edward Baranski's mother, Anna Baranski, wrote a brief biography about her family. She recorded that Edward once asked her how she wanted to die. She replied that she wanted to "be prepared," and to receive the last sacraments and be fortunate enough to die in bed. Her son replied, "Mom, I want to suffer. I want to suffer so on this earth that when I die I want to be free, I want to be in the clear."[13]

That 28-year-old Edward Baranski would get his wish in such tragic circumstances was a bitter irony. Such a scene contrived by Hollywood would have been dismissed as hackneyed and trite, but this was the evil culture of Nazi Germany at its apogee, truth more brutal than fiction.

Müller reported later, disagreeing with Thost, that he believed the following prisoners were not tortured: Jim Gaul, Robert Brown, Daniel Pavletich, Lane Miller, Jerry Mican, Nelson Paris, Tibor Keszthelyi, Joe Morton, and Margita Kockova. On the other hand the British prisoners, John Sehmer, Jack Wilson, Zwi Ben-Yaakov, and Aba Berdichev were beaten and broken by torture. Müller recalled that Berdichev was broken to the point that he was willing "to do anything."[14]

Later when Müller was detained after the German surrender, he reported to the OSS all he knew about the prisoners. He knew Daniel Pavletich was a Croatian; he had learned that Jerry Mican had been a teacher; and that Ben-Yaakov had been a fisherman. He recalled other small, personal details about the men. They discussed politics, the war, their experiences, and their hopes about the future. Müller remembered clearly that the prisoners did not fear for their lives. Interestingly, Holt Green had disclosed to Müller he had been "very angry" when so many personnel had arrived on the October 7 flight at Tri Duby from Bari, and that he insisted they must return on the next flight, a flight which never materialized. This was an issue which would be addressed by Major Walter Ross of the OSS in Bari after the war.[15]

Werner Müller had an unusual relationship with both his superiors and the Anglo-Americans. His affidavits given to the War Crimes investigators have given us a unique insight into the personalities of the *SS* staff. His account was substantiated by both Altfuldisch and Niedermayer as well as Dr. Thost. Müller revealed an atmosphere of brutality unleashed one moment followed by civility the next. Nevertheless, savage cruelty prevailed at Mauthausen in those dreadful days.

---

1 Documents from the Slovak National Archives in Bratislava show that Pavletich was brought into the jail at Banska Bystrica on December 29, 1944, and was shipped out on January 4. Presumably, he and Baranski had previously been held in Zvolen or Detva. On December 29, the other DAWES prisoners had been shipped to Mauthausen. Courtesy of Henry Siegel, Friends of Slovakia Association, Bratislava.
2 Ernst Kaltenbrunner had succeeded Reinhard Heydrich who was assassinated in 1943 in the Czech Protectorate by British SOE agents. Kaltenbrunner worked directly under Heinrich Himmler.
3 NARA, RG 153, Werner Müller affidavit, Entry 8-9, Box 116.
4 Ibid.
5 Ibid.
6 Ibid.
7 NARA, Hans Altfuldisch affidavit.
8 NARA, Werner Müller affidavit; Hans Altfuldisch verified this incident in his own affidavit, NARA, Hans Altfuldisch affidavit.
9 Ibid.
10 Ibid.
11 Ibid.
12 Ibid.
13 Anna Baranski, Unpublished manuscript, courtesy of Kathleen Baranski Lund.
14 NARA, Werner Müller affidavit.
15 Ibid.

Chapter 32

Murder, Wine, and Brandy

Mauthausen, 1945.

Whe he was captured by American troops the first week of May, *Obersharführer* Josef Niedermayer, the chief jailer at Mauthausen, was only a 24-year-old SS sergeant. The OSS interrogated him within days of the German surrender. He talked freely, knowing he faced the hangman apparently hoping he might win leniency.

Niedermayer admitted to have taken part personally in 400 executions at Mauthausen. Included among the victims were American and British military officers. Additionally, he recalled other victims who were French, Russians, Poles, Dutch, Germans, Italians, Czechs, Belgians, and Yugoslav.

Niedermayer remembered that Major John Sehmer spoke "broken German," that Sehmer had been held in cell number 17. He also recalled how 17 downed American airmen had been brought into the camp in the fall of 1944 and all shot. Furthermore, he admitted beating prisoners with a whip and sometimes with his fists. He also remembered that Holt Green and two other Americans wore Navy uniforms.

He recounted how *Hauptsturmführer* Georg Bachmayer regularly shot between twenty and 50 prisoners a week. "[Bachmayer] picked himself for this job. He was a sadist," Niedermayer remembered, lamenting that he – Niedermayer — had originally been sent to Mauthausen as a disciplinary matter and "hated" his assignment.

As the end of the war neared, orders to execute prisoners came from "so many different officers – including the physicians — at Mauthausen," Niedermayer said. "[We] just killed people whenever there was an opportunity." For these Nazi killers, there was so little time, so much to do.

Niedermayer remembered January 24 when the telegram from Berlin arrived during the second phase of the OSS-SOE interrogations, and reviewed the events of that day in detail for the OSS investigators. He recalled Franz Ziereis walking into the office of the main cell building with the message from Ernst Kaltenbrunner.[1]

Ziereis immediately ordered the prisoners returned to their cells. Then he showed the telegram to Bachmayer and the others. The prisoners were to be shot.

Werner Müller was not in the office when this occurred. After lunch, he had gone to the prison photography department to have a passport photo taken prior to the follow-up interrogations of Edward Baranski and Daniel Pavletich. While awaiting the photographer, Müller was told by a messenger he was wanted immediately in the office.

When Müller arrived back at the cell block, he noticed some unusual activity. Heinrich Arndt was waiting in the hallway with the Anglo-American prisoners, and he chastised Müller for being late. He ordered Müller into the prison office. *Kommandant* Franz Ziereis was there with several officers including *Sturmbannführer* Dr. Waldemar Wolter, Mauthausen's chief medical doctor.[2]

Ziereis ordered Müller to inform the prisoners that they must sign a paper stating they would be shot if they attempted to escape while being transferred to another camp. He asked them to sign blank pieces of paper, which they were resisting. Ziereis said they were being transferred at 5 PM, and it was necessary for them to sign the statements immediately. He was insistent.

Ziereis also ordered Müller to tell the prisoners they would have to change from their uniforms into prison clothes and undergo a physical exam.

Finally, each man signed the paper and went to another room to change clothes.

A few minutes later, when Müller and Arndt were alone, Müller asked Arndt what was happening. Arndt explained that Ziereis had just received a telegram from Kaltenbrunner in Berlin ordering the immediate execution of the entire Anglo-American group.

Müller was incredulous. He noticed the prisoners were leaving the hallway. Ziereis and three *SS* officers – Bachmayer, Altfuldisch, and Niedermayer – led them outside. Arndt told Müller again that the prisoners would be executed immediately. Müller didn't believe him.

"How and when?" Müller asked.

"Right now," Arndt replied.

Müller watched through the window as the prisoners walked onto a porch-like balcony and down a stairway. The prisoners didn't go out in the yard, but merely turned right, and walked into a basement set of rooms known as the bunker.

Müller told the OSS interrogator later that he was "terribly upset" as this was taking place.

Arndt said, "They will die an easier death than any one could wish for."[3]

Bachmayer directed the prisoners to undress in an ajoining room before being photographed and examined by the doctor. A dummy camera had been installed on a tripod in the execution chamber to deceive prisoners where Ziereis waited.[4]

Altfuldisch recalled that Schoeneseiffen stood behind Ziereis who held a small carbine rifle. In a room outside, Karl Schulz, Dr. Wolter and Willibald Proksch stationed themselves. Wolter allegedly was there to conduct the physical exams. Niedermayer and Martin Roth waited outside the room, acting as guards and set to bring in the prisoners one at a time to the execution room. Altfuldisch stood inside the door.[5]

Sehmer was the first prisoner led in. He was told they first would photograph him from the rear and then from the front. Altfuldisch testified that Sehmer noticed Ziereis was holding the carbine and hesitated. "He was frightened," Altfuldisch recalled, and attempted to say something to Ziereis.[6]

Ziereis ignored Sehmer's request and motioned with the carbine for Sehmer to move into the corner, facing the wall. The weapon, a single-shot *Mauser Wehrmanbrechse*, was a rifle normally issued to the Hitler Youth organizations.

As Sehmer faced the wall, Franz Ziereis stepped up to within a few feet of him, pointed the carbine at the back of his head, only inches away, and shot him.[7]

Other Witnesses to the Executions.

Two prisoners, Wilhelm Ornstein and Johann Kanduth, also witnessed the executions. Ornstein, a 29-year-old Polish prisoner, had been assigned in August, 1944, to the crematorium. He explained to OSS interrogators in June 1944 that it was his and Kanduth's job to remove bodies from the execution room, hose down the floor, and then burn the bodies in the crematorium. Sixteen prisoners worked in the crematorium, although seven later were murdered by the SS staff before the camp was liberated by the U.S. Army.[8]

Altfuldisch said Ziereis shot only Sehmer, after which Bachmayer shot the others. Ornstein remembered only five prisoners being shot this day, although Altfuldisch thought it was seven.[9] Ornstein remembered the following SS officers watching the executions: Karl Schulz, *Oberscharführer* Andreas Trumm, Josef Niedermayer, *Untersharführer* Willibald Proksch, and Martin Roth. Altfuldisch, who also admitted he was in the execution room, said Schoeneseiffen also was there.[10] The double door which sealed off the bunker made it impossible to hear the gun shots of the small caliber carbine.[11]

On June 28, 1945, Lt. Kelly O'Neall, USNR, an OSS interrogator, asked Ornstein to identify photos of the DAWES team. He recalled Holt

Green as the third man executed on January 24. Only five prisoners were executed this day. The remainder were shot two weeks later on February 9.

Ornstein also told O'Neall about the shooting of Holt Green:

> The first shot did not kill the victim immediately. When we brought Green to the cold storage room, Schulz told Bachmayer that there was one still alive in the cold storage room, and that he should go and give him a second shot. Bachmayer did this. The picture of that fellow remained in my memory until today, so that I am absolutely sure that he was Lt. Green.[12]

Ornstein recalled an argument between an American and both Ziereis and Bachmayer.

"I am an American officer and why should you shoot me," the prisoner argued. Ziereis and Bachmayer shouted, "*Fotografieren, Fotografieren.*" The American continued to argue, pleading. "I am an American prisoner of war and why should I be shot?"

This argument lasted two or three minutes and then the American was forcibly pushed against the wall, turned around, and shot. This victim was either Tibor Keszthelyi, Lane Miller, Edward Baranski, or Frank Perry.

Ornstein Recalls Joe Horvath's Smiling Face.

Ornstein identified Joe Horvath as one of the men executed on January 24. "I remember his smiling face [with his smile frozen in death]."

Horvath still had his dog tags on his body when Ornstein carried him to the cold storage room. Ornstein removed the dog tags, but *Hauptscharführer* Martin Roth took them. Roth was in charge of the crematorium, the gas chamber, and the so-called "shooting gallery" where the victims were shot.

Ornstein was unable to identify other victims because he believed the men had changed a great deal, having lost weight, grown beards and long hair since their photos had been taken.

He recalled another victim, a "handsome man with an unusual mark on his face along the left side of his nose, between 5'6" to 5'8" tall with dark blond hair, slightly bald-headed."

On February 9, Jim Gaul and nine others were shot. "We had difficulty with his body because it was longer than our furnace, so we had to bend his legs," Ornstein said. "This is why I still remember him. I recognize him from his photograph."[13]

Johann Kanduth, 36, had been a prisoner at Mauthausen for four years. An Austrian, his testimony substantiated Ornstein's. He stated that the dog tags he personally recovered he gave to Ornstein. The exception, he testified, was that on February 9 they were all wearing clothes.

Werner Müller, who had remained in the office while the prisoners had been taken to the Bunker, had not been able to hear any sounds. He recalled that Ziereis returned from the Bunker after about twenty minutes, sometime between 2:30 and 3 PM.

Ziereis ordered an *SS* guard to prepare a record of all those *SS* personnel who had been witnesses. He turned to the other *SS* officers and began laughing.

"I am glad to be rid of them," Ziereis said. "They were here too long. I need the cells and I might need some of their things for my men, especially the shoes."

He laughed again, and continued.

". . . this fellow Green was suspecting something. Didn't you notice how frightened he looked both ways over his shoulder when he was being examined by the doctor." Ziereis laughed again. Müller remembered the conversation clearly.

Heinrich Arndt and Müller returned to Berlin. At the *RSHA* headquarters, Arndt ridiculed Müller in front of other staff members because he had been affected emotionally by the torture of the prisoners.[14]

On June 13, 1945, Kanduth identified photos of Horvath, Baranski, Paris, Daniel Pavletich, Perry, and Charles Heller. He testified, like

Ornstein, that it was difficult to identify the victims because the gunshot wounds left the faces covered with blood.[15]

The executions and the evil perpetuated by the Mauthausen *SS* staff constitute a small episode in a vast war in which millions of people died. The Nazi regime murdered millions of people in monstrous denial of all moral values. Although the concentration camps, notably Dachau, Belsen, and Auschwitz, became well known in later years, many of the specifics of the crimes against the Anglo-Americans of the DAWES and WINDPROOF missions would be kept secret for over thirty years.

In 1946, one of the ironies regarding the fate of the Anglo-American prisoners surfaced. *Hauptsturmführer* Dieter Wisliceny, a ranking *SS* officer at RSHA headquarters in Berlin, testified at the Nürnberg military tribunal that in Berlin *Sturmbannführer* Manfred Schoeneseiffen had once showed him the RSHA file on the DAWES mission. The author has been unable to determine if Schoeneseiffen, who had prepared the interrogation questions at Mauthausen and watched in the execution room, was ever prosecuted as a war criminal.

The last paper in the file examined by Wisliceny was a request by the *Ober Kommando Der Wehrmacht* (OKW), German Army Headquarters, to transfer the prisoners to a military POW camp. Wisliceny was told by another *SS* officer that Adolf Hitler personally ordered the executions in retaliation for the alleged shooting of German officers during the occupation of Paris the previous August. Hence, the *Führer* himself apparently played a role in the Mauthausen murders of the Anglo-Americans.[16]

While it was believed originally that all the prisoners were executed on January 24, either nine or eleven of them were shot on February 9, according to the testimony of Ornstein. Additionally, Lt. Jack Taylor learned that Nelson Paris was not shot until April.[17]

Ornstein was unable to identify a photo of Nelson Paris, but he remembered the name "Paris." Paris' body and his dog tags had been covered with blood, Ornstein recalled. When the *SS* officers didn't notice, Ornstein took the dog tags. He later gave them to Lt. Kelly O'Neall during his OSS interrogation. Ornstein recalled one victim "named Miller (Lane Miller)." He removed Miller's dog tags, but Martin Roth took them.[18]

Kanduth remembered six sets of US dog tags and others that were longer and thinner, presumably British. He gave most of them directly to Roth, but at least four to Ornstein. He recalled only two names, "Nelson and Paris."[19]

Ornstein and the other prisoners, forced into the grisly business of watching murder and burning bodies, knew special crimes were being committed against the Anglo-Americans. They were determined to preserve whatever evidence they could. Ornstein secretly made notes about the January 24 and other executions and which he gave O'Neall.

Two hours after the executions on January 24, Ziereis and the staff sat down to dinner. Hans Altfuldisch was among the group of "ten to twelve" *SS* officers. Ziereis and the others "were in high spirits" after the executions, Altfuldisch recalled. Ziereis sat at the head of the table with Habecker at his right and Schoeneseiffen at his left. The dinner began with wine.

Before the meal, Ziereis presented Habecker with a dog sled for his grand son. Habecker expressed his gratitude to Ziereis for his kindness. Obersturmführer Altfuldisch recalled the scene clearly, a celebratory occasion only hours after the cold-blooded murder of the prisoners. He remembered also a speech Ziereis made about the pleasure that day of getting "rid of the gangsters."

The *Totenkopf SS* officers finished the evening with brandy.[20]

---

1   NARA, Josef Niedermayer affidavit, Box 349.
2   NARA, Werner Müller affidavit.
3   Ibid.
4   NARA, Josef Niedermayer affidavit, Box 344.
5   NARA, Hans Altfuldisch affidavit, Box 344; Martin Roth may have been the man standing inside the double door.
6   Ibid.
7   NARA, Josef Niedermayer affidavit.
8   NARA, RG 153, Entry 8-9, Wilhelm Ornstein and Johann Kanduth affidavits, Box 116.

Murder, Wine, and Brandy

9 NARA, Hans Altfuldisch affidavit.
10 NARA, Wilhelm Ornstein affidavit.
11 NARA, Hans Altfuldisch affidavit.
12 Ibid.
13 NARA, Wilhelm Ornstein affidavit.
14 NARA, Werner Müller affidavit.
15 Ibid.; Kanduth testified in November, 1945, that he once assisted Martin Roth in preparing demonstration executions for Ernst Kaltenbrunner who visited Mauthausen in 1943. Three prisoners were executed, one by hanging, one by a pistol shot in the back of the neck, and one by gassing. He recalled Kaltenbrunner laughing as he, Ziereis, Bachmayer, Schulz and other *SS* officers entered the gas chamber prior to the "demonstration."
16 Nazi Conspiracy and Aggression. Volume VIII. USGPO, Washington, 1946, PP. 606-619. Affidavit of Dieter Wisliceny, January 3, 1946, Direct examination before the International Military Tribunal, Nürnberg, Germany. Manfred Schoeneseiffen was the Berlin *SS* officer who prepared the interrogations of the prisoners. Wisliceny was executed by the Czechoslovakian government in 1947.
17 NARA, Jack Taylor report; The German announcement of the executions listed 17 persons executed on January 24. Yet, both Niedermayer and Ornstein testified that either five or seven were executed on January 24, and the rest later. Ornstein recalled Nelson Paris being executed in April. There is no way to reconcile these discrepancies.
18 NARA, Wilhelm Ornstein affidavit.
19 NARA, Johann Kanduth affidavit; There were twelve American military personnel executed, one OSS civilian (Pavletich), one civilian (Morton), three British military executed, and one British-employed civilian, Margita Kockova.
20 NARA, Hans Altfuldisch affidavit.

Chapter 33

Berlin Communiqué

January 20, 1945.

The American involvement in the Slovak National Uprising, as related in this account, started in July, 1944, when Lt. Jack Kellogg, parachuted out of his burning B-17 above the Slovakian countryside. By the end of January, Kellogg was a POW at *Stalag Luft* III, preparing to march out of the camp with 10,000 other prisoners in blizzard conditions. Norton Skinner and Sam Strode, two of Kellogg's crew, previously flown back to Italy from Slovakia by the 15th Air Force and the OSS, were back in the U.S. Virgil Stuart, awaiting the Red Army, was still hiding with a Slovak family in Hlboke village. Other American airmen had been shot down later and were being hidden by Slovak civilians and Partisans. The 40 American airmen rescued at Tri Duby in September and October were back in the States.

Lieutenants Bill McGregor and Kenneth Lain were locked up at a secret *SS* interrogation center near the Oberursel *Dulag Luft*, north of Frankfurt am Main. McGregor later remembered the center as a "castle," which the author has never been able to identify.[1]

McGregor and Lain insisted they were American airmen, but their interrogators suspected correctly that they were OSS agents. They were interrogated intensely and tortured. They were warmed by hot stoves, and then forced to stand outdoors in frigid temperatures. Neither man broke because they knew their lives hung in the balance. They finally were transferred to another POW camp and survived the war.[2]

Jan Schwartz was still in Vienna in the *Rosauer Lände* Prison, fending off his *Gestapo* interrogators. He and others there had their fingers crossed that the Red Army would arrive and liberate them before the executioner's ax fell. Schwartz, McGregor and Lain were fortunate they weren't sent to Mauthausen.[3]

George Fernandes and Jack Shafer, who like Schwartz had been captured in the *Tatra* Mountains on the *Prasiva* Range, were at *Stalag Luft* I at Barth in Northern Germany. Rumors that the Red Army was advancing toward Barth led them to believe they would be liberated with weeks or even days.

Ken Dunlevy, Steve Catlos, the two Brits, Lt. Stephan Zenopian and Sgt. Bill Davies and Maria, were in the hands of the Russians in Hungary. Nelson Deranian had been transferred to Siena, Italy, near the 5th Army front lines.

In Bari, the OSS commanders had received no news from the DAWES mission for over a month. They were still hoping their men were still eluding the enemy and would soon reach the Russian lines. Lt. Colonels Walter Ross (He had been promoted.) and Howard Chapin, frustrated and anxious, were doing what they could. On January 22, eight P-38's of the 82nd Fighter Group – the Grayson mission — flew over the *Tatra* Mountains and dropped supply canisters at the pinpointed location identified six weeks earlier by Major John Sehmer. The mission was pitifully late.

January 24, Stunning News.

Then came a shock. Berlin announced that the Germans had captured and executed American and British intelligence agents.

Eighteen members of one Anglo-American group of agents, headed by an American named Green and an Englishman named Sehmer, who posed as a major, were caught on Slovakian soil in the rear of the German fighting sector, a competent German quarter announced. Investigations revealed that they had the task to carry out acts of sabotage in Slovakia and economic and political espionage in Anglo-American interest. The agents, wearing mufti when arrested, were sentenced to death by [after a trial]. They were executed by shooting.[4]

Instantly, radio messages were flying between Bari, Caserta, London, New York, Moscow, and Washington D.C. Howard Chapin in Caserta asked Walter Ross and Otto Jakes in Bari if they had any recent word of the DAWES team. Ross asked Lt. Colonel Henry Threlfall of SOE if he had any news of Major John Sehmer and the WINDPROOF mission? The answer was negative. Three days later OSS London asked Major General John Deane, the leader of the U.S. military mission in Moscow, to inquire about what the Russians knew.

In Bari, the OSS admitted to a "strong presumption" that the German communiqué was referring to the DAWES team, concluding "…quite probably that this group [mentioned in German broadcast] included 12 to 14 of our people who were members of the DAWES and other teams, totaling 19 people."[5] Walter Ross and the rest of the OSS staff in Bari concluded grimly, but privately, that Holt Green and the others were dead.

January 31, Caserta, Italy.

Orders came down from Washington that official reports be submitted. Lt. Colonel Chapin informed his superiors that the DAWES, DAY and other allied teams flew in "openly" in B-17's on an airstrip controlled by the Slovaks, and that they were wearing uniforms. Chapin cautioned that "official silence" might lead the Germans to believe they had captured a clandestine operation. On the other hand, he pointed out that "unusual interest on the part of the U.S." might confirm or excite enemy suspicions that the men indeed had been sent in on a secret mission. Chapin stated that he was asking for "guidance" from higher authority. Chapin was leaving this tough decision for Washington.

That same day, Tony Novak, Captain Edward Baranski's DAY team member, arrived in Belgrade, Yugoslavia. He gave his report on the capture of Baranski and Pavletich. Novak passed on other rumors that other Americans were in jail in Banska Bystrica. Novak updated his report twice in the next two weeks.[6]

The Associated Press, meanwhile, took notice of the Berlin communiqué.[7] The London AP bureau had picked up the January 24 announcement immediately, and wired it to AP headquarters New York, who promptly notified "Boots" Norgaard, Rome bureau chief, to seek clarification. In Washington, the AP contacted the State Department who said simply that Joe Morton was in Slovakia, that he may have joined a partisan group and may have separated from the main party of an OSS mission. As speculation mounted, the entire event, sparked by the Berlin communiqué, had a "chilling effect" on the AP headquarters in New York.[8]

January 26, New York City.

Letty Morton, Joe's wife, contacted the AP in New York. She had seen the "London item." She wrote that she was "increasingly alarmed." Days went by, but the AP did not go public with what they knew. A month later, February 27, New York asked their man in Washington to "keep after" the OSS and the War Department.[9]

The War Department in Washington, meanwhile, wanted to know how a war correspondent was allowed to go along on an intelligence mission. Howard Chapin in Bari responded that Morton had gone along "on the authority of the 15th Air Force." Chapin said the Russians had been asked to look for the DAWES team as the Red Army advanced into Slovakia. He reported that three days earlier, the 15th AF had dropped belly tanks with food, clothing, and equipment near the Partisan headquarters of Colonel Vladimir Prikryl.[10]

March 1, Bucharest.

February went by with no news. Then, Walter Ross chanced to meet

Captain de Lannurien, the French partisan leader in Slovakia. He told Ross about Lt. Stefan Zenopian and that he had information about the DAWES team. Ross interviewed Zenopian at length and sent a report to Lt. Colonel Chapin in Bari.[11] Ross for the first time learned of Pavol Kamensky and Major Stanek, the two Slovaks who had been in the hut with Holt Green and the others.

Ross reported Zenopian's account of the circumstances of the capture OSS and SOE personnel. Zenopian accounted for all the Americans except for Edward Baranski and Daniel Pavletich.[12]

March 4, Rome.

When the AP received the news of Zenopian's report, Noland "Boots" Norgaard wired New York that American intelligence officials had interviewed a "British officer" in Bucharest, Romania. Zenopian had told Walter Ross that he had "seen" Morton and the members of the DAWES team captured in Slovakia.[13]

---

1 It may have been *Schloss* (castle) *Kransberg* where after the war the CIA set up the General Reinhard Gehlen, former *Wehrmacht* intelligence chief on the Russian front, to work for them.
2 Bill McGregor, Telephone interview with the author, April 1998.
3 Jan Schwartz, Interview with William Miller, 1983.
4 NARA, RG 226, Entry 190, Box 116, Folder 407.
5 Ibid.
6 NARA, RG 226, Entry 139, Box 29, Folder 200.
7 Larry Heinzerling, Unpublished manuscript.
8 Ibid.
9 Ibid.
10 Ibid.
11 PRO, HS 4/41.
12 Ibid.
13 Larry Heinzerling, Unpublished manuscript.

Chapter 34

Freedom In Bucharest

February 23, In and Around Hungary.

Maria and her Anglo-American group were unaware of the news from Berlin. Although they were no longer dodging the *Wehrmacht*, they were dismayed at their treatment by the Russians. In addition, they weren't reading newspapers.

During the next two weeks, the Russians hauled Maria and the others off to a variety of Hungarian locations where they were questioned by the *NKVD*, insulted, abused, threatened with imprisonment, and treated like prisoners of war. They were astonished by the shabby treatment. The new phase of their escape became a journey fraught with uncertainty, tension, and intimidation.

The Soviets locked them up in displaced persons centers surrounded by guards. They put them in prisoner of war compounds. They continually accused them of being spies. In summary, they received a vivid introduction to enigmatic Soviet political behavior and the centuries-old suspicious nature of the Muscovites. They began to wonder if they would safely escape Soviet control.[1]

During the following two weeks, they were bounced around by the Soviets between such colorful Hungarian spots as Salgotarjan, Jaszkiser, Hatvan, Jaszladany, Jaszbereny, Szolnok, and Bekescsaba. They traveled by truck, train, and foot, forced to wait long hours in unheated trucks in sleet and snowstorms. Once, they shivered by the side of the road, watching what seemed to be Marshal Rodion Malinovsky's entire Second Ukrainian Army roll by – tanks, artillery pieces mounted on caissons pulled by horses, Mongolian cavalry, and a horde of infantry pursuing the Germans and bearing down on Vienna.[2]

They spent six uncomfortable days at Jaszkiser, the *NKVD* headquarters. Maria was interrogated every night, usually around midnight. She answered the same questions over and over. Where did she meet the Americans? Who were the British? Were they spies? Who in Slovakia had sent her with the Anglo-Americans?

At Jaszkiser, the food was bad, and the Russians were hostile and rude.[3] Russian officers and soldiers were detained there, men who had been prisoners of the Germans, and now were accused of being spies. The Russians awaited transport before being sent off to prison or exile. One bewildered young officer confided his anguish to Maria. Disillusioned and bewildered, he had expected being greeted warmly when his comrades who liberated him. Instead, he had been placed under arrest.[4]

The Russians later moved Maria and the others to a POW camp at Jaszbereny, stopping first at Jaszladany for a two-hour wait during a snow storm. Soviet troops were everywhere. In the countryside, huge enclosures of Hungarian prisoners of war, living in the open, struggled to survive in horrible conditions. Hundreds of dead horses littered the roadsides.

Maria insisted to the Russians that her group should not be treated as prisoners or war, pointing out that they had voluntarily walked through the German lines to reach the Red Army. The Russians were unimpressed. Every foreign national, every stranger was considered a spy until proven otherwise.[5]

They were moved again, this time to a displaced persons camp at Tura, 30 miles east of Budapest. They actually had been dropped off at Hatvan and had to hitch-hike with their Russian guard to Tura. Here they met a Czech colonel who had witnessed the capture of Lt. Frank Perry at Dolna Lehota.

The colonel had been hiding in a barn and watched the *Edelweiss Abwehr* 218 soldiers beat Perry and strip him of his documents. Then, Perry had been forced to carry boxes of ammunition to a place where Partisans and Czech Brigade members were making a stand.[6]

The DP camp was filled with a variety of refugees. The Russians again were overbearing and rude. People from nearly every western country were there. Some had been abused by the Russian troops. Along the way, Maria and her group had met three members of a wealthy Dutch family connected to the oil industry. Two of the women had been raped by the Russians. Having spent the entire war in Budapest, this group also was under deep suspicion by the Russians. They also met several Palestinian Jews. Anyone who had had any contact with Germans was considered a spy.

After questioning Maria about her work for the Soviet Mission in Banska Bystrica, her interrogators told Maria she would be retained to work as an interpreter for the Soviets. The American and British personnel, meanwhile, were scheduled to be put on trains headed for the Black Sea port of Odessa where they would be shipped to Italy.

Maria began to panic. Bill Davies and the others decided that if Maria were married to one of them, she would be able to accompany her husband. They concocted the story of her marriage to Davies performed by Major Sehmer back in Slovakia. The story worked, and Maria was informed she would be on the train to Odessa with her husband.[7] Meanwhile, Zenopian had arrived in Bucharest on February 26 and had been interviewed by Walter Ross.[8]

March 7, Szolnok and Bekescsaba, Hungary.

The group left for Jaszladany and the following day traveled to Szolnok, southeast of Budapest, where they caught a train east to Bekescsaba. The train was overcrowded and the group was forced to stand all the way to Debrecen. Maria learned their guide, Nikolai Suslov, was not a Communist and had little sympathy for the Soviet regime. But, his orders were to accompany the group all the way to Odessa. Maria talked him into allowing them to stay over and continue the next day.

In Bekescsaba, they found decent hotel rooms. They purchased some food and Cognac, and celebrated their good fortune. During the evening, a tall Soviet captain pounded on their door and attempted to force himself on Maria. He attempted to drag her off, until Steve Catlos and Bill Davies jumped him. Fifteen minutes later, he returned, drunk, and repeated his advances. This time, he was beaten soundly. It was a dangerous incident, because at one point he drew his pistol which alarmed Suslov. A confrontation like this could have placed all of them in deep trouble.[9]

March 8, Arad, Romania.

The next day, they arrived at another displaced persons center, again operated by the Russians in total confusion. They met four American airmen who had been POW's awaiting transport to Odessa. The group had become accustomed to confusion and uncertainty. Bill Davies joked that the Russians were so incompetent "they couldn't plan a Christmas party."[10]

The group, which still included the Dutch family, the Palestinians and some British civilians, was allowed to travel to Bucharest on a luxury train that apparently once had been the personal train of the Rumanian king. The train was filled with drunken Russian soldiers.

They found a first-class compartment next to another occupied by a Soviet General and some colonels who invited them to share their food and Cognac. The Russian officers sang Red Army songs. One of the latter spoke excellent English and was extremely cordial to Maria and the others. He stayed up late and, drinking heavily, told Maria most of his life story.[11]

All these encounters, while often humorous, were dangerous. Later, when they bumped into the colonel who spoke English, he failed to acknowledge that he knew them. His colleagues obviously had convinced him that friendships with foreigners could have negative consequences. Fortunately, Maria's skill in both Russian and Hungarian, coupled with her quick wit, saved them time and again in perilous situations. By now, she also was learning to speak fair English.[12]

In Bucharest, they disembarked to change trains. The group was stalling, trying to figure out how to avoid the next train for Odessa. While waiting in the station, a young boy approached Steve Catlos. He had seen the American flag on the shoulder patch Catlos was wearing. He gave Catlos some sensational news: there were Americans in the city. Catlos immediately sought help to telephone the American mission. Within 15 minutes, Catlos was speaking to U.S. Army Brigadier General Cortland Schuyler.

"Good God, where are you?" Schuyler asked him. "Don't leave. We're coming to get you." Lt. Colonel Ross was with the OSS mission in Bucharest at the time, and the news that Catlos and Ken Dunlevy were in the city electrified the OSS staff members.[13]

---

1 Maria Gulovich, OSS Report.
2 Maria Gulovich, Telephone interview with the author, February 17, 2001.
3 Kenneth Dunlevy, OSS Report.
4 Aleksandr Solzhenitsyn, the famous political novelist, was the most notable of all Russians who were dismayed at their treatment in this situation. He later described his disgust and disillusionment with the Soviet mentality and political system. Aleksandr I. Solzhenitsyn, *The Gulag Archipelago* (New York:, Harper and Row, 1973).
5 Gulovich, OSS Report.
6 Ibid.
7 Ibid.
8 NARA, RG 226, Entry 190, Box 116, Folder 407. Stefan Zenopian, Interview with Walter Ross, March 3, 1945.
9 Maria Gulovich, Telephone interview with the author, February 18, 2001.
10 Kenneth Dunlevy, OSS Report.
11 Maria Gulovich, Telephone interview.
12 Ibid.
13 Walter Ross, Interview with William Miller, 1984.

Chapter 35

"Our Best and Bravest"

March 6, 1945.

In New York the Associated Press finally released the news that Joe Morton was a prisoner of the Germans, citing the report of an "unnamed British officer" who had witnessed his capture.[1] As a news item, it was lost in the avalanche of world events. In the Pacific, the Battle of Iwo Jima was underway, and in Europe the Eighth Air Force had just conducted a massive raid on Berlin. But the news of Morton's capture was crushing news to his family and friends.

The AP management asked their bureau chief in Rome, Noland "Boots" Norgaard, if there was any connection between the previous German story of the execution of Anglo-Americans and the whereabouts of Morton.

Norgaard replied that "It was undesirable" to speculate. In New York the AP asked the Red Cross in Geneva and Stockholm to check with the Germans to see if Morton was on any prisoner of war list.[2]

Thanks to the AP, Morton's wife, Letty, was the best informed family member of any of the missing Americans. The news of her husband's capture had "unraveled" her nerves, she wrote. She asked for more details, and recalled Joe's letter from Italy that he was after the "biggest story" of his life. Letty Morton now concluded correctly that the OSS mission must have had a greater purpose than rescuing airmen.[3]

March 10.

Boots Norgaard drew positive conclusions from Lt. Stefan Zenopian's account that he witnessed Morton's capture, and wrote to Letty Morton that he was happy to learn that her husband was still alive. This was wishful thinking. Norgaard admitted there was no way to know how long it would take to hear from her husband.

Six days later, Claude Jagger, the assistant director of the AP, wrote to her, referencing the Berlin communiqué, and explained that her husband had not been with saboteurs and that he was in uniform when captured. Jagger had not been advised by the War Department that the DAWES mission had brought in ordinance and weapons for the Slovak army.[4]

March 25, Rome.

Another two weeks went by which left Norgaard anguishing over Morton's fate. Norgaard sent a distraught message to Jagger. "I feel personally responsible for what has occurred, because I authorized him to attempt this trip without ascertaining the full circumstances under which it would be made. Lynn Heinzerling, an AP colleague of Morton's in Italy, explained those circumstances to you when he was in New York."[5]

The AP continued to wonder how Morton was allowed to accompany a secret intelligence mission. Writer William Miller questioned Walter Ross about that 29 years later. Ross told Miller,

The 15th Air Force was absolutely denying that they had approved Morton's trip on that airplane, and that they were telling their questioning officers in Washington that he was put on the plane by the OSS. That was their story, and they were going to stick to it. They didn't authorize it. They said it was Joe's own effort that got him on the flight, and the OSS maintained.[6]

Ross, of course, presumably had forgotten that Bari had alerted Holt Green on September 21, 1944, just four days after the first flight, that Morton would be coming to Slovakia on the next flight (See Chapter 8, and documents at the National Archives, 226, Entry 136, Box 34, Folder 325). When the pressure mounted, both the OSS and the 15th Air Force wilted and pointed their fingers at each other.

April went by and there still was no news of Joe Morton. The war in Europe was coming to a close as American and British forces crossed the Rhine, and the Soviets were poised to capture Berlin. In Bari, rumors circulated that some of the DAWES personnel had been seen, still in jail, in Slovakia. Others reported rumors that the men were in POW camps. Another referred to a mass grave at Kremnicka where bodies of men in American uniforms had been discovered.

In April, family members of the DAWES mission had begun receiving Missing In Action letters from the War Department. In Paris, Werner Müller, the *RSHA* interpreter, had been captured, and revealed what he knew about the grim January events at Mauthausen. He remembered clearly most of the names of the DAWES personnel. Insiders in the OSS now knew there was little hope, but nevertheless kept Müller's disclosures secret.

The AP continued to press the War Department for information. After the surrender, the OSS decided to allow the AP to conduct an investigation. The pressure was enormous. The War Department assigned to Lynn Heinzerling, Morton's longtime friend and colleague, an interpreter and provided a jeep-carrying DC-3 airplane. Jan Schwartz, who had made it back From Vienna to Italy by way of Odessa, was picked by OSS Caserta to accompany Heinzerling and ascertain the facts about the fate of the DAWES mission and Joe Morton. Heinzerling had no enthusiasm for the assignment, sensing he could only return with bad news for Letty Morton.[7]

Lt. Kelly O'Neall, USNR, an OSS investigator who began assembling evidence for the Dachau War Crimes tribunal, accompanied Heinzerling and Schwartz. They went to Salzburg and later visited Mauthausen, where they questioned Wilhelm Ornstein, the prisoner who worked in the prison crematorium. They also questioned Werner Müller in Paris. The evidence was conclusive. By July 7, Heinzerling concluded that Joe Morton and the others were dead, and he sat down to put into words the letter to Morton's widow that he dreaded.[8]

Meanwhile, the family members of the DAWES personnel, depressed with the troubling news, aggressively sought information from the War Department and other sources. How were their men captured? What kind of mission were they on? Where and how were they killed? Were they betrayed? Why did some escape and the others not?[9]

Although Letty Morton was the best informed family member, it was Jim Gaul's mother, Harriett, who most relentlessly pursued the full story. In Charleston, South Carolina, she contacted Holt Green's sister, Laura Frost, and Green's mother, Daisy Holt Green. She located Jerry Mican's widow, Mary, in Chicago.

Ultimately, she found Steve Catlos, who also lived in Pittsburgh, and Ken Dunlevy. A relative of Holt Green found Bill McGregor. Harriett located Walter Ross and Nelson Deranian. Laura Frost subsequently met with Deranian, but while he gave her a full account of the mission, he did not address the issue of sending in another 14 men into Slovakia on October 7.

Both Harriett and Laura Frost questioned Bill McGregor, Ken Dunlevy, and Steve Catlos about the fact that Holt Green had objected to the 14 men being sent in on the second mission. They apparently never confronted Deranian or Walter Ross on this issue. They did vent their feelings to General Donovan.

Daisy Holt Green Writes General Donovan.

Both General Donovan and Deputy OSS director Charles Cheston in Washington were besieged with angry letters. Daisy Holt Green wrote a scorching letter to the General, complaining about the vague answers they had been given.[10]

> All this correspondence has been unsatisfactory in that it has told little of the story and has been inaccurate in at least some particulars. I am addressing this letter to you personally in the hope that I may obtain a compete and accurate account. (Because of security,

I have refrained from making this request earlier.)
I understand that after my son went into Czechoslovakia, personnel were taken in there over my son's protest. I believe he asked for one man and fourteen were sent. I understand that he later asked that these men be evacuated both because he regarded their continued presence as a danger to the entire party and because he had been requested by the Czech forces to reduce his personnel to a minimum. I understand that it has been stated officially that the weather prevented their evacuation. On the other hand, I believe that the Russians were evacuating personnel by plane from the field near Banska Bystrica until immediately before its capture by the Germans on October 25 and that they had been flying planes in and out of there all during the week ending on that day; that the Germans were flying planes in the area and that fifteenth Air Force planes were flying during this time. [She mentions that on the 22nd 20 or 21 flyers were taken to Tri Duby; weather was clear. And bombers were seen to have passed high over the field on that day, and that Fifteenth Air Force bombers did bomb Bratislava and possibly two other cities in the general vicinity on that day.]
I feel obliged to and do feel that the unnecessary augmentation of my son's party and the subsequent failure to evacuate personnel leave (sic) directly on my son's death. Certain those two factors caused the death of many of this brave party. As these two factors are important, I feel that I am entitled and I request an explanation of the apparent abandonment of the party by the OSS base and the Fifteenth Air Force. I should like also to have a detailed account of the weather at the airforce base and a complete resume of messages which were sent by my son during the period from October 14th to October 25th, 1944, relating to the weather, the conditions of the airfield at Banska Bystrica and the evacuation of personnel.
It is to me a source of deep regret to have to feel that these brave men were given every cause to become embittered and to lose their courage because of their complete lack of support and yet it is a glorious credit to them to know that they knowing they had the courage to keep on, enduring hardships which caused even natives of that country to suffer themselves to perish in the snow.
I take particular pride in having learned that my son was always ready with a smile and a word of encouragement during this period; and which this was characteristic of him, I do not see how even with his great courage, he managed to remain cheerful and to

shut out the bitterness which he should have felt at the failure of his support.

I received some comfort from the visit of a young flier who was shot down in Yugoslavia and was evacuated from there by my son. When he read of my son's execution, he called on me to tell me of the fine treatment which he had received from my son and his little party in Yugoslavia. I have not been given any information officially about my son's work in Yugoslavia, but apparently he worked there successfully.[11]

The OSS quietly continued their attempts to appease the families. They did not, however, supply them with copies of messages sent from Bari to Banska Bystrica between October 14 and October 25. Had Daisy Green been a U.S. Senator, she might have received more satisfaction.

Charles Cheston wrote to Harriett Gaul on May 30, 1945, and included her son's Thanksgiving prayer which Zenopian had written down and turned over to Walter Ross in Bucharest. It was a moving momento for a distraught mother.[12] But the awful sense of dread which occupied the minds of the families may have been best expressed later in July when Letty Morton wrote Kent Cooper, general manager of the AP. Her poignant letter, expressing her sorrow for her loving husband, remains as a powerful statement.

"January was a long procession of sleepless nights and depressing days," she wrote... "That stark announcement on January 24 gnawed at my mind."[13]

All over America, families were wondering and asking questions about their missing men who were lost on all the fronts. Over 300,000 lost their lives, and another 100,000 were missing in action. Millions of men and women in other countries also had died. The casualties in the DAWES team were little more than a blip on the endless lists which were published daily at the end of the war. But, what nagged at the families of the men of the DAWES mission was the issue of whether the sacrifices of their men were really necessary. And they never forgave the OSS for holding back so much information for so long.[14]

Dawes Mission Failure Result of "Incomplete Planning."

The OSS later evaluated the DAWES mission and concluded that there was "incomplete planning" relative to the Slovak resistance movement. Additionally, the OSS concluded that the Uprising failed because of lack of support of the British and the Soviet Union. But, the OSS acknowledged no responsibility.[15]

In 1984, Walter Ross discussed the mission in detail with writer William Miller. Ross acknowledged there was much criticism of the "necessity as well as the planning and conceiving" of the operation afterwards in 1945. But, he said the men had volunteered for the mission and knew it was going to be a "lot tougher" than missions some had been on in Yugoslavia. ". . . nobody was forced to go on this thing at all."[16]

Yet, the decision to send in the additional men on October 7 clearly was a mistake. The fault here rests in part with Holt Green who was not adamant on the issue. A group of seven or eight men might have hidden successfully. That Nelson Deranian and Ross allowed Joe Morton to accompany the mission and also sent along a photographer, Nelson Paris, illustrates the poor judgement of the commanders in Bari.

Also, the OSS was naïve in believing that if the men were captured in uniform, the Germans would respect their rights as prisoners of war under the rules of the Geneva convention. In October, 1942, Adolf Hitler had issued the "*Kommandobehehl*," a general order in which Hitler decreed that any "commandos" captured behind German lines would be "slaughtered to the last man." This order was known to the Allies.

In Bari Nelson Deranian had failed to anticipate the problems facing the Anglo-American group in the mountains. The terrain was not as rugged as that in Yugoslavia, which meant hiding and evading could be a problem, as indeed it turned out to be.

In Pittsburgh, grief-stricken Harriett and Harvey Gaul had lost their only son, a brilliant Harvard PhD. Harriett continued to plead with the OSS for more information. At one point, she asked, "In human kindness must this suspense continue?" Finally, when informed her son was certainly dead and she had received a copy of his Thanksgiving prayer, she noted in despair that she had lost ten pounds and her hair had turned grey. She wrote to Charles Cheston about this ill-fated mission:

> The whole thing seems to be a history of narrow margins where things went wrong instead of right—so many ifs. The only thing that I am glad about is that if Jim had to die for some other country—that it was Czechoslovakia, for that is where his heart was—he was called there—a fate—and because we sold them down the river . . . in Chamberlain's day. It wipes out our shame—we did try—through them—our best and bravest—to do SOMETHING.[17]

---

1 Zenopian had not witnessed it. He had heard Pavol Kamenesky's account. See Chapter 27.
2 Larry Heinzerling, Unpublished manuscript.
3 Ibid.
4 Ibid.
5 Ibid.
6 Walter Ross, Interview (taped) with William Miller, 1984, courtesy of Marilyn Miller.
7 Larry Heinzerling, Unpublished manuscript.
8 Ibid.
9 Harriet Gaul, Letter to Hazel Frost, sister of Holt Green, October 10, 1946, courtesy of Frances Frost Hutson.
10 The author has a rough draft copy of this letter, given him by Green's neice, Frances Frost Hutson. The original may, or may not, have been sent to Donovan. The author could not find it in the files at the National Archives.
11 Ibid.
12 See Chapter 23 for the text of the prayer.
13 Larry Heinzerling, Unpublished manuscript.
14 The author supplied information from the National Archives in the late 1990's to several family members who had no idea of certain aspects of the mission and the circumstances in which the men lost their lives. In one folder, for example, the author found personal correspondence which never was delivered to the family.
15 OSS Report, Vol. 2, p. 134, NARA.
16 William Miller, Interview with Walter Ross, 1984.
17 NARA, Casualties, OSSDF.

Chapter 36

The Drama Ends

Bucharest Central Train Station, Romania, April, 1944.

Maria Gulovich, Ken Dunlevy, Steve Catlos and Bill Davies were eager to contact American or British officials and escape the control of the Soviets. Brigadier General Schuyler had alerted Catlos that help was coming, but getting away from the Russians wasn't going to be easy.

The Soviets took Maria and the others from the train station to a military guest house. They agreed to allow the travelers some rest before resuming the long train ride to Odessa. Alerted by Schuyler, American and British authorities followed the Russian convoy. Then Americans and the British left, but returned later with their own trucks and whisked Maria and the others away. The Russians were furious.[1]

Steve Catlos and Ken Dunlevy, with hardly a goodby, departed with the Americans who took them to the American mission which was across town in an old luxury hotel. Maria, stunned that the Americans left so suddenly, was taken with Bill Davies to the British mission which was housed in the mansion of a wealthy Romanian.[2]

Walter Ross and his staff debriefed Dunlevy, Catlos, and Maria the next day. Ross didn't reveal that Holt Green and the others probably had been executed. The facts had not been confirmed, and the OSS had decided for the time being there would be no announcements. Ross for his own benefit was able to confirm the story told him previously by Lt. Stefan

Zenopian. This was the news that ultimately was reported by the Associated Press.

Sergeant Bill Davies and Maria settled in at the British mission. The British colonel had leased it from the wife of Ion Antonescu, a wealthy Romanian. Maria was overwhelmed with the opulence — the marble staircase, the large, elegant baths, the stately dining room, elaborate chandeliers, and other lavish furnishings. The only things Maria had ever seen like it were in the Vienna museums. Other elegant mansions on the broad Bucharest avenue had been seized by high ranking Red Army officers. To the victors went the spoils.[3]

Colonel Harry Carter, the British officer in charge of the mission, was fascinated by Maria's story. Well aware of the Soviet desire to silence any potential critics, Carter warned Maria that she must be careful not to fall into their hands. A few nights later, he confirmed to her that the Russians were looking for her, and made arrangements for her to have a British escort whenever she traveled in the city.[4] She made day trips with Colonel Carter to the Transylvania Mountains and once went to Ploesti to view the oil refineries which had been the target of the 15th Air Force. Despite the bombings, the refineries showed little damage.[5]

Zenopian, meanwhile, had been sent back to London, and the British and Dutch civilians who had traveled with Maria and the Anglo-American group from the Displaced Persons camp were sent on to Odessa for repatriation home. Catlos and Dunlevy already were in Italy.

Soviet kidnappings of Romanian citizens were a daily occurrence. Accounts of these incidents convinced Maria that she should get to Italy as soon as possible. Maria found herself increasingly lonely as her companions faded away.[6]

May 8, VE Day, Germany Surrenders.

Bucharest celebrated the war's end in Europe with unrestrained joy. That night at an elegant restaurant, Colonel Carter took Maria and others to

The Drama Ends

a victory party. The British, Americans and Russians celebrated in grand style. Everyone was overjoyed and good feelings were shared by all. For the moment the Grand Alliance was healthy and thriving.

Maria could not believe the war was over. She was thrilled, although the fear of being abducted by the *NKVD* never left her.[7] Learning that the Soviets had to approve all exit visas, Maria concluded she might never get out of Romania. Then, In July with the help of the newly arrived Czech counsel, and also the intervention of Walter Ross, she was put on an American C-47 and flown to Bari. She last saw Bill Davies at the airfield in Bari — a tearful parting. Davies had been more protective of her than either Catlos and Dunlevy, although the two men later praised her lavishly in their own OSS Report.[8]

Maria was transferred to Caserta where she wrote a detailed account of her OSS involvement in Slovak which was translated into English.[9] Again, she was overwhelmed with the luxury of the Allied headquarters which were housed in the huge summer palace of King Victor Emanuel.[10] The palace contained dozens of offices with seemingly countless numbers of men and women manning typewriters and scurrying up and down the hallways.[11] Maria was now authorized to wear an American uniform (without insignias of rank which was customary for intelligence agents) and received a monthly salary of $50.

Most important, Maria came to know Navy lieutenant Jack Taylor who was becoming an OSS legend as a Mauthausen survivor. Taylor, a taciturn, serious officer, luckily escaped his scheduled execution, and, emaciated, was there in rags to greet the men of the U.S. Army's 11th Armored Division when they liberated the camp.[12] The former California dentist had been the leader of the DUPONT mission which parachuted into the Vienna region on October 13, 1944.

DUPONT was a risky operation. Taylor spoke no German and his fellow agents were disaffected *Wehrmacht* soldiers who had been recruited from POW cages in Italy.[13]

The mission was doomed from the start. Taylor and his men never found the canister containing their radio which was dropped with them. Worse, one of the Germans later became involved with an Austrian girl. The *Gestapo* inevitably was tipped off, and they were all arrested.

The prisoners were taken to Vienna in November, 1944, and was subsequently taken to the *Metropol Hotel* in Vienna. They were there at the same time as Jan Schwartz, Jack Shafer, Theron Arnett, and other members of Shafer's crew. Richard Moulton also was in the *Gestapo* headquarters at that time. The *Gestapo* kept the prisoners isolated, and Taylor had no idea that the OSS personnel were held in the same building. He was later transferred to Mauthausen on April 1, 1945, to await a death sentence.

Maria Learns the Fate of the DAWES Team.

When Jack Taylor learned Maria had been with the DAWES mission, he gave her the grim news — Holt Green and the others had been executed at Mauthausen. Although she already had suspected they probably were dead, she was stunned by the news. She brooded for days over the thought of her friends being brutally killed, and thought especially of Tibor Keszthelyi.[14]

Lt. Taylor had an Army Jeep at his disposal, and he and Maria drove around the Caserta, stopping for lunch or coffee at small taverns in the Italian countryside. Her platonic relationship with Taylor was warm and comfortable. Taylor had known Holt Green and Jim Gaul. Green's mission to Slovakia had started only 27 days before Taylor's DUPONT mission, and Gaul left Bari only six days before Taylor parachuted into Austria.

Taylor was eager to learn the details of the problems the DAWES team experienced in Slovakia. He told Maria he had recovered the shoulder rank boards of either Holt Green or Jim Gaul from the desk of Franz Ziereis, the camp commandant.[15]

Taylor, who weighed only 112 pounds when he was liberated at Mauthausen, told Maria how he witnessed the inmates murdering the *Capos*

The Drama Ends 311

(prisoners who worked as "camp police" who brutalized other prisoners) when the camp was liberated. She was shocked at his descriptions of conditions and the level of brutality in the camp. He described the beatings he suffered when he arrived on Easter Sunday.

Taylor opted to remain at Mauthausen after his liberation to collect evidence for use at the subsequent Dachau war crimes trial against the captured *SS* staff members. He was writing his report when he and Maria met. The evidence and witnesses he assembled contributed to the indictment of 61 *SS* Mauthausen guards and staff officers, most of whom were found guilty and executed.[16] Hans Altfuldisch, Josef Niedermayer, and Andreas Trumm were among those tried and hanged.

Maria's next few months with the OSS were a whirlwind adventure. She flew to Salzburg and later went to Pilsen and Prague. She accompanied American officials to social functions and did some interpreting. She ran into Jan Schwartz in Prague, and they had a joyous reunion. Each was eager to learn of the other's exploits, both amazed that they had survived the war. Schwartz told her how he had been held by the *Gestapo* in the same building as Jack Taylor.[17]

Taylor had difficulty reconciling why he had been sent by the *Gestapo* to Mauthausen and Jan Schwarz had not. Taylor suggested to his OSS superiors after the war that he suspected Schwartz of being a possible double agent.

On June 14, Lt. Roger Bennett, USNR, questioned Schwartz without suggesting to Schwartz that he was under some suspicion. Bennett had been told by another OSS officer that Schwartz would survive if anyone could. Schwartz told Bennett how he convinced the *Gestapo* that he was not an American OSS agent. (see chapter 21) Bennett wrote in his report that some of Schwartz' answers were not "completely trustworthy."[18] Nevertheless, there was no followup on Schwartz, and he escaped further scrutiny.

Maria observed the wild social life of some of the OSS personnel in Salzburg and Prague. Local women who had been mistresses of the Germans now were involved with American officers, much to her disgust. Maria also saw the flourishing Prague black market. Later, she traveled to Wiesbaden and then to Paris.

In September, Maria had met Allen Dulles, later the director of the Central Intelligence Agency. Dulles had been the OSS chief in Switzerland. By the end of the year, she had learned that General Donovan and Allen Dulles had arranged for her to immigrate to the United States with a scholarship to Vassar. She later met Donovan in New York in March, 1946, when she was able to thank him personally.[19]

Maria Visits Her Parents.

In the interim, Maria returned to Slovakia with Jan Schwartz. They drove a jeep from Prague to southern Slovakia where Schwartz visited his grand parents. Slovakia was now united with the Czech Republic again as Czechoslovakia. Schwartz already had been there as an interpreter for Lt. Kelly O'Neall, USNR; and Lynn Heinzerling of the Associated Press who together had investigated Joe Morton's disappearance.[20]

Schwartz and Maria then drove to Jakubany where Maria had an emotional reunion with her family. Convinced she was dead, they were stunned to see her. She told them that she could not remain in Slovakia because of the Russian occupation, and that she would be going to the United States. It was a poignant and sad farewell when they parted. She would not see them again until 1970.[21]

In the United States, Maria soon learned that her English was inadequate and that she would be on her own most of the time. She felt lonely and frightened. But she had overcome worse crises, and she would overcome this one.

Harriett Gaul, who had been contacting Steve Catlos, Ken Dunlevy, and other OSS personnel, soon learned that Maria was in the country. Mrs. Gaul had heard much about Maria from the others and was eager to talk with her. While she had accepted the fact her son was dead, Harriett sought addi-

The Drama Ends 313

tional information which would give her a more complete picture of the ordeal through which he and the others had suffered. Because of the reticence of the OSS leadership to release information about the mission and the knowledge that Catlos and Dunlevy had been ordered not to talk, Mrs. Gaul knew she did not have all the facts.[22]

Catlos and Dunlevy had not hesitated to tell Harriett Gaul and the others that they had been ordered by the OSS not to divulge information.[23] Both Dunlevy and McGregor were angry. They believed the OSS had blundered by sending in too many men over the objection of Holt Green, and also that the 15th Air Force could have flown in another rescue plane. They talked specifically about October 22 when the weather had been so clear in central Slovakia. The men had a lot to say, and their bitterness now extended to the victims' families. All this had been expressed previously in Daisy Green's letter to General Donovan.

The family members were puzzled that the Slovak officer, Jan Stanek, captured in the hut at Polomka, survived, but their men had not. They were angry that the men had been betrayed by a Slovak, Gönder. And they even wondered about Maria. Harriet Gaul met Maria and carefully grilled her. In a letter to Laura Frost and Letty Morton after a meeting with Maria, Harriet Gaul wrote, "[She] did not change the story in any way, but we went over the ground again."[24]

Harriet Gaul ultimately was satisfied that Maria had told the whole story about the DAWES mission, at least, everything which Maria knew first hand. Harriet and Maria became fast friends.

Maria struggled at Vassar. She was older than the other girls, "preppies," who mostly came from the upper middle class. Socially, Vassar was a poor fit for Maria. She was the strange, foreign "older" woman with the weird tales of espionage, intrigue, close scrapes with *Nazis*, and harrowing escapes which seemed so surreal to her fellow students. Her language handicap hurt her in her classes in which rigid instructors gave her little leeway in their grading.

Maria would later marry an attorney and have two children. She was continually promised that "her story" would be made into a best-selling book and probably into a hit movie. Her hopes were high, but it never happened.

The 1944-45 tragedy in Slovakia which destroyed the DAWES team took the lives of outstanding men and also that of Margita Kockova. Holt Green was the classic, intelligent southern aristocrat who possibly could have become a senator or governor. Jim Gaul was the creative and aggressive PhD scholar who would have made a name in the academic world. Tibor Kesthelyi, popular and intelligent, would have wound up in the CIA or in international business. Lieutenants Frank Perry and Lane Miller were talented individuals. Joe Horvath, Charles Heller, Nelson Paris, and Robert Brown were loyal, dedicated men, who would have emerged from the war with bright futures. Daniel Pavletich probably would have gone back to the merchant marine. We don't know what future Margita Kockova may have had. Jerry Mican would have returned to Chicago to teach and become a leader in the Chicago Czech community.

Edward Baranski might have found his niche in intelligence work. The dynamic and aggressive captain had formulated the FALCON plan, which although brilliantly conceived, never materialized. Bright and creative, he surely would have wound up in the CIA or some successful business. But for bad luck and a betrayal, he and Daniel Pavletich would have survived the war.

The brightest star, perhaps, would have been Joe Morton. His persistence and focus on the "big story" and his reporting skills would have propelled him into pre-eminence in the world of journalism. His murder was a sad and senseless act.

To visualize Franz Ziereis, Georg Bachmayer, and Walter Habecker – those satanic, sadistic, *SS* officers — snuffing out the lives of such people leaves one's notion of humanity shaken. Maria, meanwhile, nearly fell into the clutches of the *NKVD*, whose people were no less murderous than the *Nazis*.

Although history is replete with countless examples of base, immoral

The Drama Ends

acts and horrible murders, honorable men and women never are able to accept them.

Both Holt Green and Jim Gaul were awarded the Distinguished Service Cross posthumously.

Other members of the DAWES team received lessor awards. In a ceremony on May 25, 1946, General Wild Bill Donovan personally pinned a Bronze Star on Maria in a special ceremony at West Point military academy. Originally, she was to be awarded a Distinguished Service Cross, but because she wasn't a citizen, that was deemed inappropriate. Then a Silver Star was considered, but that too was rejected because she was a woman. Nevertheless, she became the first woman ever to be decorated on the Plain of West Point in front of the Corps of Cadets.

In 1964, the Czechoslovak government invited McGregor, Lain, Catlos, and Schwartz back to Banska Bystrica for the 20th anniversary of the Slovak National Uprising. Dunlevy refused an invitation.

The ebullient Nikita Khrushchev was there as the principal speaker. In a rare blunder, the Communists asked Bill McGregor to speak. The huge crowd, which filled the main city square, roared its approval. The small American contingent was elated. Khrushchev stormed out, furious that this unknown and insignificant American received louder cheers than he.

So it is in history when the people have an opportunity to express their allegiance to democracy and the symbols of freedom.

---

1 Maria Gulovich, Telephone interview with the author, April 12, 2001.
2 Ion Antonescu was executed as a war criminal in 1946.
3 Maia Gulovich, Telephone interview with the author, April 12, 2001.
4 Ibid.
5 Ibid.
6 Ibid.
7 Ibid.
8 Kenneth Dunlevy, OSS Report.
9 Maria Gulovich, OSS Report.
10 Maria Gulovich, Telephone interview.
11 One may see this palace in the movie, Patton.
12 Maria Gulovich, Telephone interview, April 12, 2001.

13 Ibid.
14 Ibid.
15 Ibid.
16 NARA, John Hedrick Taylor, OSS Report on war crimes.
17 Gulovich, Telephone interview, April 12, 2001.
18 NARA, HOUSEBOAT personnel folder,
19 Ibid.
20 Heinzerling gave his report to the American embassy on July 13, 1945. Affidavit, courtesy of Larry Heinzerling.
21 Gulovich, Telephone interview, April 12, 2001.
22 The author never has located relatives of Nelson Paris, Charles Heller, or Jerry Mican. It is likely that the families of Paris and Heller never learned much at all. Charles Katek presumably filled in Mary Mican with the details of what happened to her husband.
23 Steve Catlos, Interview with William Miller, 1983.
24 Harriett Gaul, Letter to Laura Frost, October 10, 1946, courtesy of Frances Frost Hutson.

Epilogue

With the war over, American families who lost sons, brothers, and husbands quietly struggled on, dealing with the loss of their loved ones. Those men who made it home set out to get on with their lives as America geared up for a peace-time economy.

Germans who survived the war faced a different reality. Their devastated nation lay in rubble, millions were dead, and untold numbers of their soldiers were missing or locked up in prisoner of war cages. As a result, Germans considered themselves victims of the war no less than the Allies. Regardless, the victors felt little sympathy for the Germans who had so enthusiastically supported their Führer and now insisted they knew little or nothing about the death camps. The Allies had been horrified by the discovery of the camps, and sought to identify and prosecute those responsible.

The British, Russians, the OSS, and the U.S. Army Counter Intelligence Corps went through the crowded POW camps looking for suspects. They pored over records they had seized, although the Nazis had destroyed many records before their surrender. Specifically, the American OSS and the British SOE wanted to catch the men who had murdered the Anglo-Americans at Mauthausen.

In Berlin prior to the German surrender, *RSHA* personnel had been given false identifications enabling them to go underground. As a result, many *SS* personnel, including *Gestapo* chief Heinrich Mueller, were not apprehended. Manfred Schoeneseiffen, Walter Habecker, or Heinrich Arndt, who had brutalized the Anglo-Americans at Mauthausen, were among the missing.

For example, U.S. Army prosecutors aggressively went after those *SS* personnel accused of murdering American POWs the previous January in Malmedy, Belgium, in the final days of the Battle of the Bulge. Those Germans arrested refused to talk which prompted frustrated prosecutors to resort to kangaroo court-style procedures, mock trials, and threats in order to breakdown the prisoners. Family members publicly accused the American guards of beating the *SS* prisoners.

In the United States, there were protests about the alleged judicial abuses, especially among German-Americans. By contrast, in the Soviet zone justice was swift. Major *Graf* Thun-Hohenstein, for example, was captured in the Czech Protectorate by the Russians, and in February, 1946 he and other *SS* prisoners were tried and executed. In the American zone of Germany, in most cases six months to over a year would elapse before the first convicted *SS* killers from the concentration camps would be tried and executed.

When Major *Graf* Thun-Hohenstein had been interrogated by the Soviets in 1945, he identified two other fellow *Abwehr* officers, Lt. Colonel Kurt Benno Fechner and Major Hans Koch. Fechner was the commander of *Frontleitstelle II - Süd-Ost*, the organization to which Major Thun-Hohenstein's *Abwehr 218* was attached. Koch commanded the Ukrainian Section of *Frontleitstelle II - Süd-Ost*.[1]

Although the Soviets tried and executed Thun-Hohenstein, both Fechner and Koch fared differently. They were captured by the Americans, but neither apparently was ever prosecuted. According to Professor Dr. Siegfried Beer of the University of Graz, Fechner immediately offered his services to his captors as an intelligence expert on the Soviets. He subsequently became the first head of the intelligence branch of the Austrian army.[2]

SS Major Hans Koch also forged a new life. He had an interesting background. After serving in Austrian Army intelligence in World War I, he had earned a PhD in theology and philosophy and became the director of the

"Eastern Institute" in Breslau, Germany in the 1930's. When World War II broke out, he became an officer in *Abwehr II* which was commanded in Berlin by Otto Skorzeny. Koch served under Fechner.

After the Americans released Koch following World War II, he joined the faculty of the University of Munich in Germany where he achieved some renown as the director of the anti-communist "Eastern Institute" similar to his old post in Breslau. He died in 1959.[3]

For the leaders of the Third *Reich* it was a different story. The 22 leading Nazis, including Herman Goering, Rudolph Hess, and Ernst Kaltenbrunner, were dramatically prosecuted. Tried at Nurnberg by an international tribunal of four judges from the United Kingdom, France, the Soviet Union, and the United States, most of the defendants were given death sentences and others received long prison terms.

Leading Nazis Tried at Nurnberg.

At Dachau in 1946, the U.S. Army also tried 177 *SS* staff members from the Mauthausen, Dachau, Flossenburg, and Buchenwald concentration camps. Mauthausen alone had an *SS* staff of 5,000 men. *Gauleiter* August Eigruber, Hans Altfuldisch, Andreas Trumm, Josef Niedermayer, and Adolf Zutter were among those tried and subsequently hanged. Over 100 members of the Mauthausen *SS* staff had been sent to prison. Following appeals, 49 were executed.[4] The DAWES and WINDPROOF victims, plus thousands of others, were partially avenged.

Lt. Jack Taylor, USNR, the OSS agent, played a key role in the Mauthausen prosecutions with the evidence he had collected following his liberation from the camp. Taylor was the first witness to testify at the first of over 400 trials at Dachau.

Nevertheless, thousands of German guards who committed murder in these camps escaped prosecution. A few took their own lives. At Mauthausen, commandant Franz Ziereis and his deputy, Georg Bachmayer, died before they could be brought to trial. Seven days before the German surrender and prior to the arrival of American troops, Ziereis fled sixty miles south to a mountain lodge he owned near Spittal.

An American patrol attempting to arrest Ziereis on May 23, 1945, shot and mortally wounded him when he resisted. The Americans took him back to the Gusen camp near Mauthausen where they had set up an evacuation hospital to care for the former camp inmates. Ziereis lived for two days and gave a lengthy, death-bed statement.

Ziereis insisted to interrogators he was "not an evil man," and that he, of course, was just following the orders of Himmler and Kaltenbrunner. After his death, the Americans released his body to the liberated prisoners who strung up his corpse in the Gusen camp grounds. A grotesque photo of that still exists.

On the day Germany surrendered, Bachmayer shot his wife, his children, and himself. Obersturmführer Hans Altfuldisch told OSS investigators he saw Bachmayer's body in the village where he lived not far from Mauthausen and helped with the burial.

Some *SS* personnel captured by the Americans were turned over to governments in the Soviet zone. *Obersturmbannführer* Josef Witiska was one example. He had been promoted in January, 1945, to Standartenführer (colonel) as a reward for his efforts in suppressing the Slovak National Uprising from his headquarters in Bratislava. Witiska had rounded up over 18,000 Jews, and his *Einsatzkommando* units had captured thousands of Partisan stragglers, many of whom were shipped to Germany as slave laborers. After the German surrender, Witiska hid first in Austria then Germany. The Americans turned him over to Czechoslovakian authorities in October, 1946, but while being transported by train, Witiska bit into a cyanide capsule.[5]

Later in 1947, Walter Habecker, who had brutalized Holt Green, Edward Baranski, John Sehmer and the others at Mauthausen, was arrested, tried and sent to prison by the British. He admitted to some of the torture of the Anglo-American prisoners, but denied that he had ordered them hanged by their arms. In January, 1949, he took his own life at Paderborn Prison in the British zone.

Allies End War Crimes Trials.

In time, the war crimes prosecutions bogged down, and even many of the American lawyers and judges lost confidence in the process. The Allies lost the political will to proceed as pressure from the German press and politicians mounted. The Germans equated the Allied bombings of Hamburg, Dresden and other German cities to the concentration camps, and this had its effect on both Washington and London.

Driven by a moral equivalency logic, the German populace was outraged that during Christmas 1948 64 Nazis awaited execution at Landsberg Prison in Bavaria. The German press raised the issue of the 8,000 children under 15 who died in the fire storms of the Hamburg air raids, and now questioned Allied postwar justice. Germans became particularly outraged during the period between October 15, 1948 and February 2, 1949, when the Americans executed 104 men at Landsberg despite the fact many were mass murderers who had committed horrendous crimes.

Nevertheless, some Allied arrests continued until 1948. Thousands of German suspects by then had been identified and arrested, although many of the earlier sentences of those convicted were reduced, much to the chagrin and frustration of the Army prosecutors.[6]

Former Army prosecutor William Denson complained years later that people, including American officials, simply did not believe the evidence. The crimes were too awful, too terrible. They were simply "incomprehensible." For instance, General Lucius Clay, US Army Chief of Staff of the occupation forces in Germany, acknowledged that he could not believe all the witnesses.[7]

In the turbulent waters of American-British-Soviet relations, the American prosecutors soon found themselves high and dry. John J. McCloy, the U.S. High Commissioner for Germany, continued to overturn or reduce sentences (reluctantly), and pressured by the State Department, finally granted clemency to two hundred condemned German prisoners.

McCloy also was pressured by the Pope, the German government and others to go further, and in 1951, McCloy, although troubled, granted a general amnesty.[8] Former Colonel Burton Ellis, at age 96, who prosecuted the Germans in the Malmedy Massacre case, told the author in 1999 he was still furious - a half century later — about the reductions of sentences, and dismissal of others, of cases he tried.[9]

Some of the clemency cases were outrageous. Dr. Hertha Oberhauser, for example, had conducted experiments on female prisoners at Ravensbrueck concentration camp, and received a 20-year sentence. One British doctor, after examining the evidence, described Oberhauser as a sadist. Granted status as a "returned prisoner," she received an early release in 1952. She later entered private practice, and was given a cash grant by the German government plus an interest free loan. Oberhauser was soon back practicing medicine.

Infamous War Criminals Released.

Other outrageous cases upset American prosecutors. Ilse Koch, the infamous "Bitch of Buchenwald," who ordered lampshades made from prisoners' tattooed skin, was released after serving four years of a life sentence. Dr. Hans Eisele, known as the "real mass murderer at Buchenwald," had been sentenced to death for medical experiments which killed hundreds of prisoners. He walked out of Landsberg Prison in 1952.

One German industrialist, who had used slave labor during the war which resulted in starvation and death for workers, was released in 1953. A free man, he commented wryly, "Now that [the Americans] have Korea on their minds, they have become a lot more friendly." The Americans were in a pickle and the Germans knew it.

General William Donovan had made a point of being in the Nurnberg courtroom when Ernst Kaltenbrunner was given the death sentence, but was undoubtedly disappointed that Manfred Schoeneseiffen and Heinrich Arndt were never found.[10]

The Allied trials finally came to an end, and the German government then took over the prosecution of war criminals. But by 1960, 85 percent of German judges had Nazi pasts. Although the German government subsequently tried 5,228 individuals, only 83 were convicted. Of those, fourteen were sentenced to death and only three were actually executed. Forgotten by many was the fact that the *Gestapo* and the *SS* had murdered millions in the concentration camps.[11]

Americans Get On With Their Lives.

Meanwhile, in the U.S., those involved in the Slovak drama moved on.

Walter Ross became a successful banker, Howard Chapin a corporate executive, and Nelson Deranian a highly successful attorney in Washington D.C. Charles Katek went to work for the CIA, operating as military attache in the American embassy in Prague.

The three West Point graduates, pilots Gil Pritchard, Fred Ascani, and Jack Gorman, became Air Force generals. Jim Cinnaman retired as a Lt. Colonel and became an airline pilot. Sergeant Bill Newton attended the University of Chattanooga and worked in industrial management. Lt. Bill Coloney left the military and became a successful businessman in auto sales. Retired, he still flies his own small aircraft doing aerial photography work. Gorman, Newton, and Coloney are still alive.

Howard Dallman retired from the Air Force as a colonel after winning the Air Force Cross in Vietnam. Jack Shafer also retired as a colonel, and Manley Fliger and Thayne Thomas retired as Air Force lieutenant colonels. Shafer, planning on visiting Slovakia the following summer, was killed in a tragic traffic accident in 1999. Jim Street became an FBI agent, and lives today in Oregon.

Don Rider, who originally was to head the DAWES mission, worked for the CIA until 1973, mostly in Latin America. In 1978 he was invited back to Yugoslavia and was personally decorated by President Tito.

Bill McGregor worked in insurance and sales during most of his career. For a time, he lived in New Zealand, and for a time raised cattle and horses in California. Steve Catlos was an administrator in the Pittsburgh Port Transit authority. Jan Schwartz became a successful business executive in Poughkeepsie, New York, and Ken Dunlevy worked in security for the U.S. Government. Dunlevy is still alive, but refuses to grant interviews. McGregor lives in Texas in a rest home.

Maria Gulovich Liu now lives in California and is a retired real estate agent. She has two children who reside on the east coast.

Theron Arnett became a teacher and administrator in the Los Angeles Unified School District, retiring as Assistant Superintendent in charge of Personnel. Robert Donahue worked as a Postal Service mail carrier for 40 years. Charlie Muller retired in southern California from the Air Force as a master sergeant after being working in special operations attached to the CIA.

Neal Cobb graduated from Indiana University and enjoyed a successful career in industrial sales. Bob Hede worked in manufacturing and sales. Howard Coleman prospered in his career in the office supply business. Howard Luzier worked for the same company for 45 years at the management level, and recently celebrated his 62nd wedding anniversary. Jack Kellogg became a vocational arts teacher and later a general contractor. Ira Corpening went into the upholstery business.

John Schianca, now retired in Connecticut, became an administrator for the Veterans Administration, while Richard Moulton, after attending Dartmouth, entered the investment banking business. He later managed a small bank, worked in the wholesale lumber business and then ran another small company. "Broker, Banker, Lumber Sales, Ceramic tile importer, sales and installation," Moulton says today with a laugh from his home in Florida. George Fernandes went to work for the U.S. Coast and Geodetic Survey, and later worked seven years on Oceanographic Research and Survey. He lives in Washington.

Frank Soltesz worked as a milk distributor, and did charity work at a local hospital for much of his life. Nick Yezdich went into the grocery business with his parents and later retired in Miami where he lives today.

In Slovakia, Jan Surovec struggled to survive as a small businessman and Josef Piontek went back to work for the Bata shoe company. Both were forced in 1948 to stop communicating with their American friends when the Communist regime tightened its grip on Czechoslovakia. Bill McGregor, Ken Lain, Jan Schwartz, and Steve Catlos were able to enjoy a reunion with Surovec in Slovakia in 1964. With the Communists still in power, Maria had to wait 25 years before visiting her family in Czechoslovakia.

---

1 Soviet interrogation report of Thun-Hohenstein, Transcript given to the author by Julian Hendy, Yorkshire Television, TV Centre, Leeds, United Kingdom, November 12, 2000.

2 Professor Dr. Siegfried Beer, E mail to the author, January 8, 2002; Some have called Fechner the "Gehlen" of Austria. General Gehlen of the Wehrmacht later worked for the CIA in West Germany.

3 *Archiv, Institut für Zeitgeschichte*, Munich, Germany, Letter to the author, February 1, 2001; The author received two obituaries of Dr. Koch from German newspapers sent to the author by the Institut, which lauded Koch's academic achievements. Neither mentioned Koch's WWII service in the *Abwehr*. The Institut had a file on Abwehr 218, but the archivist for the Institut informed the author there was no mention of Hans Koch in the file.

4 The author has been unable to learn much about three of the Gestapo officials from Berlin Schoeneseiffen, Habecker and Arndt - who interrogated the Americans at Mauthausen. A man with the same title, age, and name of Schoeneseiffen died in Cologne on June 21, 2001. The author does not know if he were ever prosecuted.

5 Courtesy of Peter Kassak citing Jan Korcek, Slovenska Republika 1943-45 (1999, Bratislava, Slovakia); Politically, Witiska was not as agile as Kurt Benno Fechner who was able cut a deal with the Americans as a source of intelligence on the Soviets.

6 Bard, *Forgotten Victims*, pp. 127-128.

7 Ibid.

8 Ibid.

9 Now deceased, Ellis left his extensive war crimes files (and $6,000,000!) to the University of Idaho.

10 The author spent hours looking in vain in the files of the National Archives for any record of arrests or trials of these two men.

11 The high number of acquittals and light sentences in the brief summaries of the German trials is depressing for most Americans.

Acknowledgements

Among the people who assisted the author in producing this book, Maria Gulovich Liu stands foremost. She not only read and re-read the manuscript, but she dug up old correspondence, wrote letters, made countless phone calls, and frequently traveled a half century back into the reaches of her memory to recall long-forgotten events. Her charm and sense of humor, as well as her keen intelligence, kept me pointed continually in the right direction.

The late Juraj Rajninec from Trencin, Slovakia, a great friend of America, helped me repeatedly before he died. He sent me documents and photos, giving me leads, but, most importantly, even before I met Maria, inspiring me to tell this story.

In the beginning, I wanted Larry Heinzerling of the Associated Press to write this book. Through his father's involvement in the story, Larry already had completed a manuscript about Joe Morton. I suggested that he widen the story to include the airmen and the OSS personnel, and volunteered to help with the research. But, as Larry moved up the ladder at the AP, the pressure of his work left him little spare time. He has graciously allowed me to quote from his manuscript.

My old friend, Dr. Jay Shivers at the University of Connecticut, reviewed my text. A consummate author himself (27 books at last count), he helped me immeasurably. Jim Jordan, my former teaching colleague weeded out many of my errors in the manuscript.

When I started my research, I mailed out three dozen questionnaires.

George Fernandes responded with a 25-page, single-spaced typewritten manuscript. His account was rich in detail and humorously written, so good in fact that I thought maybe he should write the book. We have had dozens of wonderful telephone conversations.

Colonel Jack Shafer, now deceased, was another key participant. He and George believed that their Slovakian experience was one of the great events of their lives. They shared a great passion for the Slovaks who helped them.

Julian Hendy, Yorkshire Television in Leeds, England, supplied me with a stack of documents from the British Public Records Office, all vivid and vital information. Another documentary film producer, Ulrich Koch in Berlin, helped.

Marilyn Miller photocopied for me many of her father's records and notes. A great writer at Time and Life, the late William Miller was going to write this book, but he ran out of time. His spade work among the OSS survivors and also the Slovaks in Donovaly and Polomka, where he visited, was immensely helpful.

Four family members of the DAWES mission contributed. Frances Frost Hutson, gave me information about her uncle, Holt Green. Sandy Woods, Bill McGregor's daughter, helped. Her dad resides in a rest home, and he and I had some wonderful conversations. Although his memory has been eroding over time, Bill still was able to recall details about those dramatic 1944 days. Kathy Baranski Lund, Edward Baranski's daughter, accompanied my wife and me to the National Archives in Maryland. Together we delved through the records there.

Frank and Rudy Horvath were helpful with details about their brother, Joe. Frank went with our group to Slovakia in 1998. I witnessed his poignant reunion with his cousin, Anna, now deceased, whom he had not seen since he was a boy, 63 years earlier.

Family members of OSS veterans who helped include Hatti Fitts, Mrs. Walter Ross, Buck Miller, Steve Catlos, Jr., and Mrs. Jean Arnett. Also,

Edward Papierski and Oliver Silsby, two former OSS, radiomen, helped as did Mimi Morton Gosney, Joe Morton's daughter. James Sehmer shared valuable information about his father, John. Clayton Metcalf, an old friend of Virgil Stuart, contributed.

In a stroke of luck, I located Cecilia Wojewoda in Warsaw, Poland. She recalled fascinating details about those grim days in Slovakia. She still cherishes her memories of the Americans she met in 1944, and still grieves about their fate.

Paul Strassmann and Igor Nabelek, two ardent Slovak-Americans and both veterans of the Slovak National Uprising, have had greatly productive lives in America. They shared many of their 1944 experiences with me and also kept me from making a number of mistakes in the text.

Dr. Thomas Reimer, professor history at Empire State College in New York, provided important information about the controversial issue of the ethnic Germans of Slovakia and their suffering in 1944. Dr. Reimer is a passionate critic of those Slovaks and Czechs who refuse to acknowledge atrocities committed against German civilians in Slovakia during and after the war. This general topic increasingly haunts the Slovak political scene as revisionist historians, many of them Slovaks, revisit the crimes of the war. The intellectual community is not of one mind here.

Dr. Martin Votruba, head of the Slavic Studies program at the University of Pittsburgh, read parts of the manuscript and made valuable suggestions. Colonel Jim Gabriel, USAF retired, shared ideas with me about his uncle, the late Nelson Deranian. He has allowed me to use a few of his uncle's photographs. Bella Downs, a talented artist, succumbed to her cousin's request to design the book cover.

Simon Duffee, grandson of Gordon Follas, that colorful New Zealand warrior, and Follas' daughter, Penny Paton, were an immense help.

The following World War II airmen faithfully answered my questionnaires and phone calls: Lincoln Artz, Fred Ascani, Larry Cardwell, James Cinnamon, Neal Cobb, Howard Coleman, Bill Coloney, Silas Crase, Bob

Donahue, Ed Donatelli, Manley Fliger, Jack Gorman, Bob Hede, Gene Hodge, Jack Kellogg, Howard Luzier, Richard Moulton, Charlie Muller, Bill Newton, John Pittman, John Schianca, Norton Skinner, Ethan Allen Smith, Jim Street, Henrietta Thomas for her husband, Thayne; Thayne Thomas, when he was still alive; Frank Soltesz, Mrs. Alex Watkins, Arnold Wilson, Nick Yezdick, Edwin Zavisa, and John Zebrowski.

Others included Don Rider, Franklin Lindsay, Page Pratt, Betty Mcintosh, Dr. Richard Kuhn, Edwin Putzell, General Peter Vlcko, and Jason von Zerneck.

The dedicated men of the Trencin Aviation Club helped on our 1998 visit to Slovakia. Michal Siskovsky, Matin Bubeliny, Viliam Klabnik, Roman Kruty, Dr. Marion Hrodegh, Lt. Colonel Jan Bogar, Jan Babincak, a brilliant interpreter; and Ivana and Vlad Galik all helped. Count Franz Czernin of Vienna, Austria; wrote me interesting, detailed letters about his father-in-law, Count Erwein Thun-Hohenstein.

I owe a debt of gratitude to Niels Cordes, John Taylor and Dr. Larry McDonald of the National Archives, researcher Lisa Hartjens, author Charles Kliment, author Chapman Pincher, Allen Milcic, Stuart Stein, Dick de Mildt, and Lt. Colonel Frederic Guelton, *Directeur du departement Recherches du SHAT*, French Army, Paris France; Lieutenant Jan Brockmann, *Militärgeschichtliches Forschungsamt*, The *Bundeswehr*, Potsdam, Germany; and Anton Seul of the *Bundesarchiv*, Koblenz, Germany. Also, from Israel, Chaim Chermesh, another veteran of the Slovak Uprising, assisted. Helping with translations were Erika Eisele, Pleunette Monaghan, Michael Russe, and Werner von Gundell. Thanks also to Bob Schroeder, Laurie Dunne, Marta Dunetz, Helen Hartley and my talented illustrator, Ingrid Magalinska, in Sofia, Bulgaria.

Forgive me if I have forgotten anyone.

Partial Bibliography

Bard, Mitchell G. Forgotten Victims, Boulder: Westview Press, 1994.

Brown, Anthony Cave. The Last Hero Wild Bill Donovan. New York: Times Books, 1982.

Coppi, Hans, Danyel, Jürgen and Tuchel, Johannes. Die Rote Kapelle im Widerstand gegen den Nationalsozialismus. Berlin: Hentrick, 1994.

Heinzerling, Larry, The Execution of Joe Morton, Unpublished manuscript.

Hymoff, Edward. The OSS In World War II: The True Story of American Agents Behind Enemy Lines. New York: Richardson and Steirman, 1986.

Kliment, Charles K. and Nakladal, Bretislav, Germany's First Ally, Atglen, PA: Schiffer Military History, 1997.

Lankford, Nelson D., editor. OSS Against the Reich, Kent, Ohio: The Kent State University Press, 1991.

Lindsay, Franklin. Beacons In The Night: With the OSS and Tito's Partisans in Wartime Yugoslavia. Stanford, California: Stanford University Press, 1995.

MacLean, French, The Cruel Hunters, Atglen, PA: Schiffer Military History, 1998.

McIntosh, Elizabeth (MacDonald), Women In The OSS. Annapolis, Maryland: Naval Institute Press, 1998.

Moulton, Richard, Unpublished manuscript.

Persico, Joseph E. Piercing The Reich, New York: The Viking Press, 1979.

Schlabrendorff, Fabian von, The Secret War Against Hitler. New York, Pitman Publishing Corporation, 1965.

Winks, Robin W. Cloak And Gown, New York: Quill William Morrow, 1987.

Index

Abwehr, 202, 225-27, 231, 295, 318-19.
Albright, Madeleine, 253 photo.
Altfuldisch, Hans, 248, 253 photo, 256-7, 272, 276, 279-80, 284-5, 311, 319.
AMSTERDAM mission, 58, 242, 244.
Antonescu, Ion, 315.
Arbeitskommando 768, 39.
Arndt, Heinrich, 252, 254, 271-3, 278-9, 282, 295, 323, 325.
Arnett, Jean, 328.
Arnett, Theron, 113-14, 150 photo, 171, 176-7, 180-81, 210, 324.
Artz, Lincoln, 35, 145, 330.
Ascani, Fred, 60 photo, 81-2, 86-7, 92, 95, 323, 329.
Associated Press, 83, 273, 290-91, 299-301, 304.
Babincak, Jan, 330.
Bachmayer, Georg, 150 photo, 248, 250, 253 photo, 274, 277, 279, 281.
Banska Bystrica, Slovakia, 26, 31-2, 38, 40, 41, 43, 45, 54, 56-8, 60-61, 64-66, 69, 74, 77, 82, 89, 93, 98, 99, 103, 106, 109, 111, 114, 117-120, 125, 127, 133, 137, 146, 161-2, 184, 186, 205, 241, 249, 295, 302.
Baranski, Anna, 275-6.
Baranski, Edward, 13-17, 20, 60 photo, 78, 89, 100-1, 107, 117, 125, 150 photo, 205-7, 215, 253 photo, 271, 289-91, 314, 320, 328.
Bard, Mitchell, 257, 325.
Bari, Italy, 19, 32, 47, 64-5, 67, 77, 81, 83, 85, 97, 103, 107, 116-17, 153, 161, 193-4, 196, 198, 205-6, 215, 219, 273-6, 277, 281, 289, 300, 301, 304.
Benes, Eduard, 54, 60.
Bennett, Lt. Roger, 311.
Ben-Yaakov, Zwi, 60 photo, 242-4, 245, 275.
Berdichev, Aba, 60 photo, 85, 103, 202, 213, 273, 275.
Blanchard, Huston, 89.
Bodecker, Charles, 58, 82, 92.
Bogar, Lt. Colonel Jan, 330.
Bönhofer, Dietrich, 252.

Brezova, Slovakia, 39, 42, 73.
Brinser, John, 113, 126, 187, 190.
Brockmann, Jan, 330.
Brown, Anthony Cave, 21.
Brown, Robert, 54, 61, 132, 150 photo, 180, 217, 220, 275, 314.
Bruce, Colonel David, 13, 20.
Bubeliny, Martin, 330.
Bulfin, Frank, 72, 150 photo.
Cardwell, Larry, 330.
Carter, Colonel Harry, 310.
Catlos, Steve, 80-81, 103, 109, 123, 138, 166, 195, 199-200, 209, 213, 220, 230, 232-3, 235, 238, 242, 253 photo, 259-61, 288, 297, 302, 307-11, 315-16, 324-5.
Catlos, Steve, Jr., 328
CFI, 26, 30, 45, 65-66, 69, 118, 120, 123, 125, 128, 139.
Chapin, Lt. Colonel Howard, 47-8, 59, 64, 102, 161, 220, 288-89, 223.
Chermesh, Chaim, 60 photo, 242-33, 246, 330.
Cheston, Colonel Charles, 302, 304, 306.
Chetniks, 20, 49-50, 63, 81, 101.
Cinnaman, James, 81-2, 87, 323, 329.
CIS (Czech Intelligence Service), 13-14, 24, 26, 44, 47.
Cobb, Neal, 4, 7, 8, 20, 37, 42-44, 60 photo, 64, 66, 69-71, 74, 79-81, 89, 93, 95-6, 102, 324, 329.
Cohen, Lt. Commander Edward, 16
Coleman, Howard, 6, 8, 39, 72, 150 photo, 152, 188, 192, 324, 329.
Coloney, Bill, 59, 82-3, 86-7, 92, 95, 107, 150 photo, 323.
Cordes, Niels, 330.
Corpening, Ira, 1, 2, 324, 329.
Cransac, Jaques, 243, 246.
Crase, Silas, 95, 115, 329.
Czernin, Graf Franz, 231, 330.
Dallman, Howard, 56-7.
Davies, Bill, 230, 233, 260-61, 266, 295-6, 307-9.
DAWES Mission 48, 51-2, 79, 99, 102, 118,

120, 130, 152, 155, 161, 170, 180, 215, 225, 241-2, 245, 247, 251, 256, 271-2, 275, 280, 288-9, 291, 304-5, 310, 314-15, 318, 328.
DAY Mission, 80, 289.
Deane, John, 289.
DeMildt, Dick, 330.
Denson, Colonel William, 250, 321.
Deranian, Nelson, 47, 50, 53-4, 59, 60 photo, 62, 64, 77, 79, 83, 93-4, 98-9, 102, 118, 121, 150 photo, 154, 161, 215, 220, 288, 302, 305, 315, 323, 329.
Dirlewanger Brigade, 69, 126, 131-2, 152-5.
Dirlewanger, Oskar, 69, 104, 131-2.
Dolna Lehota, Slovakia, 197-201, 214-15, 226, 244, 294.
Donahue, Robert, 44-46, 56, 60 photo, 74, 324, 329-30.
Donatelli, Edward, 330.
Donovaly, Slovakia, 125-6, 128-33, 137-8, 141, 153, 154, 169, 231, 241.
Donovan, Major General William, 11, 15, 17, 47-48, 77, 79, 99, 102, 302, 312-13.
Downs, Bella, 330.
Duffee, Simon 330,
Dulles, Allen, 312.
Dumbier Mountain, 156, 162, 183-6,190.
Dunetz, Marta, 330.
Dunlevy, Ken, 80, 87, 90, 103, 109-110, 119, 123-4, 134, 154, 158-59, 169-170, 201, 203, 212-213, 216, 217-18, 227, 230, 232-33, 235-39, 250055, 288, 297, 302, 307-313, 315, 324.
Dunne, Laurie, 330.
Edelweiss Units, 226-28, 230-31, 233-34, 295.
Eigruber, Gauleiter August, 248-9, 319.
Einsatzkommando Units, 32, 201, 226, 245, 320.
Eisele, Erika, 330.
Eisele, Hans, 322.
Ellis, Colonel Burton, 322, 325.
Engler, Anna, 211-13, 220.
FALCON mission, 14-16, 17, 100, 314.
Feemster, Clyde, 85.
Ferjencik, Mikulas, 27.
Fernandes, George, 5, 7-8, 20, 37, 40-41, 43, 60 photo, 65, 71, 73-4, 111-12, 115, 118, 122, 124, 128, 134, 150 photo, 152, 154, 158-9, 164, 167, 170-1, 184-5, 191-2, 261, 288, 324, 328.
Fliger, Manley, 43, 46, 60 photo, 89, 95-6, 98, 323, 330.
Follas, Gordon, 36-7, 42, 60 photo, 71, 74, 150 photo, 329.
French Partisans, 60 photo, 97, 169, 184-5, 243-4, 266.
Frost, Laura, 302, 313, 316.
Fuchs, Ralph, 98.
Gabriel, Jim, 329.
Galik, Ivana and Vlad, 72, 75, 330.
Galizien Brigade, 126.
Gaul, Harriett, 209, 221, 302, 304-6, 312-14, 316.
Gaul, Jim, 60 photo, 78, 80, 83, 93, 103, 105-10, 123, 125-128, 150 photo, 152, 158, 163-4, 191, 195-200, 202, 205, 210-12, 216, 218, 231, 245, 261, 271-2, 275, 281, 315.
Gestapo, 26, 117, 176, 170, 241-2, 245, 247, 251, 254, 256, 310-11, 317, 323, 325.
Glavin, Colonel Edward, 14-14, 50.
Goering, Marshal Herman, 319.
Golian, General Jan, 27, 29, 32, 61-2, 64, 77, 94, 99, 108, 123, 125, 131, 151, 155, 325.
Gönder, Bandi, 227-28, 231, 313.
Gorman, Jack, 60 photo, 81-2, 86-7, 90-93, 95, 97, 150 photo, 323, 330.
Gosney, Mimi, 329
Green, Daisy Holt, 302, 313.
Green, Earcel, 4.
Green, Holt, 47-51, 55, 57, 64-67, 69-70, 77, 80, 82, 85, 89-90, 102-3, 106, 108, 114, 117, 119, 122-3, 125, 127-30, 132, 139, 150 photo, 152, 154, 158, 162-3, 166, 168-9, 183, 186, 190, 195, 198, 200, 205-6, 213, 217-19, 227, 229, 231, 242, 245, 250, 253 photo, 254-5, 251, 272-78, 279-80, 289, 291, 302, 305, 307, 314, 314, 320, 328.
Grinava, Slovakia, 20, 36-9, 41-3, 45, 64, 71, 73-4, 82, 119.
Guelton, Lt. Colonel Frederic, 330.
Gulovich, Anastasia, 139.

Gulovich, Edmund, 139,
Gulovich, Maria, 33, 60 photo, 123-24, 127, 132-5, 137, 145-9, 153, 158, 159, 162-3, 165-8, 170-71, 184-6, 191-2, 195-7, 200-201, 203, 213, 215, 218, 220-21, 217, 230-31, 233-4, 236-7, 239, 253 photo, 259-63, 288, 293-7, 307-11, 315, 325, 327.
Gundell, Werner von, 330.
GUNN Mission, 154.
Habecker, Walter, 247, 251-6, 271, 273, 284, 320, 325.
Hartjens, Lisa, 330
Hede, Bob, 5, 7, 8, 39, 60 photo, 72, 111, 118, 124, 150 photo, 152, 188-9, 191-2, 261, 330.
Heinzerling, Larry, 87, 291, 306, 327.
Heinzerling, Lynn, 278-90, 294.
Heller, Charles, 53, 120, 128, 150 photo, 190, 282, 314, 316.
Hendy, Julian, 134, 231, 328.
Hensen, Keith, 111, 119, 150 photo, 186, 188, 253.
Hess, Rudolf, 319.
Himmler, Heinrich, 69, 78, 132, 150 photo, 234, 248, 253.
Hlinka Guard, 23-4, 133, 144.
Hitler, Adolf, 23, 53, 104, 283, 305.
Hodge, Gene, 330.
Hollis, General Leslie, 193-4.
Homolka Mountain, 213, 225, 229.
Horvath, Anna, 214, 219, 150 photo, 328.
Horvath, Frank, 150 photo, 270, 328
Horvath, Joe, 47, 54, 120, 127, 139, 149, 150 photo, 153, 157-58, 166-68, 190, 195, 198, 213-14, 216-17, 219, 227, 229, 231, 281-86, 314.
Horvath, Rudy, 328.
HOUSEBOAT mission, 48, 53, 55, 80, 120, 176-7, 206.
Hrinova, Slovakia, 145.
Hrodegh, Dr. Marion, 330.
Hruby, Blahoslav, 24.
Husak, Gustav, 25.
Hutson, Frances Frost, 47, 115, 306, 318.
Hymoff, Edward, 21.
Ingr, General Sergej, 14-16.
Jagger, Claude, 300.

Jakes, Otto, 48, 50, 65, 102, 205, 289.
Jedburgh Teams, 15.
Joyce, Robert, 18, 59, 161.
Kacaja, John, 73, 111, 150 photo.
Kaltenbrunner, Ernst, 150 photo, 248, 271, 276, 319-20, 322.
Kamenesky, Pavel, 228-9, 234, 291.
Kampfgruppe Schill, 38, 68, 119, 126, 131-3, 152, 154, 156.
Kanduth, Johann, 281-4.
Karpatendeutsche, 30-31,
Katek, Charles, 13, 20, 24, 26, 46-7, 50, 55, 77, 102, 316, 323.
Katlousky Stefan, Dr., 212.
Kellogg, Jack, 1-3, 7, 39, 74, 287, 324, 330.
Kennedy, Eugene, 83, 87.
Keszthelyi, Tibor, 50, 80, 100, 102, 123, 138, 150 photo, 154, 157-8, 163, 165-7, 186, 196, 201-2, 212-13, 218, 226-7, 238, 241-4, 251, 275, 261, 314.
Kettgen, Major Hans, 133.
Khrushchev, Nikita, 315.
Klabnik, Viliam, 95, 330.
Kliment, Charles, 32-4, 40, 70, 86, 134, 330.
Knap, Michal, 72-3.
Koch, Ilse, 322.
Kockova, Margita, 161 202, 214, 217-20, 229, 251, 275, 314.
Koniev, Marshall, 25, 28-30, 122.
Kraigher, Colonel George, 47.
Krajne, Slovakia, 71-72.
Kristiak, Jan, 268.
Kruty, Roman, 330
Kuhn, Dr. Richard, 330.
Kulka, Dr. Eugem, 73.
La Fatta, Guy, 73, 111, 150 photo.
Lain, Ken, 79, 80, 105-5, 107-8, 123, 138, 154, 166, 180, 186, 197, 218, 261, 287, 315, 325.
Langer, William, 12.
Lannurian, Captain Georges de, 46, 343, 266, 291.
Lettrich, Josef, 25.
Lindsay, Franklin, 102, 330.
Loughner, Jim, 81.
Luftwaffe, 20, 26, 74, 119, 151, 181.
Lund, Kathy Baranski, 60 photo, 276, 328.

Lussier, Betty, 79.
Luzier, Howard, 114-15, 150 photo, 185-6, 191, 324, 330.
Magalinska, Ingrid, 330.
Male Karpaty Mountains, 39, 41.
Mauthausen concentration camp, 245, 247-258, 271-285, 317, 319-20.
McCloy, John, 321-2.
McDonald, Dr. Larry, 330.
McGregor, Bill, 79-80, 85, 87, 90, 97, 102, 104-5, 107-110, 123, 127, 127, 129, 134, 137, 150 photo, 152, 154, 157-8, 165-8, 170-71, 180, 184, 186-8, 190-92, 197, 215, 221, 227, 231, 261, 287, 291, 302, 313, 315, 324-5, 328.
McIntosh, Betty, 330.
McSorley, David, 36-7, 42, 61.
McSparran, Glen, 81.
Magalinski, Ingrid, 330.
Melzer, Rudolf, 34, 231.
Menzies, Stewart, 12, 16
Metcalf, Clayton, 7, 329
Metropol Hotel, 176, 179, 182, 310.
Mican, Jerry, 54-5, 60, 103, 120, 127, 139, 166, 198-200, 211, 213, 218, 226-27, 241, 243-4, 275, 314, 316.
Mican, Mary, 61.
Milcic, Allen, 134, 330.
Hihalek, Michal, 176.
Miller, Buck, 60 photo, 102, 328.
Miller, Lane, 60 photo, 80-81, 101,102, 107-8, 123, 130, 190, 200, 205-7, 262, 264, 292.
Miller, Marilyn, 232, 328.
Miller, William, 80, 109, 134, 170, 181, 215, 221, 232, 239, 297, 300, 305-6, 316, 328.
Monaghan, Pleunette, 330.
Moravec, General Frantisek, 13, 16, 26-7, 47, 104, 110.
Morton, Joe, 47, 64, 83-5, 93, 98, 105-6, 109, 120, 123, 127, 150 photo, 152-4, 164-6, 168, 190, 195-6, 198-200, 202, 212-13, 215-18, 220, 227, 229, 245, 253 photo, 272-3, 275, 290, 298, 301, 305, 327, 329.
Morton, Letty, 290, 298-9, 302, 304, 313.
Mount Skalka, 230.

Moulton, Richard, 20, 35, 37-40, 74, 178-82, 310, 324, 330.
Muller, Charles, 90-91, 95, 150 photo, 324, 330.
Müller, Werner, 252-3, 255-6, 271-6, 278-9, 282, 301.
Myto, Slovakia, 200-203, 211, 214, 226.
Nabelek, Igor, 32-3, 216, 241-46, 253 photo, 329.
Nabelek, Ludvik, 29, 224, 241-46, 253 photo.
Newton, Bill, 60 photo, 83, 87, 93, 95, 98, 323, 330.
Niedermayer, Josef, 150 photo, 256-7, 272, 274, 276-80, 311, 319.
Nizansky, Captain, 227, 231.
NKVD, 146, 267, 293-4, 309, 316.
Norgaard, Noland "Boots," 290-91, 299-300.
Novak, Tony, 80, 107, 121, 205-9, 215, 288-9.
Novomesky, Laco, 25, 94.
O'Neall, Lt. Kelly, 280-81, 284, 301, 312.
Operation BUG HOUSE, 47.
Operation GUNN, 47.
Ornstein, Wilhelm, 280-85, 301.
Office of Strategic Services (OSS), 12.17, 27, 47-52, 68, 74, 78-80, 82, 84, 89, 93, 100, 102, 105, 120, 122, 124, 215-16, 242, 253, 257, 281, 287, 289, 300-1, 304-5, 313, 317.
Operation OVERLORD, 15
Pajedova, Terka, 195-96.
Panzer Grenadier Division Tatra, 68.
Papierski, Edward, 60, 329.
Paris, Nelson, 47, 105, 119, 123, 150 photo, 153-4, 190, 200, 212-13, 275, 282, 290-1, 314.
Parker, Andy, 4-5.
Paton, Penny, 329.
Pavletich, Daniel, 80-81, 100, 107, 150 photo, 206-8, 215, 246, 251, 271, 275, 278, 282, 291.
Pavlovich, Captain Pavel, 147-8.
Perkins, Colonel H.B., 18, 27, 193.
Perry, Francis (Frank), 81, 102, 123, 150 photo, 154, 162, 190, 198-9, 201, 227,

241, 244, 251, 281-2, 294-5, 316.
Pincher, Chapman, 20, 330.
Piontek, Josef, 106, 110, 120, 123-4, 130, 134, 158-9, 165-6, 168, 170-71, 191-2, 195, 203, 325.
Pittman, John, 82, 93, 330.
Pollack, Colonel Milan, 145.
Polomka, Slovakia, 194, 200-202, 212-13, 217-19, 237, 291.
Popov, Colonel Nicholai, 126, 147.
Prasiva Mountain Range, 155, 162, 173, 176, 183, 288.
Pratt, Page, 330.
Prikryl, Colonel Vladimir, 183, 190-91, 185-6, 198, 290.
Pritchard, Lt. Colonel Gil, 55, 57-8, 60, 81-2, 86, 93, 150 photo, 323.
Proksch, Willibald, 274, 279.
Putzell, Edwin, 21, 330.
Raczka, Ben, 73, 111, 150 photo.
Rajnenic, Juraj, 7, 75, 327.
Raubolt, Wesley, 114, 185-6.
Reik, Chaviva, 58, 60 photo, 242-44.
Reimer, Dr. Thomas, 33, 134, 329.
Reiss, Rafael, 60 photo, 242-4.
Repta, Jan, 42, 60 photo, 73-4, 111.
Rider, Don, 50-51,101, 323, 330.
Rippon, Richard, 73, 111, 150 photo.
Roberts, Frank, 73, 193.
Romania, 19-20, 33, 47, 84, 291-4, 304, 307-8.
Rommel, General Erwin, 37.
Rosauer Lände Prison, 173-8, 288.
Ross, Walter, 20, 47, 50, 59, 83-5, 93-4, 98, 102, 108, 118, 121, 123-4, 150 photo, 161, 170, 215, 220-21, 260, 276, 288-91, 295, 297, 300, 302, 304-5, 323.
Roth, Martin, 249, 253 photo, 279-81, 284.
Rowe, Hugh, 81, 86-7, 95.
Ruzomberok, Slovakia, 25.
Ryan, Colonel John, 46, 81, 83.
Sadjalenko, Alexei, 109.
Sasha, 234, 238.
Savel, Jan, 38.
Schianca, John, 4, 5, 7, 20, 41, 44-5, 59, 60-62, 74, 324, 330.
Schlabrendorff, Fabian von, 257.

Schoeneseiffen, Dr. Manfred, 150 photo, 251, 254, 271, 274, 279-80, 317, 323, 325.
Schroeder, Bob, 330.
Schulz, Karl, 249, 272, 274, 279-81.
Schuyler, General Cortland, 307.
Schwartz, Jan, 53, 60,80, 102, 109-10, 120, 128, 130-31, 134, 138, 150 photo, 153, 166, 169, 171, 180-81, 183, 197, 288, 291, 301, 310-11, 325.
Scrien, Peter, 110.
Seul, Dr. Anton, 330.
Sehmer, John, 32-33, 63, 65-6, 69, 94, 97, 103, 107-8, 124, 161, 194, 196, 198, 200, 202, 215-20, 235, 245, 250, 254, 261, 275, 277, 279-83, 289, 295, 324.
Shafer, Jack, 112-14, 118, 120, 120, 124, 150 photo, 154, 163, 166, 168, 170, 173-4, 177, 180-81, 183, 227, 161, 288, 310, 323, 327.
Shivers, Jay Dr., 327.
Shukayev, 234.
Silsby, Oliver, 329.
SIS, 12.
Siskovsky, Michal, 330.
Skalos, Josef, 230, 232.
Skinner, Norton, 2, 3, 5, 7, 20, 38, 40, 66, 69, 98, 287, 330.
Skorzeny, Otto, 225, 231.
Smidke, Karol, 25.
Smith, Ethan Allen, 58, 60, 89, 150 photo, 330.
SOE, 12, 25, 49, 68, 83, 85, 100, 103, 108, 208-9, 235, 254, 257, 315.
Soltesz, Frank, 6, 38, 40, 43, 60 photo, 64, 71, 324, 330.
Solzhenitsyn, Aleksandr, 297.
Souhrada, Colonel Jindrich, 68, 83, 85, 94.
Sperry, Colonel Williard, 55.
Srobar, Vavro, 25, 29.
Stalag VII B, 37.
Stalag VIII A, 37.
Stalag Luft I, 181, 288.
Stalag Luft III, 74, 287.
Stalag Luft VII, 91, 95.
Stanek, Jan, 199-200, 203, 214, 220, 228-9, 291, 313.
Stein, Stuart, 330.

Strassmann, Paul, 33, 115, 329.
Street, Jim, 60 photo, 83, 85, 87, 150 photo, 323, 330.
Strode, Sam, 2, 3, 7, 42, 60 photo, 254.
Stuart, Virgil, 2, 7, 287.
Studensky, Major, 122-7, 132, 136, 139, 148, 153, 156, 167, 169, 195, 253 photo.
Surovec, Jan, 44-5, 60 photo, 105, 325.
Symonds, Lt. Colonel Anthony, 242.
Taylor, Lt. Jack, 102, 249-50, 257, 283, 285, 309-14, 319.
Taylor, John, 330.
Tennyson, Henry, 63-4.
Thomas, Henrietta, 330.
Thomas, Thayne, 44, 46, 56, 58-60, 60 photo, 74, 323, 330.
Thost, Hans Wilhelm Dr., 252-3, 255-7, 275-6.
Threlfall, Henry, 68, 83, 85, 87, 90, 94-5, 97-99, 93-4, 216, 289.
Thun-Hohenstein, Major Erwein Graf, 150 photo, 170, 173-5, 181, 183, 189, 202, 225-231, 318, 325, 330.
Tiso, Josef, 23-4, 31, 117, 133.
Tito, Josef, 19, 50, 84, 100.
TOLEDO mission, 100-101.
Tomasik, Jan, 265.
Tomes, Emil, 45, 59, 80-1, 107, 206.
Toulmin, John, 49, 51.
Tri Duby Airfield, 57, 68-9, 81-2, 86, 91, 94, 97, 105, 108, 118, 120, 118, 120-24, 128-30, 133, 150 photo, 276, 287, 302.
Trumm, Andreas, 256, 274, 280, 311, 319.
Tuchel, Johannes, 257.
Twining, General Nathan, 6, 44-5, 59, 118.
Ursiny, Jan, 25, 199.
Vassar, 312-13.
Velichko, P. A., 25, 28, 60 photo, 64, 148.
Velky Bok, Slovakia, 198, 202, 212, 218, 227-8, 230, 233-35.
Vessel, Milan, 29, 242.
Vessel, Milos, 29, 242.
Vessel, Mirko, 24, 29, 93, 242.
Viest, General Rudolf, 66, 94, 107-8, 123, 125-6, 130-31, 151, 155, 157, 241.
Vlasov, General Vladimir, 170.
Vlcko, General Peter, 330.

Volnuk, Lt. Dymko, 161, 230, 233, 238.
Von Zerneck, Jason, 330.
Votruba, Dr. Martin, 329.
Vrto, Jan, 207.
VRV, 24-5, 28.
Vujnovich, George, 21.
Warsaw, Poland, 17, 67, 69, 104, 132, 329.
Watkins, Alex, 58, 82, 86, 92, 123, 150 photo, 205, 330.
Wilson, Jack, 42, 111-12, 115, 119, 150 photo, 186, 212-13, 231, 253-55, 275.
Wilson, Jake, 5, 65, 71, 73.
Winberg, George, 43, 60 photo, 64-5.
WINDPROOF mission, 63, 176, 194, 226, 245, 251, 255, 271, 320, 325.
Wisliceny, Dieter, 246, 285.
Witiska, Colonel Josef, 32, 150 photo, 175, 181, 226, 245, 251, 255, 271, 277, 320, 325.
Wojewoda, Cecilia, 106, 110, 115, 120, 124, 127, 134, 152, 158, 253 photo, 329.
Wolter, Dr. Waldemar, 278-9.
Woods, Sandy, 330.
Yegoroff, Captain Igor, 148, 156-7.
Yezdick, Nick, 5, 8, 36, 41, 46, 60 photo, 66, 49, 98, 325, 330.
Yugoslavia, 19-20, 51-2, 54, 63, 78, 83, 101, 113, 121, 273, 290, 293-4.
Zavisa, Edwin, 113, 173, 175, 181, 330.
Zenopian, Stefan, 53, 194, 197, 203, 215, 218, 220, 230, 233-6, 238, 260-5, 288, 291, 295, 300, 304, 306, 307-8.
Zebrowski, John, 330.
Ziereis, Colonel Franz, 150 photo, 248-9, 254-5, 272-5, 278-2, 284, 310, 314, 319-20.
Zvara, Vera, 206-209.